REA

**DO NOT REMOVE
CARDS FROM POCKET**

D1442388

Secret Intelligence Agent

For Isola
In memory of Freckles

The author in 1940

H. MONTGOMERY HYDE

Secret Intelligence Agent

St. Martin's Press
New York

Library of Congress Cataloging in Publication Data

Hyde, H. Montgomery (Hartford Montgomery), 1907–
    Secret intelligence agent.

Includes index.
    1. Intelligence service—Great Britain.   2. Intelli-
gence service—United States.   3. Hyde, H. Montgomery
(Hartford Montgomery), 1907–   4. Intelligence
officers—Great Britain—Biography.   I. Title.
JN329.I6H92   1983   327.1′2′0941   83-3113
ISBN 0-312-70847-5

First U.S. Edition
10 9 8 7 6 5 4 3 2 1

First published in Great Britain by Constable and
Company Limited.

2190581

Contents

Illustrations

Illustrations

Acknowledgements

MY SINCERE thanks are due in the first place to Sir William Stephenson, code-named Intrepid, under whom, with my late wife, I was privileged to serve in his security intelligence organization, British Security Co-ordination, for three years during the Second World War. He has taken a particular interest in this book since its inception and has made two important contributions to its text. My visits to his home in Bermuda, where he now lives, and my conversations with him there have been both informative and rewarding.

Secondly, I wish to thank the Hon Sir Peter Ramsbotham, who, when he was Governor of Bermuda, allowed me access to the minutes of the Bermuda Legislative Council at present preserved in the local government archives. I am likewise indebted to the colonial archivist for letting me examine files relating to the wartime censorship of transit mails and the examination of transit passengers in Bermuda.

My gratitude is also due for the help of various kinds I have received from the following: Mr Walter Bell, Mr Richard Deacon, Mr David Ogilvy, Mr H. Chapman Pincher, Mr A. M. Ross-Smith, Mrs Ann Solwey, Mr Rowe Spurling, Mr William Stevenson, and Mr Peter Wilson. From several no longer alive I have received similar help, whom I feel I should mention: notably, Guy Boulton, Sir Noël Coward, Colonel C. H. Ellis, Charles des Graz, Sir Alexander and Lady Korda, Philip Marquess of Lothian, Eric Maschwitz, Francis Ogilvy, Dusko Popov, Otto Strasser, Bickham Sweet-Escott, and Lord Tangley.

Most of the illustrations in this book are reproduced from photographs in my own collection. But several are from other copyright sources, for permission to reproduce which I am glad to acknowledge: namely, Associated Newspapers; Associated Press; the *Bermudian*; the *Book Collector*; the *Nassau Magazine*; Mrs Madeleine Ponsonby; Mrs A. V. Solwey; the Roosevelt Library, Hyde Park, New York; Gwendolen Lady Tangley; Topics; and Mrs Isola Wren.

I am most grateful to my editor Mrs Prudence Fay for her pains-taking work in preparing this book for publication, and finally as always to my present wife for typing the first draft and also making a number of suggestions for its improvement, which I have gladly adopted.

H.M.H.

Westwell House
Tenterden
Kent

Foreword

by Sir William Stephenson, CC, MC, DFC

IT WILL be readily apparent to the reader of this book that the author is an outstandingly superior individual, as were so many other members of British Security Co-ordination, the unique special intelligence organization which I created and financed in the USA to the extent of $3,000,000 and which operated throughout World War II, with headquarters in Rockefeller Center, New York. The birth of BSC was the result of a direct request from Winston Churchill to me on the evening of 10 May 1940, the day he became Prime Minister.

My friend Harford Montgomery Hyde has written an interesting, and indeed fascinating, account of his personal experiences, many of which took place during the three years when he and his deftly accomplished wife Dorothy were working under my direction in BSC. But before making any further reference to their activities, I should like to take this opportunity of putting the record straight with regard to my relations with Winston Churchill and President Roosevelt, since they have been doubted or misinterpreted, notably by Churchill's intermittent wartime private secretary, Sir John Colville.

It is also worth noting that Montgomery Hyde dissents from the charge made by Chapman Pincher in his book *Their Trade Is Treachery* that my principal assistant in BSC, Colonel Charles Howard ('Dick') Ellis, was a spy, first for the Nazis and then for the Soviets. To say that he spied for them is pure disinformation by the KGB in my view. Neither can I agree with Chapman Pincher's statement that Dick Ellis 'confessed' in 1965. If he had, I would have known about it, because I would have been the first person the Security Service in London (MI5) would have got in touch with. No documentary evidence in support of the charge against Ellis has yet been forthcoming; if it exists, it should be produced instead of relying on hearsay. Nor can I accept, as Chapman Pincher does in his generally well researched and accurate work, that the film actor Leslie Howard was engaged in carrying out 'secret war missions' for me when the Germans, having possibly been forewarned by Ellis, shot down the aircraft in which he was travelling to Lisbon. In fact, I never had anything to do with Leslie Howard.

Colville's statements about me are similarly misleading. The true facts are as follows. During the afternoon of 10 May 1940 Winston Churchill telephoned to me at my London home, 76 New Cavendish Street, telling me that he was dining that night with Lord Beaverbrook at Stornoway House and suggesting that I should propose myself and join them. I agreed, and called Max Beaverbrook who replied that he would be delighted if I would join Churchill and a few others whom he was also inviting. I should add that he welcomed me warmly when I arrived at his house. In his recent book *The Churchillians* (published in the United States as *Winston Churchill and his Inner Circle*) Colville bluntly describes my invitation as 'a clear invention'. He also states that he never heard Churchill speak of me, although my name 'may have been mentioned to Churchill' in connection with my intelligence role in North America. Finally, he says that it is more than doubtful whether I ever set foot in No 10 Downing Street. 'None of those who were there in the war can recollect his so doing.'

The other guests at Stornoway House that night included Lord Trenchard, affectionately known as 'Boom', who as Chief of the Air Staff in the earlier inter-war years of appeasement had striven to keep a nucleus of the Royal Air Force in being. There was also Bill Hughes, Prime Minister of Australia during the First World War and now Australian Minister for the Navy: he was seventy-six at this time and always carried a complicated hearing-aid with him in a small black box, which I particularly remember. Some Frenchmen were there too, among them General Maxime Weygand who commanded the French forces in the Mediterranean and was to supersede General Gamelin as Supreme Allied Commander shortly before the fall of France. The Frenchmen looked glum, as well they might, since they had no strategic reserves with which to oppose the Germans who were about to break through their lines at Sedan and overrun the country to the English Channel.

When the port and cigars appeared, Churchill rose from his seat at the head of the table and beckoned me to follow him. We walked over to the heavily draped dining-room windows. Pointing a finger directly at me, Churchill said quietly:

'You know what you must do at once. We have discussed it most fully and there is a complete fusion of minds between us. *You are to be my personal representative in the United States.* I will ensure that you shall have the full support of all the resources at my command. I know that you will have success and the good Lord will guide your efforts as He will ours. This may be our last farewell. *Au revoir* and good luck!'

We returned to the dinner table and shortly afterwards the party broke up. I went home to tell my beloved American wife Mary that we must leave London for New York as soon as possible, and I also telephoned the other members of the group who had been in Churchill's confidence, particularly on the question of securing Amercian aid. These included General Hastings ('Pug') Ismay, Churchill's Chief of Staff as Minister of Defence; Colonel Colin Gubbins, who headed the Special Operations Executive (SOE); Fred Leathers, the shipping and transport expert; Charles Hambro, the banker; Lord Selborne, future Minister of Economic Warfare; and others of the group of which I am today the solitary survivor.

My wife and I flew to Paris and thence to Genoa. There we sailed for New York. During the voyage we heard the news of the French collapse and the evacuation of the British Expeditionary Force from the beaches at Dunkirk. This heightened the urgency of my mission and I set about it immediately we arrived in New York.

Whatever may have been written or said about me by others, I can state here categorically that I never at any time claimed to provide a secret liaison between the British Prime Minister and the American President. As is now well known, from the beginning of the war, when Churchill was at the Admirality, he began a secret telegraphic correspondence with Roosevelt. This was conducted with the then British Prime Minister Neville Chamberlain's approval, and it continued after Churchill moved from the Admiralty to No 10 Downing Street in the summer of 1940. Nor was it Churchill's intention that I should supplement it in any way, save in the most exceptional circumstances. Besides setting up the nucleus of a security intelligence organization, which later became BSC, my initial task as Churchill's personal representative was to increase and enlarge American material aid to Britain during the period when Britain stood alone in Europe against the common enemy.

Consequently my meetings with the President were few, and always most discreetly conducted. The first took place a few days after my arrival in the US when I went to the White House, accompanied in accordance with diplomatic protocol by the British Ambassador Lord Lothian, whose tragic death a few months later was a dire loss to our cause. The principal topic of conversation was the aid which the United States could give Britain to replace the hardware which had been abandoned as the result of the Dunkirk evacuation. Naturally the President had to move warily, since he was faced with an election for a third term later in the same year, and while he deeply sympathized with Britain's plight he had also to contend with the strong isolationist feeling in the country which was resolutely opposed to getting involved in war. Hence I had the task of counselling Churchill to be patient when urgent action was needed, as Lord Louis Mountbatten (later Earl Mountbatten of Burma) later put it, and at the same time I had to 'urge action on the Americans who wanted any excuse to be patient'.

On the subject of security and intelligence, the President's advice was that I should work intimately and confidentially with Edgar Hoover, the FBI chief. 'There should be the closest possible marriage between the FBI and British Intelligence,' said the President. And so, as this book reveals, there was.

With regard to my initial task, the first fruits of my efforts were to secure 1,000,000 rifles and 30,000,000 rounds of ammunition for the British Home Guard, who were training with broomsticks at the time, to combat the anticipated German invasion. Other supplies of war material followed, notably 100 Flying Fortresses for Coastal Command of the RAF, as well as the secret Sperry bomb-sight. Later in the summer came the destroyers-for-bases deal in which I also played a part, along with General William Donovan on the American side. Mountbatten, in particular, described it as 'absolutely vital' for the convoying of our merchant shipping across the Atlantic and combating U-boats. As he put it, 'Big Bill Donovan and Little Bill Stephenson were primarily responsible for persuading the President' to agree to it. The deal provided, in exchange for fifty badly needed American destroyers, a grant to the Americans of British bases in the Caribbean, Bermuda, and Newfoundland.

As for Sir John Colville's statement that it is more than doubtful whether I ever set foot in No 10 Downing Street, I may say that I saw the Prime Minister frequently in the course of the forty-three visits I made from New York to London during the war, although our meetings were by no means always in Downing Street. My calls at No 10 were invariably late at night when Colville had probably gone to bed, or else was away serving with the RAF which he did between October 1941 and the end of 1943. Indeed the author of this book, who wrote my biography twenty years ago under the title of *The Quiet Canadian* in Britain and *Room 3603* in the United States, has given a detailed and circumstantial account of one of these nocturnal visits. Incidentally that biography was not commissioned by me, as Professor Hugh Trevor-Roper has written somewhere. It was a purely spontaneous effort on the part of the author, but he did it with my approval and he had access to BSC records.

The late David Bruce wrote a Foreword to *The Quiet Canadian* for its publication in 1962, when he was US Ambassador in London. I should like to quote a few sentences from it which gave me great pleasure at the time:

Stephenson's American friend, the late General William J.

Donovan, did not exaggerate when he said that British Security Co-ordination was built from nothing into the greatest integrated, secret intelligence and operations organization that has ever existed anywhere. It was Stephenson's conviction, months before Pearl Harbour, that the United States should possess a similar organization for use abroad. He hoped it would be headed by his friend. To achieve this end he brought, through subtle influences, the merits of such a proposal to the attention of President Roosevelt . . . The resultant organization was later known as the Office of Strategic Services.

I myself testify, as a subordinate of Donovan's, that I could not have carried out my own particular duties with even a tolerable measure of success, had it not been for the generous counsel and unremitting support of Stephenson and his officers.

Although Mr Montgomery Hyde joined the British Secret Intelligence Service shortly after the beginning of the war, he began by working with various transit mail detachments including the one in Bermuda, where he was in regular touch with me and where, as he relates here, he was largely instrumental in uncovering evidence from the mails of a German spy ring, whose members were the first to be tried for espionage after the United States entered the war. In May 1941 he joined BSC with his wife, whose expert technical assistance to the FBI was to prove of very great value and importance to the Bureau in Washington. For this she and her husband received Mr Hoover's warm personal thanks.

Early in 1944, much to my regret, Harford and Dorothy Montgomery Hyde left BSC, the former to join General Eisenhower's staff in Europe, where he was promoted to the rank of Lieutenant-Colonel in the Intelligence Corps. It gives me great pleasure to recommend the following account of his personal experiences as compulsive reading for all those interested in the craft of secret intelligence and 'special operations'.

Wm Stephenson

1

To War with a Steam Kettle

SECRET INTELLIGENCE, particularly British secret intelligence, has always had a peculiar fascination for the general reader and the student of history and war. The Secret Service, as the official organization is popularly called, is a perennial magnet of interest. Of course, looked at from the enemy's point of view, a secret agent is a spy, although the country which employs a man or woman on espionage and counter-espionage operations customarily refers to him or her as an agent. Such an outstanding soldier, statesman, and wartime administrator as Winston Churchill admitted to the fascination of the service and even confessed to one spy story of his own.

Writing between the two World Wars, Churchill remarked, with reference to the first of these conflicts, that:

> In the higher ranges of Secret Service work the actual facts in many cases were in every respect equal to the most fantastic inventions of romance and melodrama. Tangle within tangle, plot and counter-plot, ruse and treachery, cross and double-cross, true agent, false agent, double agent, gold and steel, the bomb, the dagger and the firing party were interwoven in many a texture so intricate as to be incredible and yet true. The Chief and the high officers of the Secret Service revelled in these subterranean labyrinths, and amid the crash of war pursued their task with cold and silent passion.

Churchill added that, although the press sometimes regarded the British authorities as 'a ready dupe of continental craft and machinations', in fact it was probable that on the whole, during the First World War, 'the British Secret Service was more efficient and gained greater triumphs, both in the detection of spies and in the collection of information from the enemy, than that of any other country, hostile, allied or neutral'.[1]

The first part of Churchill's observations was equally true of the Second World War, as I can testify from personal experience as one of countless secret intelligence agents employed by the British in that conflict. I also like to think that Churchill's opinion of the achievements of the Secret Intelligence Service in World War I was repeated a quarter of a century later in World War II.

The collection of intelligence by covert means from enemies or potential enemies in foreign countries was first officially assigned to a specially selected officer, who became the chief of a separate government department in England a few years before the outbreak of the First World War. By one of those anomalies which are characteristic of British affairs, he was a naval officer, but his department was nominally a branch of the War Office and was known as Military Intelligence 6 (MI6), originally MI1 (c). However, since the activities of his agents in the field took place abroad, particularly in Germany and Russia, his department eventually came under the jurisdiction of the Foreign Office, although it retained its Military Intelligence title. On the other hand, the counter-espionage branch, which came into existence at the same time as MI6 and was known as MI5, was nominally the responsibility of the Secretary of State for War.

Hitherto, apart from the activities of a few enterprising private individuals who kept their eyes and ears open when travelling abroad, the collection of secret intelligence had been virtually non-existent, although officially the War Office was responsible for counter-espionage. In 1907 there were still no British agents in Europe, and no plans for organizing an espionage system in time of war. 'The only consolation', a War Office official commented at that time, 'is that every foreign government implicitly believes that we already have a thoroughly organized and efficient European Secret Service.' In effect, MI6 and MI5 came into existence jointly in 1909, when a Secret Service Bureau was set up with Foreign and Home Sections, the Bureau being placed administratively under the War Office. The two sections were separated in the following year, the Home Section remaining under the War Office, while the Foreign Section was transferred to the Admiralty which was its best customer. No doubt this arrangement benefited the Directorate of Naval Intelligence, whose head, the legendary Admiral Sir Reginald ('Blinker') Hall, brought off such *coups* as the arrest of Sir Roger Casement after he had been landed by a German submarine on the west coast of Ireland, and the exposure of the Zimmerman telegram which brought the United States into the First World War. However, by the end of World War I the Foreign Section had come to be controlled by the Foreign Office and to be known as the Secret Intelligence Service (SIS), otherwise MI6. In 1921, following the recommendations of a Cabinet committee, the SIS was made responsible for espionage abroad, each service department – Home, Colonial, India, Admiralty, Air – having a representative of its own departmental intelligence branch attached to MI6.[2]

The first chief of MI6 or SIS was Captain Sir Mansfield Cumming, RN, who was fifty-one years of age at the time of his appointment in 1909. He was known within the service, as well as in official circles outside it, by the initial letter of his surname, 'C', and his successors have invariably likewise been so known, although none of them subsequently has had a surname beginning with this letter.

Mansfield Cumming, who must be regarded as the founder of the modern SIS, was also a legendary figure. He was reputed to have a great success with women and, unlike the somewhat pompous Military Intelligence chiefs, he did not mind if his agents philandered outside the sphere of duty, as he did. Like T. E. Lawrence, he had a passion for speed, and it was while driving a fast car that he was involved in an accident as a result of which he lost a leg. In fact he amputated it himself with a knife he happened to be carrying at the time. The amputated limb was replaced by one of the wooden variety, to which he used to draw attention by striking matches on it and by ostentatiously tapping it with a paper knife when he was interviewing

agents or prospective agents. One of his most successful operators in this field was Sir Compton Mackenzie, who was later to
get into serious trouble for revealing more than he should have
done in his autobiographical *Greek Memories* (1933). Curiously
enough it was during his trial at the Old Bailey on the charge of
breaching the Official Secrets Act that the judge asked when
Cumming had died. None of the Intelligence bigwigs who was
present was able to supply this piece of information, and it
remained for 'Monty' Mackenzie to do it from the dock,
although he was actually a year out in his reckoning.[3]

Mackenzie's contemporary Paul Dukes, who worked for SIS
in Bolshevik Russia, has also given a vivid account of Mansfield
Cumming in his epic account of his secret activities at this
period, *The Story of ST 25* (1938), ST 25 being his code
reference in the service. But he took care to confine the narrative to his personal adventures, and did not quote from any
official documents like those which got Mackenzie into trouble.
Nevertheless both agents ultimately received knighthoods, and
their books remain the two best about the operations of the
British Secret Service in the First World War.

By contrast with Mansfield Cumming, the first head of MI5
was a soldier, considerably stuffier than his original counterpart
in SIS. He was Major-General Sir Vernon Kell, who was known
as 'K', but in his case the initial died with him. Sometimes both
departments were colloquially lumped together and referred to
as the Security Service; however, strictly speaking security was
and still is primarily the concern of MI5.

Although MI6 and MI5 only date, as organizations, from the
early years of the present century, the operations of intelligence
and counter-espionage go back for centuries in British history.
Apart from a few conspicuous examples, it is not proposed to
detail them here. The first modern British intelligence chief
was Sir Francis Walsingham, who filled the office of Secretary of
State under Queen Elizabeth I from 1573 until his death in 1590,
being mainly concerned with foreign affairs and the collection of
relevant intelligence. 'Knowledge is never too dear', was his
favourite maxim and, far from being paid for his work, he devoted

practically the whole of his private fortune to maintaining his system of espionage at the peak of efficiency. According to an authoritative source, he had agents in thirteen French towns, seven in the Low Countries, five each in Italy and Spain, nine in Germany, three in the United Provinces, and three in Turkey. At one time he had in his pay fifty-three agents at foreign courts, besides eighteen spies who 'performed functions that could not be officially defined'. One of his most confidential associates was a certain Thomas Phelippes, a code and cipher expert. The interception by Walsingham's agents of letters which passed between the political conspirator Anthony Babington and Mary Stuart (Mary, Queen of Scots) beyond doubt incriminated the luckless Queen in a plot to assassinate Elizabeth, although the latter was only brought to sign Mary's death-warrant with the greatest reluctance after her trial and conviction.

Walsingham's most conspicuous success as a spy-master was in the matter of the Spanish Armada, despite the fact that his warnings were not acted upon. Throughout the later months of 1587 his agents in Spain kept him regularly informed, in detail, of all the preparations which the Spanish admirals were making for their great naval expedition against England: the numbers of men who had enlisted, the vessels which had been commissioned, and the horses, armour, ammunition, and food supplies which had been purchased. In the event, the Queen disregarded her minister's solemn warnings as she so often did in other respects, and refused to sanction any expenditure of money for defence against a possible invasion. The most that Walsingham and his agents could do was to persuade the Genoese bankers to withhold loans from the Spanish King, Philip II. During August 1588, when Walsingham was with the Queen at Tilbury and the Armada was in the English Channel, it was in vain for Walsingham to urge that every advantage should be taken against the enemy's ships which had been disabled by the bad weather: Lord Howard of Effingham, the English Admiral, had insufficient ammunition to pursue these and the other vessels which had been put to flight as much as by a change of wind as by Sir Francis Drake's fire-ships. It is one of the ironies of history that

England's first great secret service chief should have been brought to the verge of bankruptcy by his loyal exertions on his sovereign's and his country's behalf.[4]

Under the Protectorate of Oliver Cromwell, and after the Restoration of Charles II, at least a certain amount of money was appropriated for secret service work, about £2,000 in Cromwell's time and £6,000 under the Stuart monarch, subsequently reduced to £4,000 during an economy drive in 1668. The Lord Protector's Secretary of State Thomas Thurloe, a worthy successor of Walsingham, had such an efficient secret service that, in the words of the diarist Samuel Pepys, 'Cromwell carried the secrets of all the princes of Europe at his girdle'.[5] Thurloe also employed a brilliant cryptographer named John Wallis, an Oxford professor who could break any code or cipher known in that age, and whose *Essay on the Art of Decyphering* was deposited, along with a collection of letters deciphered by him (including many which passed between the leading Royalists during the Civil War), in the Bodleian Library, Oxford.

Charles II's secret service was administered to good effect by Sir Joseph Williamson, a distinguished public servant who helped to run the Post Office. Another expert in espionage at this period was Sir George Downing, who built the street of houses in Westminster which bears his name and which for more than two centuries has included the British Prime Minister's official residence. Downing spied for Cromwell when he was envoy at The Hague, and he stayed on in his post after the Restoration by turning his coat and luring three of the regicides to their doom in Rotterdam, whence they were forcibly conveyed to England to face trial and execution – a perfidious action for which Charles II rewarded him with a baronetcy. Downing later boasted to Pepys that while he was at The Hague he learned the most intimate state secrets from Cornelius de Witt, the head of the Dutch government, and his Cabinet colleagues; although, like Walsingham, his intelligence was not always heeded by the sovereign. In his diary Pepys describes how he went for a walk in St. James's Park one Sunday morning just after Christmas in 1668, and there met Sir George Downing, who proved most informative in this talk about his activities as British envoy in Holland.

He told me [wrote Pepys] that he had so good spies that he hath had the keys taken out of De Witt's pocket when he was a-bed, and his closet opened and papers brought to him and left in his hands for an hour, and carried back and laid in the place again and the keys put into his pocket again. He says he hath always had their most private debates [conversations] that hath been but between two or three of the chief of them, brought to him in an hour after, and an hour after that hath sent word to the King – but nobody here regarded them.[6]

A particularly ripe field of intelligence in the latter part of the nineteenth century was India, where the British suspected that the Russians had designs upon the sub-continent, and a considerable amount of espionage and counter espionage was carried out by each country against the other. Readers of Rudyard Kipling's classic novel *Kim* (1901) will recall how towards the end of the story Kim, the orphaned son of an Irish soldier and an Englishwoman, becomes attached to the Secret Service Department of the Government of India, and plays a conspicuous part in obtaining a parcel of maps and correspondence which two Russian agents have been making and gathering on the frontier when they were supposed to be shooting game. The operations of Kim and his associates against Russian, Afghan, and unfriendly powers in Northern India was known as the Great Game, and it continued in real life until the eclipse of the Tsars, first by the Japanese and then by the Bolsheviks. This may well account for the large number of British officers and others who had served in India being recruited into MI6 when that organization was formed under Mansfield Cumming, a tradition continued under his successors.

The Russians, both before and after the Revolution of 1917, had a great respect for British secret intelligence. Latterly there was one figure they particularly revered, as I discovered some years ago when I was exploring Soviet Central Asia on my own. I was staying in an hotel in Samarkand, and one evening after dinner a major in the Soviet army, who was in uniform and also appeared to be alone, ordered a bottle of wine and invited me to share it with him. In the course of our conversation, which ranged over a variety of subjects, he asked me what I did in the way of work. I replied that I was a history professor at the Punjab University in Lahore and had come up to Samarkand for a holiday, as it was vacation time at the university. I felt it unnecessary to add that I had managed to obtain a visa by cultivating the Soviet ambassador in Karachi and getting drunk with him. The inquisitive major gave me the impression that he thought I was on some spying mission, and his suspicions were confirmed when he asked me if I had served in the war and, if so, in what regiment or unit.

'The Intelligence Corps,' I replied truthfully.

'Ah!' he said knowingly. 'The Secret Service. Lawrence of Arabia!' I tried to emphasize that the Intelligence Corps was an openly recognized unit of the British army, concerned with the collection of military intelligence about the enemy for use by commanders and their staffs, and said I felt sure the Russians had something similar in their army. He dodged the implied question but went on about Colonel Lawrence, who he thought had been head of the British Secret Service. No, I assured him, Lawrence never occupied that position. On the other hand, I said, he was a great amateur of espionage, an acknowledged genius in the field of intelligence and sabotage, and one of the greatest guerrilla leaders in history, a fluent Arabic speaker who dressed and looked like a sheik and who commanded the unwavering allegiance of the Bedouin tribesmen in blowing up bridges and enemy troop trains among other 'special operations' (as they came to be known in World War II). But my Russian friend remained unconvinced that Lawrence did not really operate from behind a desk in Whitehall. We drank another bottle of wine between us, after which we parted amicably and I went to bed. He had left the hotel by the time I was up and about next morning. At least there was no sign of him. I wondered whether I was being deliberately followed and my movements reported upon, and whether the relative ease with which I had got my visa was owing, not to any alcoholic exuberance on the part of the Soviet ambassador in Pakistan, but to an authorization to grant me my visa from Moscow.

I remembered that some years previously, when I was a Member of the British House of Commons, I had visited the international Trade Fair in Poznan in Poland with the late Lord Plurenden (Rudi Sternberg, as he then was) – a man very active in promoting East-West trade at that time. I had left Poznan on the day before the fair ended, as I was booked to fly on to Moscow to join a small English delegation by invitation of the Soviet authorities. There was a KGB (Soviet secret police) agent at the Fair, and when I got back to London and saw Sternberg again he told me that the KGB man had said to him over drinks, 'I am very interested in your friend Colonel Hyde who has just left for Moscow.' 'Why?' asked Sternberg. 'Well,' said the KGB man, 'I have looked him up in your *Who's Who* and I see that he was commissioned in the Intelligence Corps in 1940, so that he must be a spy.' Sternberg argued, as I was later to do with the Russian major in Samarkand, that the Intelligence Corps was not a secret body but an openly recognized unit of the British army, and that, when I had joined up, that was the unit to which I had been assigned, perhaps because of my knowledge of foreign languages or for some similar reason. But the KGB man would have none of it. 'Colonel Hyde is a spy,' he kept on repeating. 'Well, then,' said Sternberg, 'if you are so sure he is a spy, why did your people in London give him a visa?'

The KGB man's reply was revealing. 'As a matter of fact, we quite like Colonel Hyde personally and we are willing to let him visit our country, although he is a spy.' Then, after a moment or two's pause, he added with a knowing look: 'But, of course, we always watch him very carefully when he is in the Soviet Union!'

Mansfield Cumming, who died in 1923, was succeeded as C by another ex-naval officer, fifty-year-old Admiral Sir Hugh Francis Paget Sinclair, KCB, familiarly known in the service as 'Quex'.

One observer described him as 'a little man with the face of a faintly amused frog'.[7] During his reign, which lasted until the early days of the Second World War, the SIS, partly through lack of funds, showed a marked deterioration in quality, and throughout this period successive governments paid less attention to MI6, which still recruited its senior agents through the old-boy network, than it did to MI5 and the Government Code and Cipher School (GC & CS). The latter organization, originally under the Admiralty and later the Foreign Office when it became part of SIS, was successful in deciphering the telegrams which passed between Moscow and the Soviet Trade Delegation in London, and led in 1927 to a police raid on the Delegation's premises in London, which it shared with a friendly British trading company called Arcos Limited. Mr Stanley Baldwin, who was Conservative Prime Minister at the time, stated in the House of Commons a few days after the so-called Arcos raid that the British Government's complaint against the Soviets largely consisted of information contained in intercepted telegrams, which showed that the Soviet Union was carrying on propaganda against British interests, notably in China. The Soviet Chargé d'Affaires in London protested that no *en clair* telegrams had passed between his Embassy and the Commissariat of Foreign Affairs in Moscow, and that 'Mr Baldwin must have been referring to some alleged cipher telegrams decoded by a department of the British Government'. The fact that the Russians now knew the GC & CS had broken their cipher was rather discomforting for Baldwin and his Cabinet colleagues. Nevertheless they did not shrink from taking the Soviet bull by the horns – the Trade Delegation and Arcos were closed down, and Britain broke off diplomatic relations with the Soviet Union.[8]

For the greater part of the period between the wars, MI6 was in pretty poor shape, undermanned and starved of funds which its chief Admiral Sinclair lacked the power or the influence to obtain. Also, the Admiral always seemed uncertain as to what the primary objectives of the service he headed should be, due in part to confusion and uncertainty about the Soviet Union's intentions. As a result MI6 as a body was inefficient; in its higher echelons it was staffed by enthusiastic amateurs, and it was torn by internal jealousies and wrangles between C's principal subordinates.[9]

As Sinclair's health began to deteriorate, his obsession with secrecy became almost pathological, and when he died at the age of sixty-six on 4 November 1939, just two months after the outbreak of war, his closest executives were ignorant of the location of the various dead-letter boxes for the exchange of communications with his agents. He had shared the secret with only one person, his sister Miss Evelyn Sinclair, and but for the fact that she survived him and was able to provide the requisite information, the whole of the Secret Service might have collapsed completely.[10]

Sinclair also left a devastating legacy which came to fruition five days after his death. Two of his British agents in Holland (which was then neutral) were Major H. R. Stevens, Passport Control Officer at The Hague, and Captain S. Payne Best, who ran an import-export business as cover for his SIS activities. Stevens and Payne Best had made contact with a German army officer who called himself Captain Schaemmel but who in reality was Walter Schellenberg of the Nazi Central Security Agency, the German equivalent of MI5. Schellenberg succeeded in convincing the two British SIS officers that several dissident generals in the German army were planning to capture Hitler, after which a military junta would take over in Berlin and make peace. One of the generals, whose name was not disclosed, was said to be willing to meet them with 'Captain Schaemmel' at a convenient point on the Dutch-German frontier; once in Holland, the general would be flown to London.[11]

'C has got report on interview with his German General friends,' noted Sir Alexander Cadogan, the Permanent Under-Secretary in the Foreign Office, on 23 October, probably the last time that he saw Sinclair. 'I think they are Hitler agents.'[12]

Cadogan was quite right. On 9 November Stevens and Payne-Best were lured by Schellenberg to Venlo on the frontier. There they were kidnapped while actually on Dutch territory, and driven through the border barriers to Germany, where they spent the remainder of the war in captivity. Under interrogation, although they were not tortured, they gave the Germans a more or less faithful picture of the operation of the SIS organization in London, confirming (what was in all probability already known to the Germans) that plans for propaganda and sabotage were being prepared by Section D of MI6 under the direction of a sapper officer, Colonel Laurence Grand.

Three weeks passed after Sinclair's death before his successor was officially appointed. Churchill, who had joined the Chamberlain Government in his First World War post at the Admiralty, was anxious that the naval tradition should be continued and that the next C should be a Royal Navy man. In fact, he wrote to Cadogan about it; Cadogan described it as a 'tiresome letter', adding that Churchill 'ought to have enough to do without butting into other people's business'.[13] The matter was eventually settled at a meeting in the Cabinet room at No 10 Downing Street, attended by the Prime Minister, the three service chiefs – Churchill (Admiralty), Leslie Hore-Belisha (War) and Kingsley Wood (Air) – besides Lord Halifax (Foreign Affairs) and the latter's Permanent Under-Secretary, Alec Cadogan. 'Halifax played his hand well and won the trick,' noted Cadogan briefly in his diary.[14] The Foreign Secretary, who was departmentally responsible for MI6, backed the appointment of the late Admiral's deputy, Colonel (later Major-General Sir) Stewart Menzies, DSO, MC, a thirty-nine-year-old Scotsman, ex-Guards officer and old Etonian, with impeccable social connections and a distinguished record at the Front in World War I. He was the son of Graham Menzies (a man of independent means) and Lady Holford, and had married twice into the peerage. His step-father Sir George Holford was a wealthy landowner in Gloucestershire, besides owning Dorchester House in London with its famous picture gallery which was later to come under the auctioneer's hammer; he had also been equerry to King Edward VII and King George V. His mother, Lady Holford, who had married Sir George as her second husband after Graham Menzies's death, was born Susannah Wilson, the daughter of Arthur Wilson of Tranby Croft (the Yorkshire house and scene of the celebrated

Baccarat Scandal in 1891, which implicated the Prince of Wales, as the future King Edward VII then was). Thus by birth, education and professional background, the new C, who had a more forceful personality than the luckless Admiral, seemed well fitted for what was to prove a difficult and exacting job for the next eight years.

Incidentally Stewart Menzies' surname was customarily pronounced 'Mingiss', '*gesprochen Mengis*', as the German memorandum on the organization of the British SIS put it, from information obtained from Stevens and Payne Best. The same memorandum also revealed that the SIS London headquarters were situated opposite St James's Park underground station at 54 Broadway, ostensibly the Passport Control Office, time-honoured cover for the Secret Service. A corridor on the fourth floor of No 54, where Menzies had his private office, led into an attractive period house at the back in Queen Anne's Gate, which provided C with comfortable living accommodation and also enabled him to enter and leave his official headquarters through the Queen Anne's Gate entrance without being observed by anyone in Broadway or the Passport Control Office. On the other hand, Section D under Colonel Grand had its separate offices round the corner from Broadway in the St Ermin's Hotel in Caxton Street. At first the Germans had thought that the British were responsible for the attempt to kill Hitler by a bomb planted in the Burgerbrau beer cellar in Munich the evening before the Venlo incident, but, luckily for them, Stevens and Payne Best were eventually freed from suspicion of any complicity in the bomb plot.[15]

Meanwhile MI5 was still carrying on its work under the ageing General Vernon Kell, although his days as head of the counter-espionage organization were numbered. On the eve of the out-break of war, smart new headquarters in St James's Street (con-siderably more impressive than MI6's in Broadway) were taken over to house the rapidly accumulating files and to provide space for the enlarged staff. It would have been better if MI5 had stayed there, but after the Battle of Britain the records and most of the personnel were evacuated to Wormwood Scrubs prison, which was considered a safer locality than London's West End. But it was not to be, since a chance German bomb destroyed most of the records, a very serious casualty. However, before this, MI5 brought off one important *coup* when they arrested Tyler Kent, a cipher clerk in the United States Embassy who had been leaking top secret documents to his friend, an anti-Jewish White Russian woman named Anna Wolkoff, and also to the extreme right-wing Member of Parliament Captain Archibald Ramsay, to whom Anna acted as a kind of political secretary. Anna's father, Admiral Nicholas Wolkoff, had been Naval Attaché at the Tsarist Embassy in London at the time of the Bolshevik Revolution, otherwise he and his wife would assuredly have been liquidated by the Bolsheviks. They lost all their property and other possessions in Russia, and were reduced to running a tea-shop in Kensington, where, besides Russian tea, they served what was reputedly the best caviare in London. I used to go there before the war to meet various White Russians who were helping me with my Russian language and Russian historical studies, and it was there that I met Anna, who had quite a successful dress business. She was then thirty-eight years of age. On one occasion she invited me to her flat in the same neighbourhood, where I talked with her at some length. I was struck by her violent anti-Semitism and her fervent belief that the Jews were conspiring to bring about a war for their own ends.

Tyler Kent first met Anna Wolkoff early in 1940. It has been suggested that they became lovers, although Anna was nine years older. However that may be, they were certainly on intimate terms, since for her use Kent abstracted from the US Embassy file copies of the cables which passed between the US President Roosevelt and Winston Churchill. Churchill was First Lord of the Admiralty during the first eight months of the war, and signed those cables 'Naval Person'. It is indicated by Churchill in his war memoirs that this correspondence was conducted with the knowledge and approval of the Prime Minister, Mr Neville Chamberlain, although Kent was later to state that part of it 'was devoted to questions as to how to have Churchill replace Chamberlain as Prime Minister', since Chamberlain was believed to favour a compromise peace with Germany against the views of the 'war party' represented by Eden, Duff Cooper and others as well as Churchill. Much of the Roosevelt-Churchill correspondence is still closed in the Roosevelt archives at Hyde Park, New York. However, one of Churchill's earlier messages, according to Kent, read in part:

> I am half American and a natural person to work with you. It is evident we see eye to eye. Were I to become Prime Minister of Britain, we could control the world.

Anne Wolkoff not only showed this correspondence to Captain Ramsay, but she attempted to send a letter in code to the traitor William Joyce (Lord Haw-Haw) who regularly broadcast anti-British and anti-Jewish propaganda on the German radio. These activities soon came to the attention of MI5. The officer in charge of the case, Captain Guy Liddell, was a particular friend of mine, and from him I learned its salient details. Tyler Kent and Anna Wolkoff were arrested in May 1940, and the American Ambassador Joseph Kennedy was prevailed upon to waive Kent's diplomatic immunity, with the result that Kent and Anna were tried *in camera* at the Old Bailey in the following October, when Guy Liddell was a crucial prosecution witness. Both the accused were convicted of offences under the Official Secrets Act, Kent being sentenced to seven years and Anna to ten. Meanwhile, Ramsay, who had been arrested at the same time under Defence Regulation 18B, was interned in Brixton Prison for the next four years, although he managed to retain his seat as an MP.[16]

The Kent-Wolkoff case was certainly a feather in MI5's cap, compared with the disastrous affair of Stevens and Payne Best which befell MI6.

It was in the early autumn of 1939 that I was recruited into MI6 through the old-boy network. Immediately on the outbreak of the war, my wife had joined the Fire Service. I had been practising at the English Bar for some years and was beginning

Walter Thomas ('Freckles') Wren

to build up a small but growing practice, particularly in Durham
on the North-East Circuit, where thanks largely to the influence
of the Lord Lieutenant of Durham, Lord Londonderry, the
former Air Minister, whose private secretary I had been after
leaving Oxford, I was getting a good deal of criminal work. But I
was on the Army Officers Emergency Reserve which I had
joined after the Munich Crisis in 1938, and as I was able and fit,
thirty-two years old, I felt that sooner or later I was bound to be
called up, although there was no sign of it during the early
stages of the well-named 'phoney' war. Travelling between
London and Durham became slow and difficult during the black-
out, and there was not much other work coming into my

chambers in the Temple, so that when it was suggested that I might be interested in doing a 'special' war job, I agreed that I should at least give it a trial. Dorothy, whom I had married in the previous April, was friendly with two London businessmen who were already in the MI6 organization, and she spoke to them about me. One of these friends was Walter Wren, known to his friends as Freckles, a self-made man who had done more than anyone else to popularize the Aga cooker and heater in English homes: for this achievement, by the time he was forty, he had been elected to the board of the parent company, Allied Ironfounders. The other friend was Francis Ogilvy, a director of the advertising agency Mather and Crowther, and an elder brother of David, who by a coincidence had been engaged in selling Aga cookers to English chefs, before joining Mather and Crowther and eventually emigrating to America where, after a spell in intelligence work, he was to become rich and famous with his own advertising firm and 'The Man in the Hathaway Shirt' campaign.

One Sunday morning I called, by arrangement, for Freckles Wren at his flat in Baker Street and he took me along to his office in St Ermin's where he asked me to sign the Official Secrets Act which bound me to secrecy in my future work. I was then told that I was to be attached to Section D under Colonel Grand, to whom I was introduced shortly afterwards, a tall, lean man barely turned forty, who gave me a welcoming friendly smile when he shook hands. I remember he used to smoke cigarettes through a long, elegant holder, which suggested a character out of an Edgar Wallace novel. Although I was to see very little of him, I liked what I did see and was sorry when he went back to regular duty at the War Office, when Section D as such was disbanded and its activities reshaped after Churchill took over from Neville Chamberlain as Prime Minister in May 1940. On its formation in January 1938, the task of Laurence Grand's Section had been officially defined as 'to investigate every possibility of attacking potential enemies by means other than operations of military force'. As Grand himself was to put it at a lunch which I gave for him in the House of

Colonel Laurence Grand, 'D' in MI6

Commons after the war when I was an MP, 'examining such an enormous task, one felt as if one had been told to move the Pyramids with a pin'.

As one of the office wits said at the time, the letter D stood for Destruction, which was true enough, since the projects of Colonel Grand's fertile brain ranged from blowing up the Romanian oil wells to more subtle acts of sabotage such as exploiting the mails by various means.

In practice, Section D was divided into two branches, called respectively SO1 and SO2, SO standing for Special Operations.

SO1 was concerned with covert propaganda directed at the enemy from such sources as clandestine radio transmitters designed to give the impression that they were operating from inside Germany. This branch later developed into the Political Warfare Executive (PWE) under the direction of Sir Robert Bruce Lockhart. SO2, on the other hand, was concerned primarily with sabotage, and after Grand's departure it was transformed into the Special Operations Executive (SOE) for which Dr Hugh Dalton, the Minister of Economic Warfare, was politically responsible, with a directive from Churchill 'to set Europe ablaze'. This operation was to be brilliantly and success-fully carried out far beyond the European confines by the SOE military chief, Colin Gubbins. [17]

In due course, I met Menzies, presumably because having heard of me, he wished to see what I looked like. I remember waiting in the ante-room to his private office on the fourth floor of No 54 Broadway, and being told by his secretary Miss Petti-grew that when the red light outside his door changed to green I could go in. I found him affable, rather stiff, and exceptionally discreet. Like his predecessor he had a fetish about secrecy. I was somewhat awed, perhaps a little overawed, by his presence and also by his charming manners. He did not give the impression of ruthlessness (unlike Colin Gubbins), but as I had lived for some years with the Londonderrys, I immediately felt Menzies must be *au fait* with Court circles, which was quite true since his mother Lady Holford was a lady-in-waiting to Queen Mary. I knew that he had been in the service throughout the cheese-paring days of Admiral Sinclair, but I wondered whether, as an intelligence officer of the old school, he was quite the right choice to deal with the changed face of espionage and the multitude of new men and new tasks which must be met. He was obviously uneasy about Section D, which was to become a considerable source of embarrassment to him before its eventual merger with SOE and PWE. I knew, too, that he had direct access to the Prime Minister as well as to the King, who must have been as impressed by his reputation for discretion as I was. According to a story going the rounds, he was once jokingly asked by King

George VI to reveal some of the details of the service. 'Menzies,' the King is supposed to have said, 'what would happen if I were to ask you the name of our man in Berlin?'

'I should have to say, Sir, that my lips were sealed.'

'Well,' the King retorted, 'supposing I were to say, "Off with your head?"'

'In that case, Sir, my head would roll with the lips still sealed!'[18]

If Menzies was an experienced and efficient intelligence officer, though a little old-fashioned, his Broadway headquarters struck me, from what little I saw of them, as thoroughly inefficient. The building itself looked run-down and rather shabby, while the lift to the upper floors was distinctly rickety. The exception was a nice but peculiar-looking man, with a dark office on the ground floor which matched his complexion. This was Maurice Jeffes, the Director of Passport Control, an overt organization which dealt with applications for visas and was responsible for the Passport Control Officers (PCOs) attached to British missions abroad and providing cover for their secret intelligence activities, a cover which had been known to the Germans and the Russians for years. Jeffes was a jolly, good-natured fellow who always gave me a friendly greeting when I entered the building. The curious gunmetal colour of his face was due to a doctor's having innoculated him with the wrong serum, which had turned it a kind of purple-blue that could not be changed. Once the manager of an American hotel where he had booked in wished to turn him out, on the ground that he was coloured and no coloured guests were allowed to stay there. Jeffes had considerable difficulty in convincing the manager that he was really white.[19]

Broadway was also beset with a mass of paper-work, much of it quite unnecessary, besides being fraught with internal jealousies which reached their climax in the unceasing internecine warfare waged between Menzies's two principal subordinates, Claude Dansey and Valentine Vivian. They were known respectively as ACSS (Assistant Chief) and DCSS (Deputy Chief), while Menzies himself was CSS (Chief), by

(Left) Major-General Sir Stewart Menzies, KCB, DSO, MC. He was chief of British Secret Intelligence (MI6) from 1939 to 1951, and, like his predecessors, known as 'C'. *(Right)* The house in Queen Anne's Gate where the MI6 chief lived; it backed on to Secret Service headquarters in Broadway, Westminster and was connected with it internally.

which styles they were invariably addressed in memoranda and telegrams. Dansey, then aged sixty-four and nominally Menzies's second-in-command, was a real *éminence grise*, and was spiteful, vindictive and anti-intellectual. 'I would never willingly employ a university man,' he once said. Dansey was responsible for the collection of covert intelligence, and in this capacity operated the so-called Z section which had employed the unfortunate Payne-Best in the Hague. Vivian, on the other hand, ten years younger than Dansey, was an ex-Indian police officer, son of the Victorian portrait painter Comley Vivian, and was well liked by his staff, who called him Vee-Vee. It was he who brought into the SIS organization a crop of intellectuals, including Graham Greene, Malcolm Muggeridge, Dick Brooman-White (later MP), Helenus Milmo (afterwards a High Court judge), and Hugh Trevor-Roper, (sometime Regius Professor of Modern History at Oxford and now Lord Dacre of Glanton, Master of Peterhouse, Cambridge). Vivian's particular responsibility was for counter-espionage in foreign countries. However, since Dansey had once referred to his staff as 'a lot of old women in red flannel knickers,' he detested Dansey so much that he always went on leave at the same time as Menzies so that he would not have to take orders from Dansey as acting head of the service. It was altogether a most unsatisfactory situation in the Broadway office, and in the event I was glad to be relatively so little involved with.[20]

At St Ermin's I found myself sharing a room with a most unpleasant character, Guy Burgess, who later turned out to be working for the Russians as well as his English employers, and whose dramatic flight with the Foreign Office official Donald Maclean to his Soviet homeland was to take place a dozen years later. This was after he had been tipped off by another traitor, H. A. R. (Kim) Philby, who like Burgess and myself was to begin his Secret Service career in Section D and whom I was later to meet in SIS headquarters, although I never got to know him at all well. Burgess, who had joined Section D in January 1939, was a blatant homosexual, an alcoholic, and distinctly unclean in his personal habits. But as he was out of the office more often than in it (I suspected either drinking or recovering from a hangover), his presence was not as unsavoury for me as it might have been. Anyhow, after a few weeks I was moved to Liverpool, where the Postal Censorship had taken over the huge building formerly occupied by Littlewood's Football Pools. The reason for this migration was because it had been suggested, either to Colonel Grand or by the Colonel himself, that Section

D might usefully co-operate with the Censorship. This organization, which consisted for the most part of elderly linguists who could read anything from Urdu to Chinese, was primarily interested in transit mails rather than in letters and parcels which originated in, or were addressed to, Britain, the examination of which was purely a security measure. But the mail passing between the European Continent and America, and carried by ships which were detained at Liverpool by Naval Contraband Control, might be expected to, and in fact did, yield useful intelligence when they were examined before being sent on to their destination. Normally letters and packages in transit bore labels to the effect that they had been 'examined by censor'. It was now decided to form a sub-section of Section D, known as D/L, for the purpose of operating a secret censorship, so that the recipients of letters or parcels would not know that these had been opened. My number in this outfit was D/L4.

D/L's headquarters were established in a large suite in the Adelphi Hotel, and its personnel originally consisted (besides myself) of Freckles Wren, Francis Ogilvy, and Eric Maschwitz, the theatrical producer and revue- and song-writer, later Director of Light Entertainment in BBC Television, who was then working as a parcels censor in a draughty garage separate from the main Littlewood's building. At the beginning of the war Eric had written to Admiral Sinclair, whom he had met through his actress wife Hermione Gingold, without knowing what Sinclair's real function was but guessing that as he was an admiral he might have something to do with naval intelligence, suggesting that he was just the man for a job with MI5. His letter remained unanswered, and after a few weeks Eric, in desperation, begged the Postal Censorship (then run by Mr Frank Worthington, the Chief Postal Censor) to take him on, as he had a knowledge of French and German. This time the response was quite quick and Eric was ordered to board a special train for Liverpool and to report at Littlewood's. However, his letter to C had not gone unnoticed. It eventually reached Colonel Grand, with the result that Eric was detached from Censorship and instructed to join us in the Adelphi. There he was to prove an amusing and stimulating colleague as well as a most useful one, since he provided the ideal cover for our operations. The story was put about that the others in the Adelphi suite, who included a couple of glamorous female secretaries in addition to Wren, Ogilvy and myself, were interested in the production of a new revue which Eric was writing. To lend an air of plausibility to this story, Eric actually did begin to write a revue, and when a London producer heard about it he immediately arrived at the hotel and told Eric to finish it as soon as possible. This Eric did, calling it *New Faces*. In the following April it was staged in London and one of its numbers, *A Nightingale Sang in Berkeley Square*, enchantingly sung by Judy Campbell, immediately became a smash hit on both sides of the Atlantic.

To return to the Adelphi. 'That hotel suite was a madhouse of laughing activity,' Eric was later to recall in his amusing autobiography *No Chip on My Shoulder*; 'through it passed strange visitors from all parts of the country – Post Office officials, printers, chemists, craftsmen of various kinds. We worked mostly at night and in intense cold, in the empty Censorship building and draughty sorting-stations.' Eric quite rightly described our principal censorship operation, Operation Letter Bags as it was called, as 'not only ingenious but, as it turned out, highly effective'.[21] He did not give any further details, but as more than forty years have passed since the Adelphi days no conceivable harm can be caused by revealing them now.

Briefly, it was a propaganda exercise, using mail destined for Germany which originated in the United States and South American countries whose mail bags were routed through the United States, and which were carried in ships diverted to English ports by Naval Contraband Control for examination with other transit mails. It was decided to begin activities with a New Year's greetings card emanating from the Pan-American German League (PAGL), a mythical organization with offices in New York, Chicago, Buenos Aires and Montevideo. The story was that it had been started by a mysterious Doctor O, a German-American lawyer who threw the whole weight of his brains and money into the anti-Nazi cause following the death of his favourite nephew, a young man who had been a victim of the infamous 'Roehm Purge' by Hitler in 1934 as an alleged homosexual. The greetings card took the form of a composite photograph of Hitler and Stalin dining off the mangled and bloody corpses of infants labelled Poland, Czechoslovakia, Finland, etc., accompanied by an extract from one of Hitler's Reichstag speeches in which he had declared that he would never be seen 'dining and wining with them' (i.e. the Bolsheviks). The second propaganda piece was a buff sheet on which was printed a letter from a German in South America to a friend in the Fatherland, deploring the damage done to the good name of Germany by the war crimes of the Nazi Party – particularly the alliance with the Soviet Union. The letters were inserted in sample envelopes of cocoa and coffee on their way to Germany from the leading German grocery firm of Leineweber y Cia in Buenos Aires, which was then sending several thousands of these sample packets by each mail. The letter on the buff sheet was not intended to be a PAGL activity but the work of some independent anti-Nazi with access to the mailing department of Leineweber.

To facilitate this operation, use was made of the pre-cancelled stamp, at that time known only in the USA. It was an ordinary postage stamp cancelled before purchase by being overprinted in black with the name of the city of purchase. These stamps could be bought, under licence, by firms having large mailing lists for newspapers, magazines, and circulars; since the covers did not have to go through the franking machines at the Post Office, they could be sorted and loaded direct into bags for dispatch. Also, since they bore no date of posting and had no overlapping postmark, the stamps could easily be removed from one cover to another. This was performed, without any sign of the transfer, in a secret department of the Censorship known as 'Room 99', which was under the direction of an old hand from the First World War, William Webb, affectionately known as 'Steam Kettle Bill'. Part laboratory and part dark-room, it was primarily used for the secret opening and closing of diplomatic and consular mail, and of other communications supposed to be immune from ordinary censorship. These were read by 'Special Examiners'.

Thanks to Lord Bearsted, our immediate chief in Section D who was also Chairman of the Shell Transport and Trading Co, that company provided us with addressograph machines and two operators to work them, with the result that Shell was soon able to turn out thousands of addressed envelopes a week, with addresses which we supplied from various sources, many from the mails themselves.

It was obviously necessary that the mail bags, after being loaded with propaganda, should be resealed so as not to appear to have been opened between New York and the clearing office of arrival in Germany. US mail bags are, or were at that time, closed with a strap and buckle, and were kept intact by a tin strip; this in turn was kept in position by a lead seal. When opening a bag, it was found possible to cut away the seal so as to leave the strip intact. Consequently, for purposes of resealing, it was only necessary to find a method of making a new lead seal and impressing it with the stamp of the US Post Office. This was done without much difficulty by one of the craftsmen who passed through the Adelphi suite, and presses were manufactured with which it was possible to reproduce seals undetectable from the originals. It was later found more practicable to manufacture our own cancelled stamps, a process which, like the lead seals, was carried out in Room 99. I was myself later to duplicate this remarkable 'room' in Gibraltar, Bermuda and New York; and finally, after the United States had come into the war after Pearl Harbour, to initiate our American allies into its mysteries.

The propaganda exercise was discontinued after a few months, when Lord Bearsted, having visited New York, reported on his return of its dangers should the Americans, who regarded their mails as sacrosanct, discover by some means or other that the British were secretly exploiting them for their war purposes.

Whether the propaganda operation really achieved much of value against the enemy, considering the time, trouble and expense involved, is a debatable question. Likewise, aircraft of the Royal Air Force were dropping leaflets instead of bombs over Germany at this time, and it can be argued that the RAF too accomplished little, if anything, by their experiment in overt propaganda. But these were early days and neither side had as yet taken off the gloves.

At this time a small Censorship detachment had gone out to Gibraltar, since Gibraltar, with its naval and military facilities, was considered to be a particularly suitable station for examining transit mails. Francis Ogilvy thought it might be a good idea if I were to go out there in the role of security officer attached to the Gibraltar Censorship, and carry on Section D's activities there. D, as Laurence Grand was called to distinguish him from C, gave the project his blessing. But there was one snag. Every member of SIS had to be cleared by MI5. There was no such procedure as positive vetting in those days. Brief biographical particulars were sent to the office in St James's Street with the request to reply if there was 'anything recorded against' the subject. Even Philby had passed this test easily, since there was nothing on record against him. Francis Ogilvy began to be uneasy as to the reason for my clearance taking so long to come through. Eventually after the elapse of two months and several reminders from Ogilvy, the customary sheet of paper arrived in Section D with a short sentence under the formula 'Anything recorded against'. It was simply: *Purchased a single ticket to Leningrad in 1933*. Why a single ticket? Was I thinking of becoming a Communist? And had I planned to settle in the Soviet Union? It was just the kind of damning sentence which might have irretrievably ruined my service career, had I not been given an opportunity to explain my action. Yes, I told Ogilvy and Wren, it was perfectly true that I had bought a single ticket which I used on a Soviet ship, the *Feliks Dzerzhinsky*, which sailed from London Bridge to within sight of the old Winter Palace on the river Neva in the summer of 1933. I had always been interested in Russian history, I went on, and having learned a little of the language at Oxford, I determined to see something of the country and its people under Stalin's rule. I did not buy a return ticket as I intended to come back to England by way of Finland, Sweden and Denmark, which in the event was what I did. This explanation, which obviously rang true, was accepted. In due course I was told to be ready to leave for Gibraltar as soon as possible in January, after I had made arrangements for another barrister in the same chambers to carry on my law practice. Besides tickets, I would be provided with a Foreign Office courier's passport to cover the diplomatic bag I would be carrying. Instead of mail, the bag would contain a light kettle, supplied by Steam Kettle Bill in Liverpool, for secretly steaming open letters.

One morning towards the middle of January 1940, as my wife was preparing to go off as usual to her job with the Fire Service, I was picked up at our Kensington flat in Queen's Gate by a War Office staff car, which took me to Northolt aerodrome where I was to board a military plane for Paris, the first stop on my somewhat circuitous journey to the Rock.

It was bitterly cold when we took off from Northolt. I expected we would fly direct to Paris but we unexpectedly came down at Abbeville, where snow was lying thick on the ground. There we learned that Paris was fog-bound and that we should have to continue our journey by train. In the railway carriage I found myself sitting next to Colonel (as he then was) Colin Gubbins, the future chief of SOE operations and training, who told me that he had recently been with the British Military Mission to Poland and had narrowly escaped capture in Warsaw, eventually reaching England through Hungary and the Balkans. Aged forty-four when we met, he immensely impressed me with his air of energy and vitality, and I took to him immediately. He told me that on the eve of the war Britain had sent 120 Hurricane fighters to Poland. They reached Denmark on 28 August, but were stopped there because of an unseemly squabble with the British Treasury as to who was to defray the cost of their transport, a mere £4,000. The result was that the aircraft were sent back from Denmark, whereas, had they reached Poland, the course of history might have been changed – particularly if the Poles had also withdrawn to the line of the rivers Vistula and Bug, which they might have held, at least for a time, so that Poland would in some degree have escaped her terrible baptism of fire at the hands of Goering's *Luftwaffe*.

In Paris, I dined with Maurice Petherick, a genial and loquacious Cornish MP, who was the British liaison with the French censorship. It was not too an exacting operation, I gathered, when I learned from him that it was really a police job carried out by the *deuxième bureau*, the counter-espionage organization, which, apart from keeping track of the correspondence of a few suspect individuals, made no attempt to examine the transit mails in bulk but simply held them up for a week or two on the assumption that any vital information they contained would have become valueless by the time they reached their destination.

From Paris I flew to Marseilles, where on my arrival I immediately went to the British Consulate-General, where I asked our man in charge, Sir Horace King, if he would kindly put my diplomatic bag in the consulate's strong-room pending my onward journey to Gibraltar.

'What's this?' he asked, as I handed him the bag which he realized obviously contained something lighter than official dispatches. 'A gas mask for the Governor?'

'Could be,' I replied. Tactfully he asked no further questions and put the bag in his safe.

I was held up for three days in Marseilles on the somewhat implausible pretext, so I thought, that the aircraft for Algiers could not take off because the ground at Marseilles airport was too hard, the runway being made of grass and not the usual tarmac. However we eventually made it to Algiers in three hours, thanks to a strong tail-wind. In Algiers the Consul asked no questions about my bag and I went off for the night to the Aletti Hotel, which was soon to become a nest of spies and informers.

Next morning, when I was due to fly on to Rabat and Tangier, the pilot of the French plane announced that he must go to Casablanca where the flight would terminate. 'Why?' I asked.

'Exceptional weather conditions over the Atlas mountains,' he replied.

'Weather conditions in flying are always exceptional,' I countered.

While waiting in a café in Casablanca for the bus to take me to Tangier, someone switched on the radio, and I recognized the voice of Édouard Daladier, the French Radical-Socialist Prime Minister and former exponent of the policy of appeasement, pleading for closer Anglo-French co-operation in the war. 'We shall win because we are the stronger,' he said. He sounded un-certain and vacillating, so that it came as no surprise when his government, riddled as it was by personal intrigues, fell shortly afterwards, to be followed by the German invasion of Belgium and Holland and the fatal breach in the seemingly impregnable Maginot Line. Daladier's defence, when he was subsequently tried on a charge of 'war guilt' by the Vichy regime, was that the National Assembly had placed excessive confidence in the judgment of elderly soldiers like Marshal Pétain and General Weygand. However, Daladier was to survive his trial, imprison-ment in a fortress, deportation to Germany, and a further spell of captivity in a Soviet prison in the Alps, before being released alive. The next time I heard the voice of France's 'Man of Munich' was at close quarters in the early 1950s in the Chamber of the Consultative Assembly of the Council of Europe (as the European Parliament at Strasbourg was then known) to which we were both delegates. Although a member of the National Assembly under the Fourth Republic, he had never again held ministerial rank, and by the time he reached Strasbourg he was a stout, red-faced, solitary man living on in a world in which, as one obituary notice eventually put it, even Munich was little more than a distant name.

My bus landed me in Tangier just in time to miss the thrice-weekly ferry to Gibraltar, so I had to spend two more nights in an hotel, this time in Tangier's opulent El Minzah, then under British ownership. When I finally reached the Rock on 31 January, I reckoned that the journey had taken me more than a week, so that it would have been much quicker to go by sea. However, my instructions were to go the long way round.

Gibraltar was then, and still is, a Crown Colony under the rule

The Rock of Gibraltar from the south-east, in 1940. Harbour and dockyard are on the left; part of the racecourse can be seen on the extreme right – this was later converted into an airfield. Beyond is mainland Spain.

of a British Governor, then assisted by a Legislative Council, now the House of Assembly, and a local ministerial government. The territory, which has belonged to Britain since 1704 when it was ceded to the Crown by Spain, has an area of just over two square miles with a population of approximately 26,000, and is part of the Spanish mainland. It has been a perennial source of dispute between Britain and Spain, although before the Spaniards closed the frontier with La Linea the situation favoured Spain, since 5,000 Spaniards who lived on the Spanish side came over every morning to work in the naval dockyard, returning home every evening, while many Gibraltarians also had their homes on the Spanish side, coming into their offices in Gibraltar every day. However, I soon discovered that the natives of Gibraltar are passionately attached to the British Crown and have no desire at all to be ruled by Spain.

On my arrival in Gibraltar I found that the Censorship detachment which had come out from England to examine the transit mails numbered about 200. It was headed by a soldier of the First World War, Captain Humphry Cotton-Minchin, whose personal assistant in effect I became, in addition to my secret work. Cotton-Minchin was extremely pleasant to work with and I eventually shared a house with him and his second-in-command, a brilliant linguist named H.M. ('Steve') Cowtan. Once, when I had to leave Cotton-Minchin to return to England to make a short progress report, he wrote to me: 'I miss you because you see things large as I do and because you are a delightful companion.' The majority of the censors, officially known as examiners, were women, and extremely efficient some of them were. In particular I remember Alethea Hayter, then an attractive and talented girl in her late twenties, who had previously worked for the British Council and who later wrote a couple of prize-winning literary biographies.

The Governor, General Sir Clive Liddell, was a firm friend to Censorship throughout our time on the Rock, as was his wife; and both Cotton-Minchin and I were frequent guests at Government House.[22] Gibraltar was a military garrison besides being a Royal Naval station, and although the Governor was in theory Commander-in-Chief of the forces, in reality they were commanded by a Brigadier and staff at Fortress Headquarters. As the Postal and Telegraph Censorship, overseas as well as at home, was under the control of the War Office at this time, the military authorities in Gibraltar at first wished us to be subordinate to them in every respect. However, shortly afterwards overall control was transferred to the Ministry of Information, upon which Fortress Headquarters became much more co-operative, on one occasion spontaneously providing a military guard after we had seized $800,000 in notes consigned from New York to Switzerland. The Censorship staff were also allowed to use the somewhat inadequately stocked garrison library. But relations could never be called cordial between the censors and the officers, as is illustrated by the following incident. Two of the censors happened to be in the gentleman's cloakroom of the library, when they overheard one officer remark to another: 'Gibraltar was quite habitable before the Censorship started up. Now you can't move without running up against some of these beastly censors!'

The two censors said nothing but waited in the passage outside for the officers to emerge. When they did so, one censor said to the other in a loud voice: 'What curious uniforms the lavatory attendants wear in this place!'

The naval authorities on the other hand, particularly the Contraband Control branch, were quicker to appreciate the importances of our work in examining the transit mails, and of course we were dependent on them for help in removing the mail bags from passing ships for examination. Here we had an invaluable liaison with the navy in the person of Edgar Kirby who I kept pressing should be given a commission in the RNVR, although I do not think he ever got it.

The majority of the Censorship staff worked in the King George V Memorial Hospital, which had recently been built and which was commandeered for the censors. It was a fairly convenient building, as it overlooked the south end of the inner harbour, the Royal Naval Dockyard, and the lunatic asylum from which frenzied outcries intermittently disturbed the more sensitive of the Censorship examiners. Some time later we had at very short notice, for some military reason, to move the main body of examiners and the secretariat from the Memorial Hospital. We found temporary quarters in the adjacent Loreto Convent, being allowed by the Catholic Bishop of Gibraltar to occupy the whole of the ground floor. The nuns were relegated to the upper (structural) regions, but the Bishop, who gave the double migration his blessing, made it a condition that no male member of the Censorship detachment 'should have access to the nuns'. When Cotton-Minchin and I had seen these good ladies, we had no difficulty in reassuring the Lord Bishop that he need not be unduly worried.

My immediate task was to get together a small team of Special Examiners to deal with diplomatic mail which could be secretly

Photographed in May 1940 on the roof of the King George V
Memorial Hospital, which was then serving as Censorship HQ in
Gibraltar: *(left to right)* the author; Mr H. M. Cowtan, Deputy Chief
Censor; Capt. H. Cotton-Minchin, Chief Censor; General Sir Clive
Liddell, KCB, DSO, Governor and Commander-in-Chief, Gibraltar.

opened, and to set up a miniature Room 99, on the Liverpool
model, in the porter's lodge of the Hospital. The most outstanding of the Special Examiners whom I chose was a remarkable
young woman of twenty-four, named Myrtle Winter, who had
been brought up in India, and could read and speak German,
French, Italian, Spanish, Dutch, and Persian. She was also an
expert photographer, a strong swimmer and a fine rider. At the
last race-meeting in Gibraltar before the racecourse was
converted into an airport, she astonished everyone by coming

second in the principal race. Peter Wilson, subsequently a most distinguished Chairman of Sotheby's, eventually came out from England and took charge of the Special Examiners, with valuable results.

An initial achievement was the execution of the Liverpool propaganda exercise in reverse, with, I imagine, a more useful outcome. At this time the Germans were sending a mass of anti-British and anti-Allied propaganda abroad, in English, to the United States, and in Spanish and Portuguese to Central and South America. It was mostly routed through neutral countries, notably Spain and Italy, where the covers were appropriately franked. After a number had been picked out by the ordinary examiners and quite rightly condemned, I asked Cotton-Minchin to have all future material of this kind held in their covers, which were now easily recognizable, and set aside for our use. What we did then was to have considerable amounts of anti-German propaganda printed in England (in those respective languages) and sent out to me. The letters with the original propaganda were secretly opened, our own propaganda was substituted, the letters were resealed as if they had never been opened and then sent on their way with their new contents. Thus, besides having an effective method of distributing our own propaganda, we had the satisfaction of knowing the Nazis were paying the postage for its delivery!

One diverting incident I remember concerning a letter which for some reason had been secretly opened. It was from a German girl in Germany to her boy-friend in Argentina. In addition to her undying love, this *fraülein* enclosed a reminder of herself to her loved one. It took the form of several pieces of her pubic hair. Somehow this amatory token got lost in Room 99. The question was, what to do now? My eye fell on a broom standing in the corner of the room. I suggested picking a few twigs from the broom and inserting them in the letter as a substitute for what had been lost. I sometimes wonder what the recipient of the loving missive thought about this curious change in his beloved's anatomy!

Many diplomatic bags passed through our hands, but although

Mr Peter Wilson, CBE, head of the Censorship 'Special Examiners' in Gibraltar and Bermuda; later chairman of Sotheby Parke Bernet.

we could open them, if necessary with the help of a trustworthy and expert lock-picker, we could not do much with the contents, the dispatches and letters usually being sealed with wax seals. We lacked the equipment to make replicas of the seals with plaster of Paris – with such equipment the seals could be melted and then reconstituted, the necessary impression being done with the plaster of Paris replica after the contents had been read and noted. Steam Kettle Bill in Room 99 in Liverpool had promised to train a girl and send her out as soon as possible. But, on her arrival, her training proved to have been too rapid, or else she had been unable to assimilate it in the time available; also she was of rather delicate physique and indulged in strenuous exercise both on the tennis court and in bed, where she carried on affairs with two married men at the same time. At all events she was not a success, at least in the Gibraltar Room 99. In the end we got the top expert in Liverpool, Mrs Davis who had done such work during the First World War. Unfortunately, she arrived so late that she only got down to work shortly before the Italians came into the war on the Nazi side and the Gibraltar Censorship detachment was ordered home. However, thanks largely to Mrs Davis's efforts, we did secure some most valuable intelligence of enemy plans before we had to leave the Rock. Meanwhile my wife had gone through an intensive course of training in Liverpool and proved a first-rate operator, but her talents were not destined to be employed in Gibraltar.

During the time that the Postal and Telegraph Censorship was under the War Office, the Controller was naturally a military man, a friendly bachelor Irish Brigadier from County Cork in his mid-sixties named Charles French, who had been on retired pay since 1924 and had now been 'dug out' for the Censorship job, to which the War Office did not seem to attach very much importance.[23] However, as soon as Censorship was put under the Ministry of Information, Edwin Herbert, later Lord Tangley, then aged forty-one and a partner in a well-known firm of City solicitors, assumed control as a civilian.[24] Brigadier French was consoled for the loss of the top Censorship job with the impressive title of Inspector General of Overseas Postal and Telegraph Censorship, and partly, perhaps, to get him out of the way when other changes were taking place in the higher echelons of Censorship at home it was decided that the first place the Brigadier should inspect would be Gibraltar. At the same time the headquarters organization was moved from Liverpool to London, to the Prudential Assurance Building in Holborn which had been taken over for the purpose. About the same time Frank Worthington retired as Chief Postal Censor, his place being taken by his Deputy, Charles des Graz, the then Chairman of Sotheby's.[25]

Brigadier French was accompanied on his mission by two other officers, of whom one was his ADC and the other was Freckles Wren, who now had the acting rank of Major. They arrived in Tangier by air on 8 April 1940, and as Cotton-Minchin and I anticipated that they would miss the Gibraltar boat, as I had done, we both went over to meet them. To our consternation we saw that they were in uniform when they stepped off the Air France plane, and we immediately urged them to change into civilian clothes, since Tangier at that time was an international zone and the place was a hotbed of German and Italian espionage, many of the agents being Spaniards. The Brigadier and his two companions immediately did as we suggested, but it was too late to escape notice, since the local Spanish agents reported to their employers in Berlin and Rome that the British had sent a reconnaissance mission to prepare the way for a British invasion of Spain. When we learned of this, Wren was rather uneasy that it would cause trouble with his MI6 superiors at home, but the rumours soon died down and the affair blew over. We were all comfortably accommodated in the El Minzah, and filled in the time waiting for the next boat by having general discussions on the work at Gibraltar and also learning something of the conditions in Tangier which, as Brigadier French described it in his subsequent report, 'was an international area where peaceful, but mutually suspicious, feelings are entertained by the Powers represented in that delectable area'. So far as local conditions went, we were well briefed by the British Consul-General for Tangier and the Spanish Protectorate of Morocco, Mr (later Sir) Alvery Gascoigne, who was afterwards British Ambassador in Moscow. While French and Cotton-Minchin talked with Gascoigne over dinner, Wren and I were able to sample some of the night-life of Tangier, which had its own peculiar character.[26]

When we reached Gibraltar, Brigadier French, who stayed in Government House went thoroughly into every aspect of the Censorship operations. He recommended that the detachment, whose importance he appreciated, should be increased to 600 strong, and because of the shortage of accommodation on the Rock should live and work on a ship which would serve for both purposes. The *Franconia*, a large liner, was earmarked for this, but before she could arrive Italy came into the war, consequently making most of the existing Censorship staff unnecessary and leading to their return to England. In the report which he submitted to the Director when he got back to the Prudential Building, the Brigadier was good enough to write in more flattering terms about myself than I felt I deserved, and he endorsed the War Office proposal that I should be given a temporary commission as a Captain and act as Military Adviser to the detachment and also as Security Officer, in liaison with the Security branch of the Gibraltar garrison. In the event, my commission did not come through until after I had got back to England, and it was to take a rather different form.

When we were at the El Minzah in Tangier, I noticed a woman hanging round the bar whom I guessed was a Spaniard and who seemed to be taking a particular interest in the presence of the Brigadier. Anyhow she aroused my suspicions, and as soon as French, his aide, and Wren had left Gibraltar, I took advantage of a week-end's leave to go over to Tangier and see if she was still around. She was, as I quickly discovered when ordering a drink at the El Minzah bar on the evening of my arrival. As I had surmised, she was a Spaniard, and in the course of our conversation, which was in Spanish, I gathered she had strong pro-Nazi sympathies which she made no attempt to hide. In due course I asked her to have dinner with me. She accepted the invitation eagerly but said she must first go to the Café Universal, as she was expecting a letter there. So I went along with her and sure enough she did pick up a letter, which she showed me. It offered her an engagement to appear as a cabaret dancer in a Gibraltar night-club provided she could get an official entry permit from the local police. By this time I was convinced she was a German agent, while she accepted my assurance that I was a southern Irishman who had been allowed to visit Gibraltar.

Over dinner she begged me to help her to get the permit, as I seemed to have some influence with the Gibraltar authorities. I told her I would do what I could. After an excellent meal washed down with Spanish brandy, she suggested I should go back with

her to her flat. Needless to say, I agreed and eventually we went
to bed together.

I woke up early, crept out of bed, while she was still asleep, and
went through her bag and other belongings, where I found clear
evidence that she was working for the Germans. I remember her
full name, but I need not reveal any further details except that she
was married, was a reasonably well-educated woman, and that her
first name was Encarnación. She was still sleeping when I left her
flat. I did not see her again. But a week or so later she turned up
in Gibraltar by the ferry, fully expecting to be allowed ashore.
The Immigration officer, who had been warned about her,
politely expressed his regrets that he had received instructions not
to let her have a landing permit. Sadly, she was obliged to return
to Tangier. Poor Encarnación, I thought, when I heard what had
happened. She had tried so hard!

Freckles Wren and I were both very sorry to miss the first night
of Eric Maschwitz's revue *New Faces*, which opened at the
Comedy Theatre, London, on 11 April, two days after Hitler
invaded Denmark and Norway. But my wife was there, as well as
others from the Liverpool Adelphi days, and some weeks later,
when things were beginning to 'hot up' on the Rock, I wrote to
Eric having heard details of how the opening had gone, particularly Judy Campbell's smash-hit *A Nightingale Sang in Berkeley
Square*. For Eric it must have been a wonderful night, since a year
earlier he had thought that his brief career in the theatre was at an
end.

I must congratulate you most warmly on the success of *New
Faces*, which I see from the papers which reach us in this
imperial outpost, after inordinate delay, is proving a
tremendous success. I gather too that you have a really
glamorous collection of lovelies. I must say that it does full
justice to what I shall call 'your flair for selecting such as are
easy on the eye', of which we had some proof in Liverpool!

I hope too that the Box Office receipts are as enormous as
you could wish and that you are living up to them. If it is the
break that I sincerely trust that it is, you certainly deserve it.

What about coming out here for some local colour for your next? Tangier, you will find, has definite possibilities, for apart from being the gateway to Africa, there is a nice little business always going on in spies, dope and white slaving. Also there is no Income Tax and your furniture would be safe from the distraint of the most pressing landlord!*

Of course by the time you receive this I may be back in England, since we have been instructed by the authorities here to stand by to be evacuated (horrible word which always reminds me of castor oil at school!), or it may be French Morocco or even Madagascar. We just don't know.

I won't bore you by writing shop. In any case I expect Freckles has shown you all my letters on official matters. It would be a pity in some ways if this detachment does close down – particularly from the point of view of our own little show, because with the long deferred advent of Mrs Davis we were getting down to things nicely. Even if the flap here does die down (the military wings are still beating hard), it seems that this place will lose much of its importance, as we are giving the Italians so much soft soap in that their principal ships are now passing through the Straits without detention and any mails being removed . . .

The change in the treatment of the Italian ships mentioned in this letter came about as the result of a change of policy at Cabinet level. The Italians had been complaining vociferously for some time at the diversion of their ships by Contraband Control in Gibraltar and the examination of the mails they were carrying. On 8 May – two days before the German invasion of Belgium and Holland, followed by the fall of the Chamberlain Government and the appointment of Winston Churchill as Prime Minister – Cotton-Minchin and I called on the Italian Consul General, the

---

*Eric Maschwitz had been in arrears with the rent of his London flat and his landlord had tried to seize his furniture in payment, but this had been prevented by the emergency legislation passed by Parliament where 'hardship' could be shown.

Marchese Theodoli, at his urgent request. The Marchese glowered furiously at us both as we entered his office. I happened to be carrying a black briefcase, and as soon as he caught sight of this he turned to Cotton-Minchin and said: 'I see you have brought your lawyer with you. I know what that means, I was ten years at Geneva!' Cotton-Minchin admitted that I was a member of the English Bar.

The Marchese began by saying that he had asked us to come because he was 'deeply concerned' at the manner in which mails were being removed from Italian ships and being detained and examined by the British Censorship in Gibraltar. 'I have to make a report to my Government,' he added somewhat naïvely, 'and I would like to know your reactions and observations so that I can avoid putting forward any argument to which there is a complete answer from you and your Government.'

'We are simply here to carry out instructions,' Cotton-Minchin replied. 'I am not at liberty to furnish information on any specific point, nor am I in a position to discuss the nicer legal points involved – but on this Dr Montgomery Hyde may have something to say.'

The Marchese thereupon flourished a piece of paper in my face which turned out to be an extract from the Hague Convention of 1907, guaranteeing the inviolability of the correspondence of neutrals or belligerents, and stating that in the event of a ship being detained the correspondence should be forwarded 'with the least possible delay'.

I pointed out that things had changed to some extent since 1907, and that both in the Great War and in the present one censorship of mail had been carried out by belligerents. As to mails carried in neutral vessels ordered by patrols into British ports like Gibraltar, or removed from ships on the high seas by the Royal Navy, the British Government had always claimed the right to examine all postal packets to search for contraband, and to see whether they contained anything which did not fall within the category of 'genuine postal correspondence'.

At this point the Marchese appeared to be boiling over with rage. 'Then why do you stop harmless postcards?' he asked, holding up a card. 'You cannot put any contraband in a postcard. You cannot put any gold there!'

My retort to this was that the examination of mails was regarded by the British Government as part of the exercise of the right of 'visit and search', and that all genuine postal correspondence was sent on by the next ship. I added – and here Cotton-Minchin supported me warmly – that a case could be argued for the proposition that Italian ships came into Gibraltar voluntarily, and therefore became subject to municipal law, thus falling entirely outside the scope of the Hague Convention article.

'Come in voluntarily!' the Marchese shouted. 'Not at all! Do you think Italian ships lose twenty-four hours here whenever they call just to get a view of the bay? Believe me, they have something better to do!'

In response to this outburst I observed quietly that in point of fact most Italian vessels came into Gibraltar of their own accord and therefore might be said to be 'voluntarily diverted'.

'What you mean,' said the Marchese, 'is that they come in because they know that, if they did not, they would be brought in forcibly.'

'That may well be,' I remarked. 'But I submit with the greatest respect that a case for voluntary diversion can be made out.'

'It is splitting a hair,' spluttered the irate Marchese.

'Yes,' Cotton-Minchin could not help adding, 'but rather a good hair!'

'You have the key of the gate,' said the Marchese in conclusion, meaning the Straits. 'It is *force majeure*. It is part of a series of pinpricks. My people won't stand for it much longer.' He then rose from his chair, thus bringing the acrimonious interview to an end.

A week later, after he had become Prime Minister and Minister of Defence, Churchill sent Mussolini a friendly message of goodwill hoping to persuade Italy to remain neutral. However the Italian Duce sent a cold reply reminding Churchill how the British Government had organized sanctions against Italy at the time of the invasion of Abyssinia. 'I remind you also of the real and actual state of servitude in which Italy finds herself in her own sea,' he added ominously. 'If it was to honour your signature that your Government declared war on Germany, you will understand that the same sense of honour and of respect for engagement assumed in the Italian-German Treaty guides Italian policy today and tomorrow in the face of any event whatsoever.'

The Admiralty, with Churchill's assent, now signalled Gibraltar to stop diverting Italian ships, both inward and outward bound. But such soft soap tactics were to prove of no avail, since the die had already been cast in Rome. On 13 May Mussolini told Count Ciano, his son-in-law and Foreign Minister, that he would declare war on France and Britain within a month. A fortnight later he was to let Hitler know that he would do so on any date after 5 June which was most favourable to the Führer. In the event Hitler asked that the declaration should be made five days later, and this was to be done.

One of the private letters which I wrote home at this time was to my kinsman Sir Mayson Beeton, whose mother Mrs Isabella Beeton was the authoress of the celebrated *Book of Cookery and Household Management*, the Victorian housewife's great standby and that of many of her successors. I had a great affection for Mayson Beeton, cemented by the fact that we were both members of the same Oxford College (Magdalen), and he had allowed me to go through his parents' papers with a view to writing a biography of them. I had spent many weekends at his house on St George's Hill near Walton-on-Thames in Surrey, and when the war broke out I asked him if I could leave copies of the six books I had written with him. He agreed, and we buried the books in a container in a hole which I dug in his garden. The rest of my private library, several thousands of books, I deposited in a London warehouse. Remarkably enough, all the books in the warehouse were to escape the ravages of the Blitz entirely and were in perfect condition when I collected them after the war, while the six copies of the books I had written were spoiled by the damp which had somehow impregnated the container in which they had been stored.[27] Incidentally it was on the strength of these six books that my name appeared for the first time in the British *Who's Who*, that invaluable work of reference which I have always thought should be regarded with some caution since the entrants are invited to write their own biographies. However undistinguished or obscure you subsequently become, your name always remains in successive editions unless you go to prison, when it is taken out, or until the time comes for your name to be transferred to *Who Was Who*.

The following extracts from my letter to Mayson Beeton give a fairly clear view of local conditions as well as of my overt activities with the Censorship:

4 Secretary's Lane, Gibraltar, 24 May 1940 . . . You may care to know a few things about the Censorship here. Up to the beginning of April we were examining Eastbound mails only – from North and South America. Since then we have been working on Westbound mails, it having taken the Cabinet exactly seven months to give their permission for this to be done. We examine neutral transit mail first, e.g. USA to Italy, as we cannot hold this up for long. Mails to and from Germany, on the other hand, we cannot handle here owing to the lack of necessary staff and we send them to England by the first available boat. All letters which we examine have in theory labels attached to show that they have been opened at this point, but we have from time to time in the interests of policy to let certain letters go forward without bearing any external signs of censorship . . . We detain and condemn a certain number of letters, but I personally, viewing as I do the Censorship from the Intelligence as well as the Security stand-point, am in favour of letting as much go forward as possible once the relevent information has been extracted. At the moment we have a staff of about 230, but this number is decidedly inadequate for dealing with all the mails we should like to handle . . .

Of course, if Italy relinquishes her neutrality, we shall cease to have any value as a censorship point. Already certain sections of the civilian population have been compulsorily evacuated, some to French Morocco and others to England. Whether we shall all eventually go is a question . . . From reports which we receive the Italian people are most adverse to the idea of fighting.

There is little which I can tell you about this part of the world, as you have a fairly intimate knowledge of it. I have ridden into Spain a few times but have not made any extended excursions. That country is, so far as we can judge here, in anything but a happy condition internally. There is a great shortage of food and grave discontent in many quarters. There are at least 10,000 German troops there, and some of them openly wearing uniform. At Algeciras there is a German Gestapo agent who seems to have his headquarters at the Christina Hotel, whence he reports all comings and goings to his Government. The Germans seem to be more or less in charge of the aerodromes at Seville and Malaga, which are uncomfortably close to us for a bombing attack.

French Morocco presents a rather more pleasing picture. I have been to Rabat and Casablanca besides flying across Morocco to Oran and Algiers, and have seen something of French methods of administration. I must say they have done wonders. The Sultan has been left with all his former prestige, while his power is exercised by the French, who have introduced most up-to-date public services and other economic and material improvements.

Gibraltar by contrast is no great credit to our colonial administration. Much of its unattractive complexion can be traced to the fact that it has been a fortress and garrison town too long. Fortunately it is a healthy station . . . There is not a good bookshop in the place, although the population is considerably larger than that of Oxford, and the Garrison Library does not go much beyond military manuals, *Leaves from a Staff Officer's Diary*, and so forth.

The Chief Censor and myself share a house in Secretary's Lane which is quite close to Government House. It is between the Colonial Secretary's residence and Fortress Headquarters. It is a fine colonial mansion built about the time of the 'Great Siege' of 1779–83. We have two beautiful fireplaces of which I am very covetous. You would like them.

It is of course rather depressing to think that we have been in occupation of this place for nearly 240 years and yet few of the natives can speak English. I am quite certain that were the French to take over for five years everyone would be able to speak French.

At the moment we are living in a definite state of tension . . . We do not know what our fate will be, but presumably if and when we move, it will be as a detachment.

About my other work I can tell you nothing for obvious reasons, except that it is intensely interesting and very different from what I have been doing in the past few years . . .

I used to ride early in the morning on the racecourse, besides sometimes going into Spain. One morning, a few days after I had written to Mayson Beeton, I went out with one of the Censorship girls who was a good rider, but unfortunately we did not realize that work had begun to convert the racecourse into an airport. As we galloped along we suddenly saw a large cavity which had been dug in the middle of the course and we could not avoid it, with the result that we went in full tilt. It was a miracle that the horses' legs were not broken, but as luck would have it they escaped without injury and were not even lamed. As for me I got up with a broken collar-bone. But it was a perfectly clean fracture and apart from the bother of having my right arm strapped up I could carry on with my work just as usual. On the other hand my companion was rather badly concussed, and had to lie up for ten days in a darkened room, but she eventually recovered and was none the worse for the experience.

Meanwhile the mails were running very short. 'The *Rex* has had her outward bound sailing this week cancelled,' I wrote to Freckles Wren on 1 June, 'and with her and all the other Italian ships either tied up in their own ports or in South American waters, it rather looks as if the zero hour is approaching.' My surmise was correct. On 10 June 1940, Italy declared war on France and Britain. Within two hours of the official announcement, orders were received from Censorship Headquarters in

London to evacuate the Gibraltar detachment and proceed by the first available boat to England.

'We had some wild excitement in the town last night after the news about Italy had circulated,' I wrote to Freckles Wren on 11 June:

> One Italian ship, a tanker, scuttled herself in the bay, and a good proportion of the crew managed to get off in the lifeboats to Spain. Another vessel, carrying a cargo of timber, was set alight by the crew, but the conflagration was eventually put out. Both incidents, I think show shocking negligence on the part of the Port authorities. Then, Andrews, [one of the Special Examiners] whom you met here, was shut up in his flat which happens to be above that of the Italian Consul. He had a lady dining with him and she was obliged to spend the night in the apartment. Although they made a pretence of embarrassment, I do not think either of them really objected to the enforced incarceration!

There was a ship already in the port of Gibraltar, the *Al Rawdah*, 3,500 tons, which the local authorities thought might be suitable for the embarkation of the Censorship contingent, and we sailed in her two days later, the day before the Germans entered Paris after the fall of France. On our last day, while I was busy packing up the Room 99 equipment, Cotton-Minchin had lunch *en famille* with the Governor and Lady Liddell. 'It was plain that Sir Clive was ill at ease about the boat,' Cotton-Minchin told me afterwards, 'but as I had not seen her, I could only assure him that my people were as able to take orders as anyone else. If either the naval or military authorities had put forward any other alternative, I know that the Governor would have been both relieved and delighted.' In the event Cotton-Minchin's fears were amply confirmed. 'It can hardly be refuted that the military authorities were so keen on getting rid of us that they cared not a jot for any other considerations,' he wrote later. 'The ship was not a proper one for the transport of some 175 civil servants who on account of their qualifications could not easily be replaced. Even the ''Q'' officer responsible for transport at Battle Headquarters, as Fortress Headquarters had now become, was appalled at the conditions, but it was only later that I knew that we were almost entirely unprotected and were dependent on the collective safety of being one of a convoy.'

The *Al Rawdah* was about thirty years old and had originally been used for carrying pilgrims to Mecca in the service of an Egyptian line. At the outbreak of the war she had been converted into a troop-ship, had been brought to Gibraltar with the object of evacuating the civil population to Casablanca, and had been used for this purpose. She did not look to me to be particularly clean, and I soon discovered abundant evidence of what might be euphemistically described as 'foreign bodies' on board. In addition she was a curious mixture, flying the French flag, commanded by an English Master (Captain Harvey) with English officers, and worked by a Lascar crew. She had accommodation for only 50 first-class passengers, but in fact there were more than 200 passengers on board, of whom 175, including 58 women, belonged to the Censorship detachment. They included a retired Royal Naval Commander, G. L. Browne, who had recently come out to Gibraltar as the detachment's naval adviser, and on this terrifying voyage his advice and assistance to the ship's Master were to prove invaluable. The women naturally occupied the cabins and most of the men slept at night in hammocks slung on the troop-deck, that is, when they could get any sleep. Fortunately I had been given a cabin, partly because my right arm was still strapped up following my riding accident. The ship possessed no guns or other armament, and she had not been 'degaussed', i.e. rendered impervious to magnetic mines.

We sailed in convoy, twenty-one ships in all, the convoy on its departure from Gibraltar being escorted by one destroyer and one sloop. The progress of the convoy – six knots an hour – could be clearly observed from the Spanish coast. It seems likely that the German Gestapo agent in Algeciras passed on this information either to his own people or to the Italians. Indeed the convoy's route may even have been known to the enemy in advance, since submarines were waiting to attack the convoy at two points on the route.

For the first four days the voyage was uneventful, except that it blew quite hard and most of the passengers were seasick, including the ship's doctor who found it difficult to attend to his duties in these circumstances. Nevertheless those of us who knew French – and most of us did – were greatly heartened to hear the news over the radio of General de Gaulle's dramatic escape from France to England, followed by his moving broadcast to his fellow countrymen and women to resist the common enemy. 'The flame of French Resistance must not and shall not die,' he said. He was forthwith to make himself head of the Free French and he was to be immediately recognized as such by the Churchill Government. So it happened, on the same day as the aged Marshal Pétain signed the humiliating armistice with the Germans.

During the evening of 18 June when we were about 120 miles west of Cape Finisterre, the first alarm was given on the *Al Rawdah*. Our destroyer escort had disappeared some time in the previous night, presumably having received orders to return to Gibraltar. As our sole protection we were left with the sloop, which only carried a few guns on her upper deck. This later struck me as rather curious, since it was known that enemy submarines were operating in this particular area and a distress message had been received by our ship's radio operator from a lone vessel which had been torpedoed and sunk at this very spot twenty-four hours earlier.

I went below about 11 p.m., and as I was undressing I heard a signal given by one of the other ships in the convoy on her siren. I did not know what it meant, but a few minutes later Edgar Kirby, the detachment's liaison with Contraband Control, came into my cabin and said that a submarine had been sighted by the vessel, which had sounded her siren and indicated that a torpedo had been seen on her starboard bow. Meanwhile the Commodore in charge of the convoy signalled all the vessels to make an emergency turn to starboard. Very lights were sent up but there was nothing further to report, as the submarine had disappeared.

About midnight the return to normal course was signalled, and the convoy had scarcely come round to that course when the ship immediately ahead of us was struck by a torpedo. I heard the explosion very clearly from my cabin and immediately afterwards our own ship's alarm sounded.

Everyone went to boat-stations in an orderly fashion, while speed was reduced. We had previously increased to full speed – twelve knots, the maximum of which the *Al Rawdah* was capable of doing – when the ship ahead of ours had been hit. The passengers all stood by the lifeboats with their lifebelts on, but the order was not given to get into the boats as we expected. It was a bright night, the moon being almost full and the water calm, an ideal night for a submarine attack. After a while, as nothing more was seen, we were allowed to go below but not to turn in, and we were also told to keep our lifebelts on.

About 1 a.m. the Quartermaster on the bridge reported the track of a torpedo crossing astern from the port to the starboard side of our vessel. But no one else apparently saw it. However, about an hour later Captain Harvey and several other officers on the bridge, including Commander Browne, sighted the wake of a torpedo crossing our bows from the starboard side at very close range. There can be no doubt that it was aimed at us, since a few minutes afterwards it struck a ship to port of ours. I heard the explosion quite clearly. Then the signal was made on our siren and the alarm sounded. We all went again to our boat-stations, and many of us could see the torpedoed ship sinking rapidly; she went down in about three minutes. Soon afterwards we passed a large patch of oil on our port beam and we heard agonizing cries from people struggling in the water. But we were not allowed to stop, and could only pray that some survivors would be picked up by the sloop.

For the next hour and a half we stood by our boat-stations while the ship went through a complicated series of manoeuvres in an attempt to avoid being struck by another torpedo. At first the order 'Full steam ahead' came from the bridge, but very soon afterwards the order was given to reduce speed. Since we had got up a lot of steam, it was necessary, in order to obey this order, to let the steam escape to prevent the ship's boilers from bursting. The noise of the escaping steam added to the terrors of that unforgettable night.

My lifeboat was No 3 on the starboard side, but at intervals during the alarm period I walked about the deck and from the raised portion above the engine-room I got a view of what happened to port. I had just clambered up to this position, about 2.40 a.m., when I saw one of the ships in the convoy being torpedoed at very short range. The torpedo exploded with an enormous red flash on contact and practically blew the ship out of the water. Immediately there was another terrific explosion, probably owing to the boilers bursting, and she literally split in half. The ship went down in about a minute. Again I heard voices of distress coming from the water, but it was not possible for us to stop and look for survivors.

One of the censors with whom I had become friendly in Gibraltar was convinced that the next few minutes would be his last. He came up and solemnly shook hands, saying, 'It is a great pleasure to have known you. I just wanted to say good-bye for the last time.' I replied simply, 'Never say die!'

We had altered course to about south by compass when the Commodore rather belatedly, I thought, gave the signal 'Convoy Scatter Chased By Submarines'. Commander Browne, who was on the bridge throughout the attack, advised Captain Harvey to resume our previous northerly course. This we did, in a zig-zag manner. With the exception of two or three other ships, the rest of the convoy continued to go south. After a while we altered our course to westward and made a considerable detour into the Atlantic, increasing our speed to the maximum twelve knots. During the remainder of that day, 19 June, nothing of any consequence was seen. In addition to the normal ship's watch, members of the Censorship detachment volunteered to keep a look-out for submarines and floating mines. Two were posted fore and aft each day for the remainder of the voyage.

Before the convoy sailed from Gibraltar, a rendezvous had been arranged in the event of an enemy attack, or in case any one of the ships became separated from the convoy for any reason. The rendezvous had been fixed for 12 noon on 21 June at a point approximately 150 miles south-west of Ushant island off the coast of Brittany. At the appointed hour we were sixteen miles due west of the rendezvous. Our Captain was at first inclined to make direct for the rendezvous on the chance that we might meet with some of the convoy who might also be late. Commander Browne, on the other hand, was for steering a converging course, pointing out that, whether any of the other ships were late or not, we should in all probability be able to catch up with them later in the day. Commander Browne's advice was followed. Providence indeed seemed to be watching over us, since we heard a few hours later over the ship's radio that three of the ships which turned up at the rendezvous shortly after the appointed time were attacked by submarines, who were lying in wait for them. Apparently they must have heard of the location of the rendezvous through a leak in Gibraltar. One of the three ships was torpedoed and sunk, but the other two succeeded in escaping towards the English Channel. The Captain now decided to make for the nearest port consistent with safety, which was Milford Haven in Wales, although our actual port of destination was Liverpool. We were considerably cheered by this news, and still more cheered the same evening when we sighted a British bomber aircraft on a reconnaissance flight; as the aircraft circled round our ship we were able to exchange signals.

All was well until about 1.20 p.m. on the following day, 22 June, when we were about half-way across the Bristol Channel. I was at lunch in the forward saloon when the alarm suddenly sounded. Once more everyone went to boat-stations, the reason for the alarm being that the periscope of a submarine had been sighted about 700 yards off our starboard bow. It seemed to those on the bridge that the submarine would attack us at any moment. The Captain gave the order for passengers to get into the boats. This was done and the lashings were cut away preparatory to lowering the boats.

It was a bright, sunny afternoon with little wind, and the sea was quite calm. We increased speed to the maximum, keeping on a zig-zag course, although we expected the impact of a torpedo at any moment. The Captain now wished to abandon ship and was on the point of giving the order when Commander Browne, who was on the bridge with him, persuaded him not to do so, or at least to defer the order for some minutes. The Quartermaster later told me that he actually saw the submarine's conning tower, which gave him the impression that the U-boat was about to fire. Everyone was remarkably cool and there were no signs of panic anywhere. Cotton-Minchin, who very properly decided, with the Captain's approval, not to get into his boat until it was in the water and the other members of the detachment safely in their boats, walked about the deck and bridge with his camera, taking photographs of the bizarre but nevertheless rather frightening scene.

After about seven minutes the periscope disappeared from the surface, but we remained in the boats for a little over an hour, still expecting to be attacked. I imagine the reason we were not attacked was because the submarine commander thought that we were armed. We were then allowed to get out of the boats, but were asked to remain on deck with our lifebelts on. There we remained until Milford Haven was sighted and we passed the harbour boom.

Some thirty years later I was strongly reminded of this incident in the voyage, when I went out to the West Indies on a German ship chartered by the Geest Line which sailed from the nearby port of Barry. After we had gone through the Bristol Channel with a pilot, the German Captain remarked to me: 'You know, I didn't really need a pilot for that stretch of water.'

'How is that?' I asked.

'Well,' he answered, 'I happen to know the Bristol Channel very well as I commanded a German submarine during the last war and for the greater part of four years I lay in the bed of the channel waiting to torpedo British merchant ships!'

Looking back, I could not help wondering whether the dread periscope which was sighted in the afternoon of 22 June, 1940, belonged to his U-boat.

To return to Milford Haven. On our arrival, the Captain sent a signal to the Chief of the Naval Staff ashore requesting instruc-

Sir Edwin Herbert (later Lord Tangley), Director-General of Postal and
Telegraph Censorship 1940–45.

tions. About two hours later we received a message that we were
to proceed the same night to Liverpool, which was our port of
destination. This caused general consternation, since the Captain
was naturally anxious not to risk another night at sea with such a
large complement of passengers with their particular talents.
However, he gave orders that we were to be ready to sail at midnight after we had taken a pilot on board to guide the ship
through the boom. Whether it happened by accident or design I

do not know, but the pilot failed to appear. Nor was there any sign of him by ten o'clock the following morning, when we were still tied up in Milford Haven harbour. However, shortly after this, fresh instructions were signalled from ashore to the effect that the passengers should be disembarked later the same day.

In the early afternoon Cotton-Minchin asked Commander Browne and myself to go ashore in advance of the main party, which we did. On landing we reported to the Chief of Naval Staff and he informed us that a special train was being dispatched to take the whole of the Censorship detachment to London. In due course we boarded the train and arrived at Paddington Station at 4.30 a.m. on 23 June. There we were met by Edwin Herbert, the Director, and a number of wives, whom the Director had kindly forewarned. It was a happy reunion for all of us.

2

The Bermuda Triangle

AFTER a few days' leave at home, I returned to St Ermin's and also kept in touch with Censorship Headquarters in the Prudential building. Following the heroism of the British expeditionary force on the Dunkirk beaches, the fall of France and the division of the country into occupied and unoccupied zones, it was clear that Hitler's next objective would be Great Britain. Indeed the Führer issued a directive to the German armed forces to this effect on 16 July, 1940:

> As England, in spite of the hopelessness of her military position, has so far shown herself unwilling to come to any compromise, I have decided to begin to prepare for, and if necessary to carry out an invasion of England . . . if necessary the island will be occupied.

Preparations for the invasion were ordered to be completed by the middle of August, and the operation was given the code-name 'Sea Lion'.[1]

Meanwhile this directive had been anticipated by Laurence Grand, and a good deal of time was taken up at St Ermin's in preparing to organize 'left behind' parties which would carry out sabotage and otherwise harass the enemy – assuming the occupation operation succeeded. While Grand was able to convince the military high-ups that this kind of guerilla warfare was fully justified, events moved with such swiftness that there was insufficient time to build up an effective sabotage organization, although a few members of Section D were sent to key spots. One of them was Francis Ogilvy, who was dispatched to Scotland and wrote to me privately from Perth, inviting me to join him as his assistant. Reluctantly I refused, as I greatly liked Francis. I replied on 3 July from St Ermin's, 'We *must* have the best man possible to help you, and quite frankly I do not think that my local knowledge could be held in any way to justify my coming to you.' I went on:

If it were Northern Ireland I should be very much more suitable, since I know that part of the world intimately and have many connections there, official and otherwise. My visits to Scotland have been confined to staying in a few people's houses, and brief holidays, golfing, etc. I really don't know the country and its people as you do and as your assistant undoubtedly should.

At the moment I am spending my mornings in the Censorship and my afternoons here trying to get out a diverting propaganda story, or rather to supply the material for the story which Val Gielgud is going to write. There is a possibility that I may go to Bermuda as Cotton-Minchin is taking a Censorship Detachment out there, but nothing has been decided yet. There is also an idea that I may be kept in London to do the work that Norman Hope has been doing before his disappearance. He is still missing.

Val Gielgud was the actor John Gielgud's elder brother and was Head of Sound Drama at the BBC for many years, besides being a dramatist in his own right. Norman Hope, another member of Section D, had gone over to France to rescue Madame de Gaulle, and having got her to England he returned to France on a similar mission, from which he was never to return. He was Section D's first casualty.[2]

What Norman Hope had been doing before his Scarlet Pimpernel excursions I have forgotten. However, in connection with Francis Ogilvy, I do remember that, as another colleague put it, one of D's emissaries arrived, 'complete with black hat and striped trousers, in a remote Scottish village, and, on asking the post-master if he would accept a parcel of stores, was promptly handed over to the police'. It was shortly after this, in fact on the same date as Hitler's invasion directive, that Churchill put Special Operations under Dr Hugh Dalton as Minister of Economic Warfare. The new operational chief was Sir Frank Nelson, a successful business man and former Conservative MP, and it was announced that Section D's activities should in future be shared between him and Laurence Grand. This arrangement obviously could not last long, and after a few days Grand returned to his sapper duties, in which he was to end up as Director of Fortifications at the War Office.[3] Section D thus came to an end, while its activities were absorbed in the new SOE which had its headquarters at 64 Baker Street.

In view of my work at Gibraltar and the experience I had gained there in the censorship of transit mails, it was eventually decided that I should join the detachment Cotton-Minchin was taking out to Bermuda early in August. At the same time I was commissioned in the Intelligence Corps with the acting rank of Captain, and duly collected a steel helmet and a revolver from the War Office, so that I could, if necessary, appear in uniform in my newly designated post of Security Officer attached to the Censorship in Bermuda, where we expected to play a much bigger and more important role than we had done in Gibraltar.

Laurence Grand's departure, which coincided with the abolition of Section D, was largely due to the machinations of Claude Dansey and his assistant David Boyle at MI6 headquarters in Broadway, and their dislike of Grand extended to many of his henchmen who now found a haven in Baker Street. I seem to have been originally earmarked for SOE, and for some time I found myself getting a salary from both SOE and SIS, in addition to the army. However, in view of my approved position as liaison with the Bermuda Censorship, I was told that officially I still belonged to MI6 and should report directly to David Boyle. I met him briefly in the Broadway office for final instructions before I left England. He struck me as a somewhat unctuous character who worked hard to ingratiate himself with Dansey and C.

I had heard that a new Passport Control Officer had been appointed in New York, a Canadian called William Stephenson, code name Intrepid, with a wide-ranging brief from the Prime

Minister himself; at the same time he was to represent SOE, and later MI5 as well as MI6. When I asked Boyle whether I should repeat to Stephenson any secret information of Anglo-American interest which I discovered from Censorship and Contraband Control sources, Boyle replied that I must on no account communicate with Stephenson without his (Boyle's) express authority. I said nothing, but I gathered from Boyle's manner that he disliked Stephenson as much as his chief Dansey did. C himself was also wary of Stephenson whose appointment had been forced upon him by the Prime Minister; hence C attached a full-time professional MI6 officer Colonel Charles Howard ('Dick') Ellis to Stephenson's embryo organization in New York. He hoped that Ellis would keep Stephenson 'on the right lines' in accordance with the traditions of the service of which the un-orthodox Canadian, a millionaire who was doing the job without pay, had hitherto not formed a particularly high opinion. The only MI6 representative in New York before Stephenson's arrival was Walter Bell, about the same age as myself, who had been an Acting Vice-Consul there since 1935. Many years later, after Ellis had died, the journalist Chapman Pincher suggested in a controversial book, *Their Trade is Treachery*, that Ellis was a double agent who worked for the Germans, and also for the Russians whose language he spoke fluently.[4] But more of this later.

On 5 August, our party (numbering 108, and later to be considerably enlarged) embarked at Liverpool on board the RMS *Mataroa* of the Shaw Saville Albion line. I was glad that Peter Wilson and Myrtle Winter were included. We expected to sail the same night but for some reason did not weigh anchor until 10 o'clock next morning. Meanwhile an awkward matter of discipline arose. One of the male censors came on board drunk, having been noticed in this condition by one of the Immigration officers in port, and he behaved in a most unpleasant manner during the night in the cabin which he shared with another male censor, insisting on smoking a pipe and refusing to have the fan working so that the cabin was without ventilation. Both Cotton-Minchin and I visited him in his cabin, where we found him babbling away incoherently. It was obvious that he was unfit for duty and that he would be the cause of grave difficulties if he were allowed to continue on the voyage. This was reported to the Captain, who told us that he had orders to call at Milford Haven to pick up some cargo and we could put him ashore there. When the censor was told of this decision, he made no objection and assured us that he was willing to work anywhere, even at Milford Haven, if this was necessary. What happened to him after he was landed I never discovered, but he would have certainly proved a liability if he had come on with the rest of us to Bermuda.

We then went back to the Irish Sea, and steered a northerly course. Some depth charges were dropped, and I was told by one of the ship's officers that there was a submarine in the neighbourhood. Throughout the whole of that day we were escorted by several RAF fighter aircraft, since it was thought that we were being followed by Nazi planes owing to the fact that the *Mataroa* was carrying a considerable cargo of aircraft to New Zealand, whither she was due to proceed after disembarking our contingent at Bermuda. Since we were not sailing in convoy, the ship was able to maintain a good speed, although we zig-zagged a lot. At all events the voyage was uneventful, and we dropped anchor in Hamilton harbour, Bermuda, on the morning of the 21st, just a fortnight after leaving Milford Haven. The approach to the capital, past the smaller coral islands and reefs in the Great Sound, is a breathtaking experience for every traveller who makes it and sees Shakespeare's 'still vex'd Bermoothes' for the first time. I know it was for me. On disembarking we were told that we had just missed the Duke and Duchess of Windsor who had spent the previous week on the island, having stopped on their way to the Bahamas of which the Duke had been appointed Governor. Their stay, I gathered, had been something of an embarrassment at Government House, where fifty-eight pieces of luggage and three dogs had had to be accommodated, besides the royal visitors. 'We have so much baggage,' wailed the Duchess 'but it doesn't contain the right things.' I was later to meet the Duke and Duchess in Nassau, where their baggage had been reinforced by fourteen additional pieces, including a trailer. 'Every refugee

Government House, Bermuda, 1940. It was completed in 1886, when
the capital was transferred to Hamilton from St George's.

has a trailer,' was the Duchess's sage comment.

The Governor and Commander-in-Chief of Bermuda at this
time was Lieutenant-General Sir Denis Bernard, a bachelor Irish
landowner from Galway, who had been to Eton and Sandhurst
and who was a professional soldier with a very distinguished
record in the First World War. Now rising fifty-eight, this was
to be his last official appointment, as he was shortly due to
retire. From the outset he was to prove as helpful and coopera-
tive with the new arrivals as Sir Clive Liddell had been in
Gibraltar.[5] To meet us at the quayside, he sent his twenty-one-
year-old ADC Lieutenant Frank Giles, who was later to leave
the public service for journalism and is now editor of the London
Sunday Times. He was to prove equally helpful. We were also
met by the second military officer, Colonel Roger Swire, who
combined the post of Commander of the Royal Engineers with

that of Chief Censor. He had a small staff who were censoring the local terminal mails, but they had proved quite incapable of dealing with the transit mails which were on board the Pan American Clipper seaplanes calling at Bermuda, besides the ships of the American Export line and other neutral vessels which called for the purpose of contraband control. Swire appeared to be under the impression that he was to be in charge of the 'imperial' detachment. Fortunately Charles des Graz, who had recently become Chief Postal Censor for the Western Area, was in Bermuda, having come down from his headquarters in New York, and he also welcomed us. In addition, des Graz tactfully explained to Swire, who knew nothing of the technique of examining transit mails but nevertheless was Chief Censor, that while there was no objection to his being nominally in charge, he (des Graz) hoped that Cotton-Minchin would be given a free hand to get things going without interference, that the Director Mr Herbert would soon be visiting the island, and that a senior and highly experienced civilian censor would also be coming out from England and would be taking control. Swire, who might have proved difficult, eventually saw the point, and if he lacked enthusiasm and a sense of humour at least he gave us little trouble.

Bermuda's inhabitants were proud of the fact that the island, or rather the collection of small islands which made up the Bermudas, as they were first called, was Britain's oldest colony, with a popularly elected House of Assembly going back over three centuries. Unfortunately its economy depended almost entirely on the tourist trade from the United States and Canada, being a particular favourite with honeymoon couples, and tourism had virtually ceased on the outbreak of the war. Consequently the influx of the censors from England, increased by subsequent reinforcements, was to prove of considerable benefit to the colony's languishing economy. Part of Bermuda's old-world atmosphere, which was not altogether an unmixed blessing, was that there were no motor-cars. Apart from an electric tram which traversed a part of the main island, public transport was limited to ferries and horse-drawn buggies (which were very

(On the rostrum) Charles Geoffrey des Graz, CBE, Chief Postal Censor and Director of Censorship in the Western Area during the war. He was chairman of Sotheby's from 1949 until his death in 1953.

expensive) and push bicycles (which most of us used). Indeed my earliest and keenest memory of Bermuda, which has never left me, is that one always seemed to be pedalling up hill against the wind. The islanders were also dependent on rain-water, since there were no wells, and the water was drained off the houses' characteristic sloping white roofs into catchments. When there was a drought, which sometimes happened, fresh water had to be imported from the United States. Although Bermuda consists of more than a hundred islands, of which only twenty are inhabited, the total area covered is only just over twenty square miles, with a population of about half a million, the majority of whom are black. When we arrived, the local cedar trees were prolific and were much used in boat- and ship-building, but during the war they were almost entirely destroyed by blight. When I had any time off, I used to sail a small dinghy which was made of this wood.

Besides the House of Assembly with its forty MPs there was a Legislative Council, a kind of Upper House of eleven nominated members presided over by the Governor, which had the power of initiating legislation, but more often approved or rejected the measures which originated in the House of Assembly. As the second military officer and CRE, Swire was a member of the Legislative Council, as were the Colonial Secretary (Mr E. T. Dutton), the Colonial Treasurer (Mr Eldon Trimingham), and the Attorney General (Mr Trounsell Gilbert). During my time in Bermuda I had a good deal to do with the last three, particularly Gilbert, who was later Chief Justice of Bermuda, and with whom my friendship was to last until his death.

Cotton-Minchin and I had our first taste of Bermudian hospitality a few days after our arrival, when Mr Tucker, the manager of the Bank of Bermuda, gave a large lunch party for us at the Yacht Club, where we met the Speaker of the House of Assembly and half a dozen other members, as well as Mr Eldon Trimingham and Mr Howard Trott, who both belonged to the Legislative Council and were later knighted. Howard Trott was, besides, a rich man who owned the Princess, Inverurie and other hotels on the island. Somewhat pointedly, I thought, Colonel Swire had not been invited, and in the course of the lunch quite an outspoken attack was made upon him. As Cotton-Minchin remarked afterwards, 'it was only too evident that the company then present was very far from satisfied with Censorship in Bermuda'. However, I was not unduly worried about Swire as I knew that his nominal control over the censorship of transit mails would soon be terminated, as indeed it was. Personally I had no difficulties with Swire as the colony's senior military officer, and when it was suggested that I should be invited to sit on the Intelligence Committee, which met weekly under the chairmanship of the senior Naval Intelligence officer to consider local defence security matters, Swire welcomed me along with the other members, who included the Commissioner of Police

Front Street, Hamilton, Bermuda in 1940: many ships (such as the one here belonging to the Furness Withy Line) docked off the street for customs and mail examination.

and the Chief Immigration Officer. After a while this Committee became rather unwieldy and ineffective, and the Colonial Secretary, who guessed or had been told that I was working for MI6 in addition to my other duties, approached me to know whether I was prepared to conduct confidential investigations on my own account with the assistance of the local police, and report direct to the Governor. This I agreed to do.

At first we were accommodated both for work and living in the Inverurie, a long, low, two-storey hotel across the Sound in Paget, while we had our meals in the Belmont Hotel in the neighbouring parish of Warwick. This was not at all satisfactory, since the meals in the Belmont consisted for the most part of outsize steaks more suited to American tourists than ration-conscious English. From my own work point of view, I found the Inverurie quite tolerable. 'I am very satisfied with my own particular show,' I wrote to Freckles Wren at the end of my first week there. 'We have got three rooms interconnecting which accommodate Special Examiners, Room 99 with photography, and myself . . . Charles des Graz is very pleased that we have come out and are already under way . . . I think we are going to get some good stuff out of the mails and we are all very enthusiastic.' However, as a whole the Censorship staff was so cramped for space in the Inverurie that Swire reported to the Legislative Council that we should be moved to the more commodious Princess Hotel in Hamilton for work. The move was made on 22 September, after a month in the Inverurie, and it coincided with the arrival of 200 more Censorship examiners from England. At the same time the Bermudiana Hotel was taken over for living quarters and meals, except for those, like my wife and myself and a few others, who preferred to live in rented accommodation. At first we shared a house at Salt Kettle near the Inverurie and the ferry to Hamilton. Eventually Dorothy and I found a charming furnished house in the Pitt's Bay Road called Granados, a few minutes by bicycle from the Princess, and we moved in. This move was to be the prelude to many exciting adventures and experiences during the next three-and-a-half years.

During the months immediately following the outbreak of the war, the United States protested strongly at Britain's claim to examine American mails and divert American ships to British ports for the purpose of examining their cargoes to see if they contained any contraband articles ultimately destined for Germany. Many acrimonious discussions on this subject took place between President Roosevelt's Secretary of State, Cordell Hull, and the British Ambassador in Washington, Lord Lothian. 'British censorship of American mails proved a lively focus of contention,' Cordell Hull wrote in retrospect. 'We admitted

The Princess Hotel in Hamilton, Bermuda, which was the headquarters of the Bermuda Censorship 1940–44. The part on the right
has been considerably rebuilt since then.

Britain's right to censor mails normally passing through the
United Kingdom for transmission to their final destination, but
refused to admit her right to interfere with American mails on
American or other neutral ships on the high seas, or to censor
mail on ships that were forced by British warships to enter their
ports. Britain contended that both parcel- and letter-post were
being used to convey contraband and military intelligence to
Germany, and that the only way to uncover them was to
examine the mails.'

 With regard to ships' cargoes originating in the United States,
a compromise was eventually agreed. This was the genesis of the
so-called navicert system, which Hull claimed that he suggested
to Lothian at one of their talks, 'whereby British representatives
would examine cargoes prior to their departure from the United
States and issue certificates that would prevent the ships from
being stopped on the high seas or taken into British ports for
examination'. One of the conditions which the Secretary of State
insisted on was that when the applicant for a navicert had his
application rejected 'a clear, concise statement of the reason for
rejection should be given' to him. But this was not always done,
and sometimes the application was rejected by the British

Embassy or consular representative in the US without any reason being given, which led to further recriminations.[6] However, the navicert system worked well on the whole, and after the fall of France, when Britain stood alone, United States neutrality became more benevolent towards Britain, and American public opinion became more sympathetic – with the exception of the hard core of isolationists, led by Senator Burton K. Wheeler and the trans-Atlantic aviator Colonel Lindbergh. Eventually Cordell Hull came to acquiesce in the examination of the mails carried by the Pan American Clippers and the ships which called at Bermuda.

When Charles des Graz was in Bermuda on our arrival, he suggested that I should send Mr Stephenson, the Passport Control Officer in New York, any information I could obtain from censorship and ships' examination relating to 'Fifth Column and similar activities in the USA'. I told him what my instructions were from Boyle, but he advised me to go ahead, saying that the Director of Censorship Edwin Herbert would see Boyle and everything would be all right. My censorship work included being present at the arrival of the Pan American aircraft at Darrell's Island in the Great Sound about a quarter of a mile from the Warwick shore. This was the seaplane airport, which had been constructed three years previously at a cost of one million dollars, and my work there consisted of supervising the removal and loading of transit mails, and assisting the Customs in examining passengers and their effects. This procedure also applied to neutral vessels who usually lay off Hamilton, notably those of the American Export lines which plied weekly between New York and Lisbon. 'Let Stephenson have as much as you can for the Federal Bureau of Investigation,' des Graz wrote to me from New York at the beginning of September. 'I am most particularly anxious to impress them with the idea that we may be very helpful to them.'

About the same time as I heard from des Graz, the *Exorchorda* from Lisbon stopped in Bermuda, and I discovered among the effects of an American passenger named Frank van Lew evidence that he was engaged in pro-Nazi propaganda in America. The

Granados, the author's house in Bermuda 1940–41, where many local intelligence operations were planned.

Dorothy in Bermuda, 1940

documents he was carrying were seized, but the passenger was allowed to proceed, since there was no legal reason for detaining him. I therefore sent a brief report to Stephenson, addressed to the Passport Control Office, then located in a small office in the British Consulate-General in downtown Manhattan. I also advised Boyle of what I had done. Before leaving London Boyle had promised to let me have a high-grade cipher for urgent communications, and I had practised how to use it in his office. I wrote to him on 9 September:

I hope you will be able to let me have the cipher shortly. I should like to be able to use it if necessary for the purpose of communicating with the PCO in New York. Information is extracted from the mails almost daily which that office should have. Passengers are continually passing through the Island on the Clipper or in ships who, for one reason or another, are suspect on account of Fifth Column or pro-Nazi propagandist activities, and there is at present no rapid or effective means of advising the PCO so as to be able to take any steps which may be considered necessary before their arrival.

I had previously written to Wren from the Inverurie:

The Chief Censor, who is incidentally CRE, is quite a good fellow, but unlike our friend Cararra [the Chief Censor in Gibraltar], he is most unwilling to be anything in the shape of a figurehead. He insists on having all the cabling arrangements under his control, and as the enciphering is done at his private office which is some considerable distance from here, it is going to make urgent communications very difficult if not impossible for me. I would therefore like you to urge on Boyle in as strong terms as possible the advisability of my having his High Grade Cipher so that I can get messages through to you as well as himself. I practised with this particular High Grade Cipher under instruction when I was in London and the technique is quite clear to me.

Three weeks later Boyle replied: 'The fruits of your work have already shown that Bermuda is a key position, and some of them have been most valuable.' But he made no reference to the cipher and I never received it. Instead the Governor allowed me to use his top-grade Foreign Office cipher as a temporary measure, since the ordinary Censorship cipher was not thought to be sufficiently secure, besides which Swire read all the Censorship messages first and I had originally been told by Boyle before I left London to use the Censorship cipher in the meantime.

Early in October 1940, the Censorship Director Edwin Herbert came out from London and spent a week in Bermuda on his way to New York, being joined by des Graz. During his stay Herbert attended a meeting of the Legislative Council where he was asked to explain how important Bermuda was in the scheme of things from the Censorship point of view, and this he did with his customary lucidity. Prior to the collapse of Norway, Denmark, Holland, Belgium, and France, he said, the majority of the censorship of mail had been done at Gibraltar and in various places in England. Now, however, the majority of this would be done in Bermuda. In England, he went on, they were doing more or less security work only, as there was now very little mail which passed through there destined for European countries. It was in Bermuda, and also in Vancouver, that the effective work was being done by Censorship, in the examination of mails to and from Europe. Herbert also explained the importance of the navicert system in the context of Contraband Control, whereby neutral vessels called at certain ports and thus avoided the risk of being taken long distances off their course to places like Freetown and Falmouth, the latter being in the combat zone.[7]

What was perhaps the greatest haul of contraband landed in Bermuda during the war took place on the eve of Herbert's visit, in the shape of 500 French Impressionist paintings and sketches worth hundreds of thousands of dollars. It was a *coup* in which I played a leading part as Security Officer with Contraband Control and Censorship, and it merits some description here. The collection had been formed by the well-known French art dealer and collector Ambroise Vollard, and included 270 paintings and drawings by Renoir, thirty paintings by Cezanne, twelve by Gaugin, seven by Degas, and many works by Manet, Monet, and Picasso. Some of the works were in various Paris museums, but the majority were in Vollard's spacious Paris house in the Rue de Martignac, near the Invalides, where he was in the habit of mounting exhibitions.[8]

Information was received from a reliable secret intelligence source that the collection had been seized by the Germans and consigned to a Paris art expert in New York named Martin Fabiani, with the object of selling the treasures and thus raising much-needed dollar currency for the Nazis. 'British authorities had good reason to believe Fabiani was being used as a German agent,' the Ministry of Economic Warfare stated afterwards. 'The Germans apparently recognized the commercial value of what they officially describe as commercial art.' The collection was shipped aboard the American export liner *Excalibur*, which sailed from Lisbon with the valuable cargo on board without having previously obtained a navicert. A British warship, HMS *Belfast* then stationed in Bermuda, was accordingly instructed by the Admiralty to intercept the *Excalibur* in the course of her voyage and bring her into the Great Sound.[9] This was done, much to the *Excalibur* captain's annoyance, and she dropped anchor in the Sound on 3 October. Meanwhile instructions had been received from London to remove the cargo as contraband, and it fell to me to carry out this operation, with the help of the energetic Chief Customs Officer in Bermuda, Rowe Spurling, and his able assistant Ralph Gauntlett, as well as several officers of naval contraband control.

On boarding the *Excalibur* with my companions, I was taken to see the Captain, to whom I explained the purpose of my mission and asked him where the pictures were stowed. He pointed to the ship's strong-room and remarked that he could give me no assistance in opening it since, besides being locked, it was welded round the sides with strips of steel. 'Excuse me a moment, Sir,' I said, and spoke to the senior contraband control officer who had also come aboard. I requested him to send a signal to the Royal Navy Dockyard on the south side of the Sound and ask for an expert shipwright-welder to be dispatched to the *Excalibur* as quickly as possible. About a quarter of an hour later the welder, whose name was Edward Pearce, arrived in a lighter with his oxy-acetylene burning gear and electric welding equipment, accompanied by the dockyard foreman. The Captain and the rest of us stood outside the strong-room as the welder prepared to begin his work, with a preliminary caution, 'Stand well back, gentlemen, please!'

The welder burnt off the steel strips as neatly as he could, since he had been told that the strips would have to be welded on again. I then asked the Captain for the key of the door which at first he refused to hand over. 'Very well, sir,' I said. 'We shall now burn a hole in the door large enough to remove the contraband articles, and this is likely to take some considerable time.'

The Captain, who was already furious at his ship's being held up, did not relish the prospect of a further delay of the length I had indicated. He promptly had second thoughts, produced the key with a show of ill-grace, and at my request opened the door. All the wooden crates containing the pictures were easily identified from their labels bearing Martin Fabiani's name and New York address. They were then lowered over the side one by one to the deck of the Customs boat which had been standing by; in due course, with myself on board, this headed for Hamilton, where its valuable cargo was unloaded and put into safe storage under my supervision.

Meanwhile, the welder had re-welded the strips round the strong-room door, and he and his foreman were then hustled off the ship, far less carefully than the crates, as Shipwright-Welder Pearce later recalled. 'In fact our little lighter was nearly capsized as the liner Captain was so annoyed at being held up and delayed that he started up the propellers almost before we had cast off. However, we got back to the Dockyard safely, and as I look back I like to think that though my war service was not too spectacular – just long hours and hard work – I did at least play my part in diverting untold millions of dollars away from the German war chest.'[10]

Next day I spoke to the Attorney-General, Trounsell Gilbert, and told him that I assumed that the pictures would be the subject of prize court proceedings and that they must, in the light of our knowledge, eventually be condemned as prize. We also agreed that it would be unwise to keep the pictures for very long in Bermuda, owing to the island's humid climate which would be bound to damage them. In the event they were condemned as prize, and were sent to Ottawa, where they were kept in the Canadian National Gallery for the duration of the war.[11]

'In case you should see any sensational press accounts of the removal of part of the S/S *Excalibur*'s cargo when she was here on Thursday,' I wrote to des Graz, 'I enclose a copy of my report to the Chief Censor which will explain the true facts. I had hoped to be able to add to this my impressions of Leon Feuchtwanger, who was one of the passengers, and the most interesting conversation which I had with him, but this must wait, I am afraid . . .' Feuchtwanger was the German Jewish novelist, best known for *The Ugly Duchess* and *Jew Suss*; he was fifty-eight at this time, and had succeeded in escaping from Germany when Hitler seized power in 1933, and had latterly been living in the unoccupied zone of France. Unfortunately I kept no record of my 'interrogation' of Feuchtwanger, but it was mainly concerned with conditions in France under the German occupation and the Vichy regime of Marshal Pétain. Other writers whom I similarly 'interrogated' included Antoine de St Exupéry, mistakenly believed to be pro-Vichy, and W. Somerset Maugham, who gave me a dramatic account of his escape from Cannes in a collier bound for Gibraltar and his eventual arrival in England still covered with coal dust. It was the first time I had met him, and I was interested to do so as I knew he had been a secret intelligence agent working in Russia at the time of the Bolshevik Revolution: he considered himself a failure for having been unable to stop it, although he had been given a vast sum of money to help the rival Mensheviks and prevent the Bolsheviks from seizing power. I gathered that he had received his instructions and his funds from Sir William Wiseman, the head of British Intelligence in America in the First World War, who did the same job as William Stephenson (Intrepid) was now doing in the Second.

'You can have no idea what a disadvantage my stammer was to me when I was a secret agent,' Maugham said. 'One morning in the autumn of 1917 Kerensky sent for me and gave me a message for Lloyd George.[12] It was so secret that I couldn't put it in writing. But when I got back to London I wrote the message down because I knew that when I came to tell it to the Prime Minister I'd begin to stammer. Lloyd George was in a hurry when I met him, so I just handed him what I'd written out. And he only glanced at the note. If I'd read the memo out to him it might have made all the difference. And perhaps the world today might be a very different place. But I made a hash of the whole business. And that's why I consider myself a failure.'[13]

Somerset Maugham arrived in Bermuda by Clipper from Lisbon. I had to ask him how much money he was carrying, since English passengers were only allowed to take £10 out of the country with them and many were suspected of smuggling out large sums. (This was indeed the case, since some of these funds were later seized by Bermuda customs.)

Maugham produced three US dollars from his pocket, which was all the money he had, he said, although he knew he could get as much as he wished from his publisher in New York. He flew on there and I later heard that the first thing he did with the money on landing at Idlewild (later JFK) airport was to order an Old-fashioned cocktail.

Before leaving Bermuda with des Graz to continue his journey, Herbert suggested that it might be a good idea if I were to come up to New York and meet Stephenson, perhaps going on to Washington as well to establish personal relations with the FBI. I agreed to do this a little later in the month when I could get away from my current work. Meanwhile my old chief in Section D, Lord Bearsted, arrived from London to spend a few days with his niece, who was married to the best-selling English novelist Robert Henriques, then on active military service, and who had been evacuated with their children to Bermuda. When Bearsted heard that I was planning to visit New York, he said he was going on there too. He proposed that we should travel together, and since it was my first visit he kindly invited me to spend the night of our arrival as his guest in the Waldorf Towers, at that time New York's most luxurious section of the Waldorf Hotel where he had a suite. I gladly accepted his invitation and I can never forget the thrill of the drive from Idlewild and my first glimpse of the mid-town skyscrapers and Fifth Avenue, with the city lights burning all night and no thought of the black-out three thousand miles away in blitzed London.

Walter Bearsted, whose father, the first Viscount, founded the great Shell oil combine, was a most likeable person and it was a pleasure for me to be, and to work, with him at all times.[14] After dinner he suggested taking me to see Harlem, where he seemed to know his way around. I was feeling tired and far from well – in fact, I was sickening for influenza – but I did not wish to disappoint my generous host and so we went to a kind of nightclub in Harlem where Bearsted was most interested in seeing the coloured dancers. Although neither of us ventured on to the dance-floor, it was an instructive spectacle, though I should have enjoyed it more if my eyelids had not been drooping. Eventually we returned to the Waldorf about 2 a.m. Next morning I felt terrible and, disguising my condition as best I could, I thanked Bearsted for his hospitality and took a taxi to the Westbury Hotel at 68th Street and Fifth Avenue where I had originally arranged to stay. There I went straight to bed, where I spent the next few days, until I reckoned my temperature had dropped to more or less normal and I felt strong enough to call up two Americans, husband and wife, who were friends of Dorothy's. It was a Sunday, and they came for me with their car and showed me a little of New York, driving out to the World Fair for what I think was the last day.

William Stephenson, the nominal Passport Control Officer, had only recently agreed to represent MI6 and SOE, after some prodding from Winston Churchill with whom he had been on friendly terms for a good many years, feeding him with important industrial intelligence through his business contacts in Europe, particularly Germany. On his appointment Stephenson had taken one look at the cramped and depressing quarters of the PCO in an annexe to the British Consulate-General in Exchange Place, and decided that this was no place for the headquarters of the security-intelligence organization he had in mind. This he was eventually to find on two upper floors of the International Building in Rockefeller Center. Meanwhile he had taken a large apartment in Hampshire House, on the south side of Central Park, where he was living with his wife and which he was also using as an office. Charles des Graz had given me his address and telephone number, so that when I called him up a soft voice with a slight trace of a Canadian accent replied that he had heard all about me from des Graz and invited me to have a drink with him that evening at his apartment. This was to be my first meeting with my future Intelligence chief, whose biography I was later to write. The biography appeared more than twenty years afterwards under the titles of *The Quiet Canadian* in England and *Room 3603* in the United States. With some changes and additions, the American edition, *Room 3603* (which has frequently been reprinted on both sides of the Atlantic and among other languages has been translated into Romanian and Serbo-Croat), no doubt owed its success, at least in part, to the fact that it carried a foreword by the late Ian Fleming, whose character James Bond, while fascinating in himself, bore little resemblance to my own real-life portrait of Stephenson.

A small, wiry man with penetrating blue eyes and an engaging smile, William Samuel Stephenson was a Canadian from Manitoba. Although only forty-four years old at this time, he had already had a fantastic career both in the First World War and in the years between the wars. In the former he had been badly gassed while serving with the Royal Canadian Engineers, and had been invalided back to England in 1915. While convalescing he had applied for a transfer to the Royal Flying Corps, quickly learning to fly and afterwards as a fighter pilot shooting down twenty-six German aircraft before himself being shot down and taken prisoner, eventually escaping and making his way back to the British lines. This gained him the MC and DFC from the British and the Légion d'Honneur and Croix de Guerre with palm from the French. Meanwhile he had taken up boxing, with character-

Sir William Stephenson, MC, DFC, Companion of the Order of
Canada, code-named 'Intrepid' by Sir Winston Churchill. He was
Director of British Security Co-ordination, New York, in charge of
wartime security intelligence and special operations in the western
hemisphere, 1940–45.

istic enthusiasm, and had become amateur lightweight world
champion.

After the war Stephenson began to experiment with wireless
telegraphy and acquired an interest in an English company,

which under his impetus was the first to manufacture cheap radio sets for the ordinary householder. He continued his experiments with the transmission of pictures by W/T, taking out patents for his inventions which were to revolutionize pictorial journalism besides pointing the way to television. Hence he had become a millionaire by the time he was thirty, while the royalties on his patents brought him in an average of £100,000 a year until they expired eighteen years later. By the early 1930s he controlled a score of companies manufacturing a variety of products from cement and plastics to aircraft and car bodies. At the same time he kept up his interest in flying and in 1934 he won the King's Cup air race with a Monospar, the machine he had designed and built in one of his factories. He also encouraged the aircraft designer Reginald Mitchell to complete the Spitfire fighter, and he later put up the necessary finance to enable Frank Whittle to perfect the turbo-jet aircraft, after this novel concept of flying in a machine without propellers had been turned down by the British Air Ministry.

These details of his career were fairly common knowledge when the Second World War broke out. It was in the course of the many conversations I had with him that I learned of the covert side of his activities between the wars. During his visits to Germany in the 1930s to buy steel for his company Pressed Steel, he first became interested in secret intelligence, he told me, when he discovered that German steel production under the Nazis had been largely turned over to the manufacture of armaments and munitions. Through an introduction to MI6 he began to supply this organization with relevant data, as well as passing them on to Churchill, then almost a lone voice in the House of Commons pleading for an expansion of the Royal Air Force, and also to Churchill's friend Major Desmond Morton who ran the official Industrial Intelligence Centre. However, one matter was so secret that, although I knew about it, I dared not use it in my biography of Stephenson for fear of unpleasant repercussions under the Official Secrets Act. This concerned Enigma, the cipher machine which had been invented by a German engineer and marketed commercially by its Swedish manufacturer as a 'secret writing mechanism' for use by companies 'to frustrate inquisitive competitors'. In 1937, through his contacts with the German communications industry, Stephenson discovered that a revised and portable version of Enigma was being manufactured near Berlin for use by the German armed services. Partly as a result of his information, a prototype of the machine was obtained by British SIS with the aid of the Polish Intelligence Service just before Poland was invaded in 1939, thus enabling the 'most secret Ultra' enemy signals to be deciphered throughout the greater part of the war.

This was the man whom I met for the first time on what was for me a most memorable evening in Hampshire House, and whom I, with a host of other friends and co-workers, were to know affectionately as 'Little Bill'. Along with the American Colonel William Donovan, a former Republican Attorney General and the future chief of the Office of Strategic Services (OSS), and with the British Ambassador in Washington, Lord Lothian, Stephenson had already played an important part in negotiations which were to result in President Roosevelt's agreeing to transfer fifty American destroyers to the British in exchange for the right to establish American bases in the Caribbean, Bermuda, and Newfoundland. The liaison which Churchill had urged Stephenson to establish with the United States President had already been facilitated by the President's confidential legal adviser, Ernest Cuneo, a friend of Stephenson's with a growing international law practice in Washington, the object being to establish a secret collaboration between the FBI (in the person of the latter's Director J. Edgar Hoover) and the British SIS (in the person of William Stephenson). For the time being no other US Government Department, not even the Secretary of State, was to be informed of it. In due course Cuneo reported to Stephenson that the President had welcomed the idea enthusiastically. 'There should be the closest possible marriage between the FBI and British Intelligence,' the President had said. Later, by way of confirmation, the President repeated these words to Lord Lothian in the British Embassy.

In fact, Stephenson had already met Hoover informally

through their mutual friend Gene Tunney, the American world-champion boxer. But when Stephenson broached the subject of security intelligence collaboration, Hoover explained that he was unwilling to take any step which might be interpreted as a breach of American neutrality without a direct order from the White House. Once that order was forthcoming, Hoover proved most co-operative. He welcomed the suggestion that information from the Bermuda Censorship, where it concerned American national security, should be passed to him. He also appreciated the need for protection of British shipping in American ports where arms were loaded on to British ships for transport across the Atlantic to the war zone, and which were in danger of being sabotaged by dock labourers and stevedores who could be recruited without difficulty from the local German, Italian, and Irish communities who hated Britain. In fact, it was Hoover who suggested to Stephenson that the new all-embracing security and intelligence organization which was already in process of being formed should be called British Security Co-ordination, or BSC for short.

In view of my special position in Bermuda, Stephenson told me he thought it would be a good idea if I could accompany Herbert and des Graz to Washington where he would arrange for us to visit Hoover in his official headquarters. This we duly did on 30 October, meeting in Hoover's impressive office, where Herbert carefully explained the workings of censorship, particularly in relation to the examination of transit mails. He did not initially refer to the Room 99 procedures, although the FBI was later to be let into the secret of the various techniques of opening mail. Hoover was a heavy-set bachelor, a year older than Stephenson, and during the past sixteen years as the Bureau's head he had developed it, from a feeble body during the period of the scandal of President Harding's administration into a first-rate law enforcement agency which had seen many gangsters, hoodlums and 'Public Enemies No. 1' put behind bars, if not shot in confrontations with FBI agents. Like Stephenson, Hoover was a man of outstanding personal courage. Once when a Senator implied that he was afraid to make an arrest himself, Hoover proved that he was as good as any of his agents. A group of FBI agents surrounded a house in New Orleans where a dangerous criminal was known to be hiding. On the man's eventual appearance, after he had been warned to come out, Hoover sprang from his car and promptly over-powered him. (Incidentally, Stephenson similarly immobilized a sailor on the New York waterfront who was known to be passing information about British convoy routes to the enemy.) Likewise, a few weeks before the outbreak of war in Europe, the nation's most-wanted criminal, Louis ('Lepke') Buchalter, head of Murder Incorporated, had surrendered in a New York street to Hoover, who was alone and unarmed, through the intermediary of the New York *Mirror* columnist and broadcaster, Walter Winchell.

One domestic drawback, to which Hoover drew our attention, was that owing to a recent Federal legal judgement, telephone intercepts or 'wire-tapping' had been declared illegal, and this was a great handicap in tracking down possible German agents who were violating American security. We did not ask what steps, if any, he was taking to counter this. However he expressed considerable gratitude for any help which the Bermuda Censorship might contribute. Herbert then suggested that Hoover should send one of his agents down to Bermuda to see the censors in action, which the FBI chief said he would gladly do. We were also introduced to Hoover's assistant directors, Clyde Tolson and Edward Tamm, and were invited to inspect the whole of the headquarters, including the finger-printing and forensic medicine departments. Herbert and des Graz had to get back to New York that evening, but as I was staying over in Washington for several more days it was agreed that I should return next day, which I did.

I was duly shown round the various laboratories and the fingerprinting department, which had a complicated apparatus for turning up any wanted individual's or suspect's prints with computerlike precision. I appeared suitably impressed and made some complimentary noises. All went well on my guided tour until we reached a corridor, at the end of which was a door sufficiently open to reveal to my then practised eye an interesting piece of gadgetry. I immediately asked my guide what went on in that room. 'Oh,' he said with feigned casualness, 'that's just a lecture room for instructing new agents.'

'Come off it!' I replied. 'I know what you've got in there, as I've just seen a bit of it. That's a wire-tapping apparatus!'

At first the agent denied this, but after some further questioning by me, he eventually came clean and admitted that I was right. Nevertheless he looked a little scared, as he repeated what Hoover had told us the previous day, namely that wire-tapping was illegal under a recent Federal court ruling. However, he added, FBI agents were doing it surreptitiously; and as I seemed to know about it, he took me into the room and showed me how the necessary gadgets were fitted into a suitcase which the agent could take with him on an assignment. The telephone could not be tapped from an exchange, since the American telephone system was a privately run company, so the only way to tap an individual's telephone was to attach a hidden piece of mechanism to the receiver and wire it up to the next room where the agent could record any conversations the suspect might make. Thus the surveillance was severely limited and depended upon the agent's installing himself in an adjacent room, either in an hotel or an apartment block. The suitcases which the agents used for this work were of a distinctive brown colour, resembling those cases commonly carried by aircraft passengers at this period.

This episode had a curious sequel a few days later. On my way back to New York, I stopped off at Princeton to spend the weekend with David Ogilvy, Francis's younger brother, who had joined the Audience Research Institute of Dr George Gallup, whose right-hand man he was in process of becoming. Among the crowd of fellow passengers who had got off the train I spotted two unmistakable FBI agents, staggering under the weight of two brown suitcases whose contents I had no difficulty in guessing. I later sent Hoover a message through Stephenson to the effect that if he dispatched agents on a certain assignment, the agents ought to carry the cases as if they were going to catch an air flight and not as if the cases were full of bricks. No doubt some adjustments were subsequently made to the weight of the equipment.

Before leaving Washington I wrote my wife a letter which she could show to her co-workers in Bermuda:

British Embassy, Washington, D.C., November 2, 1940.
. . . Mr Hoover was quick to realize the potential value of our assistance in Bermuda in recording the activities of enemy agents operating in the United States, and expressed appreciation of the material which we had already sent him through our recognized liaison in New York. We told him that with all the eastbound Clippers now calling at Bermuda as well as increased traffic in shipping, coupled with additions to our own staff, we hoped to be able to put him in possession of considerably more information under this head than hitherto.

As we were taking our leave, I asked Mr Hoover if he would let me see through his laboratories which have now become almost world famous, and he immediately detailed the officer in charge of these laboratories to take charge of me and let me see everything I wanted. I have been in the laboratories every day since then, and I may say that Mr Hoover's instructions have been most carefully carried out.

What strikes the visitor at first sight is the vast quantity of elaborate and expensive equipment for doing jobs which we have been in the habit of doing with homemade apparatus. The impression gained is almost one that the operators in the laboratories are more pleased with the magnificent equipment at their command than with the actual results of any particular piece of work. They have, for instance, at least thirty different kinds of cameras including one whose lens is about eight feet in diameter. Their photographic equipment is probably the most complete and uptodate of that in any police laboratories in the world, but then they photograph many more objects and documents, notably wanted individuals and their fingerprints of which many thousands of copies are printed off each day. In the matter of contact printing they were able to give me a few hints, and they showed me apparatus containing bulbs of 1000 watts which can print through paper of almost any thickness direct instead of having to print back. This seems to me to depend upon having adequate power bulbs and therefore suitable sensitized paper.

As I think you already know, the FBI people concentrate on the negative side of our work – what is most properly performed by the testing department. They have a useful test for secret writing in which iodine vapour is used and I shall bring back the formula for this with me.

Similarly they use the ultra-violet lamp on seals to ascertain whether any changes in the composition of the wax has taken place since the original impression was made. When I get back to New York I am hoping to arrange for a complete ultra-violet unit to be purchased at a reasonable cost and sent to Bermuda. The ultra-violet light would probably also reveal traces of plaster but the opinion is that an ordinary microscope is more effective for this purpose.

An additional use of the iodine test is for the development of latent fingerprints which we might try out in the case of letters from agents going through known intermediaries. For where an agent writes to his principal through an intermediary leaving his communication unsigned, this method should prove of great value in determining his identity.

The FBI people know something of the positive side of our work, but little of the detail. Their knowledge to date has been obtained in a manner which for us has been somewhat unfortunate. During the last war Dr S. W. Collins, who is now in charge of the testing department in London, came over here at the request of the Department of State and gave instruction in all secret branches of censorship and cryptography. Unfortunately the officer who was in charge of the American organization, Major Herbert O. Yardley, wrote a book called *The American Black Chamber* some years after the war in which he divulged a good deal of information which had been imparted by Collins to the people here in confidence. This book has been to some extent utilized by the enemy, and it is a great pity that so much is actually known. On the other hand certain aspects of our work are only very briefly described and not in great detail, and besides all that we have made some improvements since then. They are of course now very much ashamed of this book, and for that reason are most anxious to help us in every way possible.*

One subject of which they know nothing at all is chamfering [invisible mending of letters which have been torn or slit open]. Herbert and des Graz have agreed that there is no objection to describing our technique. Would you therefore draw up detailed instructions on the processes, explaining exactly the necessary equipment? In the meantime I am sending you some specimens, which I would like you to get to work on without delay. These might be returned when the instructions are complete.

Mr Hoover is seriously considering the possibility of sending one or more of his agents down to Bermuda. With the approaching construction of an American air and naval base, FBI agents will obviously be necessary for reasons of security. I have suggested that a suitable young woman in the guise of a secretary or stenographer might be attached to one of the agents, and that we should be very glad to train her in our craft.

Summing up then I would say that on the negative side we do not lag far behind the FBI if at all, even with our inferior equipment. On the positive side we are greatly in advance of anything they know or are doing. By the way, they do play about with postmarks and stamps, and in this respect their technique is not dissimilar to ours. On the police laboratory work they are somewhat in advance of us I should say and in methods of interrogating and searching suspects and prisoners they are by reason of the previously disturbed state of this country extremely adept. I have had some very useful hints on search and interrogation (call it third degree if you like) and also that pertinent task of telephone tapping and concealed recording of conversations. Our positive work, I repeat, remains untouched, some very flattering things have been said about one or two of the jobs we have done recently,

The American Black Chamber was published in 1933 by Bobbs-Merrill in the US and Faber & Faber in England, and recently reissued.

and I hope you will tell everyone in Room 99 how pleased I am with the way they have been doing their job.

On the same date I also wrote from the British Embassy to Rowe Spurling, the energetic Chief Customs Officer in Bermuda:

You will probably have heard from the letters which I have written to Simpson and Boulton how delighted everyone is here with the good work that you have been doing at the airport and on the ships. You may also have learned that Hamish Mitchell is giving up his job with the British Purchasing Commission in New York and coming down to Bermuda to take charge of several sections of our work there. I think he will prove a most valuable asset to our organization, and I am sure that you will cooperate with him very closely. . . . He will probably have reached Bermuda by the time you receive this letter, but he is not, I understand, to embark upon any executive undertakings until my return which I am hoping will be about next Saturday or Sunday.

It has been agreed here that from now on we should take a very lenient line with the Swiss couriers in transit at Bermuda. Clear instructions have been given to the Swiss Legation who have transmitted them to their authorities in Berne about the exact manner in which the couriers' papers should be drawn up. Unless we are acting on strong advance information or there is some other reason attaching suspicion to any particular courier I think that in future we must not delve to find any technical flaw in their papers but to let them go through. There is no objection however to their continuing to avail themselves of the admirable arrangements which you have introduced at the airport for the safe custody of their documents.

With the Vichy people, on the other hand, the policy will be to leave them vague which will give us a pretext of jumping on them whenever we want to. You will, I know, use your discretion in this matter. Brousse, the man with whom you remember we had words on the *Exeter*, made a

certain amount of fuss here in the newspapers, but no one in
the Embassy has attached the least significance to what he has
said and of course cannot do so until a formal protest has been
received from the French authorities and this has not yet
come in.

My work was retarded by an attack of influenza in New
York, so that I must return there next week to finish up what
I started in the first day or two of my visit. Here, on the other
hand, I managed to see everyone I wanted, particularly at the
Federal Bureau of Investigation where all doors have been
opened.

Three points in this letter need a few words of explanation. First,
Hamish Mitchell, a Scotsman who had been security officer with
the British Purchasing Commission, was married to Elsa Mott,
the wealthy daughter of the head of General Motors, and had a
most attractive house in Bermuda. Secondly, Spurling had a
positive obsession with diplomatic couriers (whom he used to
call 'curriers') and I feared his zeal in trying to find excuses for
relieving them of any documents they were carrying might get
him into trouble. His great forte was persuading them to leave
their diplomatic bags or pouches over-night at the airport in a
strong-room which he would ostentatiously lock in their
presence. Of course they were usually opened during the night
by a team of experts in Room 99 and the contents unsealed,
photographed, and resealed. Finally, the M. Charles Brousse
referred to was the Press Officer at the Vichy French Embassy in
Washington, and more will be related about him in the course of
this narrative.

Concerning the incident on the American Export liner *Exeter*,
in which I participated with Spurling, what happened was
described in a letter from Brousse in New York to his mother in
Perpignan, dated 21 October, 1940, which the Bermuda
Censorship intercepted and copied before sending it on its way to
France. The following is a translation of the relevant passage:

In Bermuda, against all diplomatic regulations, the authorities seized from me my two packages which, by the way, were not of great importance. It is a gross violation of diplomatic privilege. I refused to give up the papers without getting a receipt signed in the presence of the ship's Captain. The papers here are full of it. My photograph appears everywhere and dozens of reporters and photographers boarded the ship while still at sea, before docking, to interview me. I gave them the necessary information and I gave it to them in the right way. When the English make mistakes, they make them big, without a doubt.

Although Brousse was travelling on a diplomatic passport, the material which we seized was neither official nor addressed to the Vichy French Embassy in Washington; it was therefore strictly speaking not covered by diplomatic privilege. The reason why Brousse was able to exploit the incident with such effect in the American press was that he had considerable knowledge of press matters since, besides being his country's Press Attaché in Washington, he had previously worked for the French news agency Havas, and in addition his family owned the principal newspaper in Perpignan.

I returned to New York for the closing stages of the Presidential election, in which Roosevelt was running for a third term against Wendell Willkie, the lawyer from Indiana, still on the right side of fifty, who had unexpectedly won the Republican nomination on the sixth ballot. I had never seen a campaign button before, and I was intrigued by some of the legends on those worn by Willkie's supporters, such as *No man is good three times* and *Elliot's a Captain. What are You?* (Elliot was the President's son). Although in the count Roosevelt secured a plurality of only five million votes, by the United States electoral system, which differed so much from the British, he defeated Willkie in the electoral college by 449 votes to 92.

Immediately after the result of the election was announced, Willkie made a nation-wide broadcast in which he called on his Republican followers to support Roosevelt, and which I heard in a friend's house the night before I returned to Bermuda: 'He is your President and he is my President.' Willkie was a big man both physically and spiritually, and always a strong proponent of all possible aid to the Allies before the United States came into the war. Shortly afterwards he passed through Bermuda on a visit to England, which he made at President Roosevelt's special request prompted by Stephenson. I enjoyed talking with him and was saddened to learn of his tragic death before the war ended. He had written a fine book, *One World*, in which he pleaded persuasively for post-war co-operation among all nations. By an ironic twist of fate he died from a virus contracted from another book which he had been reading.

A few days after getting back to Bermuda, I received a message from London that Lord Lothian, our Ambassador in Washington who had played a conspicuous part with Stephenson in negotiating the destroyers-for-bases deal with the American President and his Cabinet, would be returning from leave in England by Clipper which was expected at Bermuda airport on 23 November. The eleventh Marquess of Lothian, born Philip Kerr, was a man of outstanding ability and breadth of vision, whom the first Director of the Institute of Advanced Study at Princeton, Dr Abraham Flexner, described at the time of his appointment in 1939 at the age of fifty-seven, as 'the first British Ambassador since Bryce who has not been a diplomatic clerk'. He had once been Lloyd George's confidential secretary and was later for many years secretary of the Rhodes Trust in Oxford, which had given him a profound knowledge of American academic life; while on the other hand American journalists described him as 'a super salesman for the British Empire' and as looking 'more like an American businessman than a British aristocrat'. He was withal a most attractive and brilliant personality in spite of his somewhat erratic religious beliefs – he was a Roman Catholic turned Christian Scientist, to which latter creed he had been converted by his friend Lady Astor. I had known him in England and had been a guest at Blickling Hall, his beautiful Jacobean house in Norfolk, where he had given me the run of his magnificent library and allowed me to copy certain historical manuscripts in which I was interested. Thus I thought it would be a courtesy which he would appreciate if I were to meet him when his plane touched down at Darrell's Island, which it did about 7 a.m. on the 23rd.

I thought he looked a little pale when he stepped ashore, but the colour soon returned to his cheeks as he tucked in to the unexpected breakfast of bacon and eggs which I had ordered for him at the airport restaurant. With him, also bound for the embassy in Washington, was Peter Smithers, who had been appointed Assistant Naval Attaché and was later to be a Conservative Minister and finally Secretary-General of the Council of Europe, for which he was deservedly knighted. Peter shared the meal with us and listened, as I did, to Lothian's vivid descriptions of scenes in the air-raid shelters, of life in London generally during the Blitz and of the remarkable courage and good humour with which the inhabitants were taking it. The Ambassador would have stayed on talking away happily for another hour if the passengers had not been summoned aboard the Clipper, which they were shortly after 8 o'clock.

A fortnight later I heard that he had been taken ill, and this was followed a few days later by the dreadful news of his death during the night of 11/12 December. Because of his Christian Science beliefs he had refused to have a doctor, contenting himself with the services of a faith healer from Boston. In fact, Lothian was suffering from uremia, a kidney complaint which could easily have been cured by conventional medication. His death was an appalling tragedy for Britain, since it proved impossible to find an immediate replacement with his talents. Stephenson lobbied hard for his friend Beaverbrook, but the latter was busily engaged as Minister of Aircraft Production and any possibility that he might be persuaded to fill the gap was frustrated by his breakdown in health. Churchill's eventual choice was another aristocrat, Lord Halifax, but although he was to have a considerable success with the American government and public, Halifax lacked the unique qualities of Lothian, who had always been *en rapport* with Stephenson. Halifax remained nervous and apprehensive on the subject of British Secret Service activities in the United States.

Lord Lothian, British Ambassador in Washington, shortly before his sudden death in December 1940.

Philip Lothian, for whom I had an unbounded admiration, was accorded the rare honour of having his ashes interred in Arlington National Cemetery, although after the war his remains were to be exhumed and conveyed in an American warship to the Lothian family vault in Scotland. 'If you back us you won't be backing a quitter,' he told an audience in Baltimore in a speech that was read for him the day before he died. 'The issue now depends largely on what you decide to do. Nobody can share that responsibility with you. It is the great strength of a democracy that it brings responsibility down squarely on every citizen and every nation. And before the judgement seat of God each must answer for his own actions.' It was his farewell message to the American people. [15]

A few days after Lothian's brief but unforgettable stop-over in Bermuda, another incident occurred involving the bearer of a French diplomatic passport. The person concerned was the Countess Josée de Chambrun, whose father Pierre Laval, Vice-Premier and Foreign Minister in Marshal Pétain's Government at Vichy and arch-collaborationist with the Nazis, had arranged the meeting between Hitler and the Marshal at Montoire. She was returning to France and her passport carried a British diplomatic visa from the British Embassy in Washington, a courtesy which the Embassy was bound to grant since Britain was not at war with Vichy France, although no diplomatic relations existed between the two countries. Countess de Chambrun, whose husband was a lawyer temporarily on the staff of the Vichy French Embassy in Washington, had also been provided with a safe-conduct from the British Embassy covering any documents she might be carrying, provided that they were destined for un-occupied France. She was not accompanied by her husband Count René de Chambrun, who had arranged to follow on later; because of his descent from the Marquis de Lafayette, the French states-man and general who had served in the American forces during the War of Independence, René de Chambrun enjoyed dual nationality, American and French. The Vichy French Ambassador to the United States was Gaston Henry-Haye, a former Mayor of Versailles, and he had had a cool reception from Cordell Hull when he presented his credentials two months previously. 'It is due to you to know,' the Secretary of State told him on this occasion, 'that your Government is anti-British and pro-German when it goes beyond the requirements of the spirit or the letter of the armistice agreement,' having 'virtually signed away its navy to Germany.' About the same time Stephenson had received a report that a kind of Gestapo was operated in the Vichy French Embassy, designed to report on the activities of the supporters of General de Gaulle's Free French Movement in the United States and to threaten their families at home with reprisals such as depriving them of their citizenship – which was in fact done, after their names had been sent to Vichy.

I went along to the airport on Darrell's Island in the afternoon of 28 November, shortly after the east-bound Clipper from New York had stopped to refuel, as I wished to have a word with one of the passengers who was an official of the British Library of Information in New York. While I was speaking to him, Rowe Spurling came up and told me that the Countess de Chambrun was among the other passengers, and at that moment a telephone call was coming through for her from Washington. I immediately telephoned the Bermuda Chief Censor, Mr J. R. Blair-Leighton, who had replaced Colonel Swire, and asked him to have the Countess's conversation carefully monitored, which was done. Spurling then told me that the Countess was carrying three sealed packages addressed to the Ministry of Foreign Affairs, one to Vichy and the other two to *Paris*, together with about forty letters addressed to various individuals in both the occupied and un-occupied zones. I promptly telephoned the Colonial Secretary Mr Dutton, and requested his authority to detain the two packages addressed to Paris, pending instructions from the interested authorities in London. To this he agreed, and the Countess was accordingly informed.

Josée de Chambrun, whom I now proceeded to interrogate, was a smartly dressed brunette, who looked quite like her father and was also, so I noted, not lacking in sex appeal. The two large sealed envelopes addressed to Paris were no doubt intended for Vichy, but they were old printed envelopes from the Embassy stock in Washington and in preparing them the clerks in Ambassador Henry-Haye's office had not (as they should have done) crossed out the word 'Paris' and substituted 'Vichy'. She admitted to me that a mistake had been made and added: 'It is a little mistake, but now you are making a big mistake.' She went on to say that, although the two packages of which I was about to relieve her, 'might and probably did contain documents destined for Paris, the civil servants in Paris and in other parts of France were subject in all things to the instructions of the Government at Vichy, and furthermore that couriers travelling from Vichy to Paris were not interfered with by the German occupation authorities.' I did not believe her, and I had no scruples in taking advantage of the technical error.

'Unfortunately, Madame, the British Government has no means of verifying your statement,' I told her, 'and my Government does not recognize the existence of any government in Paris. The only French Government on French territory, the existence of which the British Government recognizes, is at Vichy.'

Her eyes blazed with anger as I took the two large envelopes from her. 'There may be a mistake on the part of the French officials in Washington,' I added, 'but if indeed there has been a genuine error, the packages will no doubt be forwarded to Vichy with the seals unbroken.'

Her suitcase, which at my request, had been removed from the plane, was then brought into the interrogation room and opened in her presence. In it I found twenty-seven letters addressed to various individuals in occupied France, including one to Herr Otto Abetz, Hitler's ambassador in Paris, from Jean Musa, Henry-Haye's personal assistant in Washington. I informed her that I must also seize these, but that the sealed envelope addressed to Vichy, together with the other letters addressed to the un-occupied zone, would not be detained and she could take these with her. She was obviously furious with me at her treatment, although this had been quite correct and polite; and she continued to protest as she boarded the Clipper.

All the correspondence which I had seized was taken to Room 99, where it was appropriately dealt with: the valuable information which it contained was copied and where necessary the contents were photographed. The letters were then sent on with the seals apparently unbroken, the letters bearing no trace of having been secretly opened. A suitable note was afterwards dispatched to the Vichy-French Embassy in Washington apologizing for the 'mistake'.

A few days later Stephenson and Donovan arrived in Bermuda en route to London. It was Donovan's second visit, and this time President Roosevelt had agreed that he should go on to the Mediterranean, where the danger to British shipping and communications had recently been increased by the Italian invasion of Greece. It was also agreed that he should travel as the official representative of the US Navy Department, and on his return should report directly to the President as well as to Frank Knox, the Navy Secretary. Before leaving the US, Stephenson, who arranged to travel with Donovan as far as London, cabled Menzies at SIS headquarters to the effect that it was impossible to over-emphasize the importance of Donovan's visit. 'He can play a great role, perhaps a vital one, but it may not be inconsistent with orthodox diplomacy nor confined to its channels,' Stephenson urged. 'You should personally convey to the Prime Minister that Donovan is presently the strongest friend we have.'

Bad weather in the Azores, which was the Clipper's next stop, delayed the onward flight for nearly a fortnight. However, irritating as the hold-up was in a sense, it gave me a chance of getting to know both Stephenson and Donovan well and it gave them a chance of seeing the Censorship in operation.

It so happened that while they were in Bermuda, a letter with a New York postmark dated 20 November 1940 and addressed to a Herr Lothar Frederick in Berlin was reported to me by one of the Censorship examiners. It contained a list of shipping observed by the writer in New York harbour and gave details of their arrivals and departures, together with information about their armament. The letter was signed 'Joe K', and the fact that the word cannon (German *Kanone*) was used for guns suggested that the writer was a Nazi agent, particularly as I recognized the Berlin address as a cover address for the Gestapo Chief Heinrich Himmler. I showed the letter to Stephenson and Donovan, and they both expressed considerable interest in it. We all three shared the feeling that this letter might well lead to the revelation of widespread German espionage activities in the United States. Such indeed was to prove the case, as will be seen in its proper place in this narrative.

Stephenson and Donovan eventually got away about the middle of December and reached London safely, Donovan saying afterwards that he 'had never been treated in such royal and exalted fashion,' and that 'the red carpet had been thicker and wider than he thought it possible to lay,' thanks to Stephenson's prior arrangements with the Prime Minister through Menzies.

Thus the year 1940 drew to a close for me in a very different manner and in very different surroundings from those in which it had begun. However I was encouraged by a note which I received from David Boyle at this time. 'Just a line to say I have heard a lot about you from Herbert, and from Stephenson, apart from your memos and letters to me,' he wrote on 26 December from MI6 head office. 'I'd like you to know that everyone concerned thinks that you are doing a grand job of work, the results of which are already most valuable. Various questions are now being thrashed out which may lead to further work and activities; if so, more power indeed to your elbow.' What these activities turned out to be, the following year was to reveal.

A clue to the 'further work and activities' mentioned by David Boyle was given by Lord Lloyd, the Colonial Secretary in London, in a circular telegram dated 4 January 1941, and addressed to the Colonial Governors in the West Indies and Bermuda, informing them of the appointment of two Intelligence officers of army field rank or its equivalent in the navy, who would jointly represent MI5 and MI6 in the Caribbean area. One was to cover Trinidad, Barbados, the Windward and Leeward Islands, and British Guiana (now Guyana), with his headquarters in Port-of-Spain; the other was to cover Jamaica, the Bahamas, and British Honduras (now Belize), with his headquarters in Kingston. These two officers were to be responsible for the distribution of security intelligence material to the colonial governments in their respective areas and to be available for consultation by the Governors when required. They were to maintain liaison with each other and also with me in Bermuda, while for administrative purposes they were to be subject to the general direction of Stephenson in New York, who had now officially become Director of British Security Co-ordination in the Western Hemisphere, with headquarters in Rockefeller Center.[16]

There was some delay in the officers taking up their appointments. I was delighted to learn that my old friend and colleague in Section D, Freckles Wren, had been chosen for the Trinidad area, and I wrote inviting him to spend a few days with me and my wife in our house in Bermuda. His departure was retarded by the fact that he was still recovering from a serious injury received in an air raid on London three months previously. 'I have just heard,' I wrote to des Graz on 2 October 'that Wren, poor fellow, has been badly burned by an incendiary bomb which fell clean through five stories into the cellar where he and his wife were sheltering. His wife was also burned and Captain Ellis (I don't know whether you met him – he was in our Paris office) was so badly injured that he is not expected to live.' Fred Ellis, not to be confused with Colonel C. H. ('Dick') Ellis, Stephenson's principal MI6 assistant in New York, actually did survive, but his face was so badly disfigured that he had to be invalided out of the service. Wren suffered mostly in his hands and rather less in his face, but he was unable to leave London until the third week in January and did not reach Bermuda via Lisbon until 1 February 1941.

The officer who had been chosen for the Jamaica area was a barrister, Lieutenant-Commander J. C. D. Harington, RNVR, later a county court and a circuit judge. He did not accompany Wren, and for some reason he was not expected to come out for at least another six weeks. Consequently Stephenson, who gave me the news of the appointments when he passed through Bermuda on his way back to New York in the middle of January, told me that, because of Harington's delay, it had been agreed with Boyle and Herbert that I should go round the West Indies islands with Wren but that we should first come to New York for briefing by him and des Graz, and that I should prepare a report of the tour on my return to New York.

So as to give Wren a short rest in my house, I made reservations for us both by Clipper on the morning of 3 February. But the weather was too rough to enable the seaplane to take off either on that day or the following morning. Since it looked as if the bad weather would continue for several more days, Major Wren, as he had now become, agreed to my cancelling the flight reservations and transferring to the Grace Line *Santa Rosa*, which had arrived from New York and was due to sail on the return voyage the same afternoon, although because of the weather the ship could not enter St George's harbour but was obliged to anchor in the shelter of Grassy Bay. We went aboard by tender from Hamilton and as the ship was quite full I had to share a cabin with Freckles. About 6 p.m., shortly after the ship had sailed, Freckles told me that he was going down to the bar where I agreed to join him after I had unpacked some of my things. This I did, an action which was to be the prelude to one of the most unpleasant experiences of my life.

On entering the bar I went to a table in the corner where Wren was sitting alone, having just finished a whisky and soda. When I sat down I beckoned one of the bar stewards and ordered another whisky for Freckles and a White Lady cocktail for myself. It was ten minutes or so before the drinks arrived, but I attributed this to the bar's being very full with other passengers having drinks.

I took a sip of the White Lady and immediately detected a distinct flavour of peppermint. However, I thought that the bar had run out of Cointreau, which is the main ingredient of the cocktail, and had substituted Créme de Menthe. I finished the drink and a few minutes later returned to my cabin to change for dinner, while Wren ordered himself another whisky.

As I was taking off my jacket, I began to feel giddy, but as the ship was rolling a lot and the cabin seemed rather stuffy I put this down to the motion of the vessel. The sense of giddiness became more pronounced, and I lay down in my berth. I felt my muscles beginning to relax, and I knew that I could not get up and dress.

I remembered nothing more until I came to, fourteen hours later. Freckles Wren, who came into the cabin after dinner to go to bed, told me afterwards that I appeared to be sleeping very heavily, but as he imagined I was feeling the weather, he thought no more about it. Next day I felt so weak that I was unable to leave my berth and could eat nothing except for a little soup.

The ship should have docked in New York the following morning but owing to the rough weather did not do so until the afternoon. Meanwhile I managed to get up about noon and to dress, still feeling very groggy, and sat for a short time on deck. Fortunately the US Consul-General in Bermuda had forewarned the Immigration officials of our expected arrival, so that the formalities were quickly completed and I was able to get away to our hotel, where I went straight to bed. I had to get up several times during that night with violent attacks of diarrhoea.

In the circumstances there was no doubt that my drink in the bar of the *Santa Rosa* had been deliberately doctored with the peppermint knockout drops usually known as a Mickey Finn, which, according to the strength of the dose, is calculated to incapacitate the drinker for any period up to twenty-four hours or longer.

Why should I have been singled out for this treatment alone, and not Freckles Wren as well? The only reason, I imagined, was that some weeks previously I had gone on board the *Santa Rosa* when she was tied up in St George's harbour and, along with the Customs and Censorship officials, had assisted in carrying out the examination of the passengers and their effects. I knew from the Grace Line agents in Bermuda that this passenger examination was greatly resented, not only by the agents but also by the members of the ship's company. I concluded that I had been recognized from the previous occasion, and I may also have been associated with the decision of the Bermuda authorities not to allow the crew to go ashore while the ship was in port. On the other hand, Wren had only just arrived in Bermuda by air from England and was quite unknown to the Grace Line agents and to the officers, crew, and stewards of the *Santa Rosa*.

Naturally I reported the matter to the British Consul-General in New York, who was Mr L. H. Leach. At first he spoke of making a strong complaint and having the suspected culprit 'stood off'. But on reflection, having no doubt discussed the matter with his colleagues, he wrote to me that 'as you did not call in a doctor on board, I should be in a weak position to take the matter up with the company,' since 'it would be so easy for them to maintain that you were entirely mistaken in your symptoms and so completely impossible for us to produce any effective reply'. In fact, I doubt very much whether the ship carried a doctor on such a short run and in any event I felt too ill to make any inquiries among the other passengers, besides being unconscious for most of the voyage. Of course, Wren might have done so, but he merely thought I was seasick. Anyhow in view of the Consul-General's letter the matter was dropped. The only result was a long-term one. I have never drunk another White Lady since.

After I had recovered and we had had some discussion with Stephenson and des Graz, Wren and I eventually took off by air via Jamaica and Colombia to Trinidad, which we reached on 18 February. The previous night we spent in the Colombian port of Barranquilla which appeared to be a hot-bed of Nazism, there being 1,100 Germans living there out of a total of 4,000 in the whole country. We stayed in a local hotel, the Prado, which had an English manager who was clearly under the influence of his Austrian mistress, a lady of avowed Nazi sympathies who was the hotel housekeeper. I hoped that the manager had not been weaned away from his British loyalty by his mistress and begged the British Vice-Consul, who was also Reporting Officer to the Naval Intelligence Centre in Jamaica, to do what he could to secure the manager's loyalty and at the same time make use of any information that he could obtain about the many Germans who were in the habit of frequenting the hotel.

It is unnecessary to go into any details in regard to the matters we talked over and the action taken with the local governments in Trinidad and the neighbouring island of Barbados, which Wren and I visited together a few days later. However, measures were initiated to afford increased protection to the Trinidad oil fields and to prevent any attempts at sabotage from the nearby Venezuelan mainland. Barbados I found particularly enchanting, and the memory of my first early-morning swim from the beach opposite the hotel outside Bridgetown, where we stayed, still lingers with me after forty years.

Our official meetings took place in Government House, a beautiful early eighteenth-century building completed in 1703, where the Governor, Sir John Waddington, entertained us and the local notabilities on our first night to an excellent dinner. I recall that the port circulated generously in accordance with tradition, and the King's health was drunk with the Governor remaining seated as His Majesty's representative in the colony.

Wren and I were surprised to learn that, since the outbreak of the war, more than 300 aliens, the majority German and many of military age, had been allowed to pass through Barbados by boat without any effort being made to examine or detain them, an omission which we both regarded as deplorable. 'There is no question that the local authorities have had the security of the colony at heart,' I wrote in my subsequent report to Stephenson, 'but their attitude has, as in the case of other British West Indian Islands, been governed by a desire to expedite the movement of any enemy alien or other suspicious in-transit passengers to any point outside their own colony. Instructions have now been given for enemy aliens to be removed for interrogation and search, and if necessary detention.'

On our return flight to Trinidad, where I parted from Wren, one of the engines in the twin-engine aircraft cut out and I thought we should come down in the sea. However, the pilot somehow managed to get the machine back to Piarco airport in Trinidad on one engine, a remarkable feat in the circumstances.

I was sorry to say good-bye to Freckles Wren, who was a congenial companion. I felt sure that he would do a good security intelligence job in Trinidad and in the event he did so. During the following five weeks I went on to visit Puerto Rico, Haiti, Jamaica, and Cuba, ending my tour in the Bahamas where the Duke of Windsor had recently become Governor.

The liaison which I had established with FBI Headquarters in Washington paid off at my first port of call which was San Juan,

Puerto Rico. I was met at the airport by the local FBI chief agent, Mr Dwight L. McCormick, and by his chief assistant. They had obviously been instructed by Mr Hoover to pay me some attention, since they went out of their way to show me every possible consideration and to hold back on nothing in the way of information on any matter in which I expressed an interest, besides arranging for my accommodation in what was then the best hotel in the Puerto Rican capital, the Condado (now the Holiday Inn). The FBI agent also introduced me to the officer in charge of US Naval Intelligence for that area, which included the American Virgin Islands, and at the officer's invitation I addressed about thirty of his junior officers on the workings of postal and telegraph censorship as part of a course of instruction which they were undergoing at the time.

I sensed a strong anti-American as well as anti-British feeling in the island. The natives of Spanish descent were ardent Falangists and supporters of General Franco, and they hoped that a German victory would result in the restoration to Spain of her old empire in Latin America. At the same time the local Nationalist Party, led by a certain Senor Medina Ramirez, declined to recognize the sovereignty of the US Government, refusing to acknowledge any other citizenship than that of Puerto Rico, and urging all those who were affected by the provisions of the draft (the US Selective Service and Training Act) not to register. A prominent centre of subversive activity was the University of Puerto Rico in San Juan. There at least the situation did not change, since when I revisited the island forty years later the students were still acting subversively, this time protesting against the current increase in university fees and the local government's withdrawal of their share of the gaming profits in the casinos. By this time, of course, Puerto Rico enjoyed a measure of devolved local government.

The island's situation in the Pan American Airways network made San Juan an important clearing house for passengers from Cuba, Haiti, Santo Domingo, and the French West Indies, of which the latter supported Vichy rather than de Gaulle's Free French movement. Passengers were also in transit at San Juan from South America, and there might be occasions when for some reason they and their effects could not be examined at British control points such as Trinidad and Jamaica. Mr McCormick told me that, if he were to receive any advance information of this kind from any British control point, it would be quite easy for him to arrange with the Immigration officials at the airport to make a thorough examination of any particular passenger and his effects, and if necessary to detain him pending further inquiries. I gladly undertook to put this proceeding into action which I subsequently did with useful results. In fact, as I noted, FBI agents were already carrying out such investigations in the guise of Immigration officials.

I also took note of the fact that all passengers disembarking at San Juan airport, including those in transit, were obliged to have their body temperatures taken by the Port Medical Officer. As I subsequently reported to Stephenson in New York, this proceeding presented 'interesting possibilities'.

It would be quite easy for the medical officer, having previously been taken into confidence, to say to any passenger (such as a courier with a diplomatic bag or pouch), 'You have a high temperature and must go to bed immediately!' This the passenger would do, and meanwhile his effects would be carefully searched and, in the case of diplomatic correspondence, secretly opened and photographed, as we were doing in Bermuda. Next day the traveller's temperature would be found to have fallen to a degree which would make it quite safe for him to proceed on his journey, and he would accordingly be sent on his way. The FBI was grateful for this advice and lost no time in putting it into operation, with useful results. I mention this as one of the small ways in which the British co-operated with the Bureau during the period of United States neutrality, thus contradicting the charges that British Intelligence was acting illegally and without the knowledge of the FBI, not to mention of President Roosevelt.

My next stop was in Haiti, France's former slave colony and at the time of my visit a corrupt Negro republic, recently occupied by the United States whose government still controlled the republic's revenues.[17] The Immigration official to whom I presented my passport when I landed at Port-au-Prince obviously could not read English, since he studied the document upside-down for several minutes and eventually affixed an immigration stamp to it in the same position. This was long before the days of the infamous Papa Doc Duvalier, but his predecessor when I was there, the dictatorial President Stenio Vicente, was just as bad, though in a different way, since, although ostensibly pro-American, he and his ministers were largely dominated by the German Chargé d'Affaires, who was bribing the Voodoo priests to preach the doctrine of German might, blackmailing the inhabitants by threats against their relatives in France, and proclaiming that the decline in the export of coffee, the country's staple industry, was owing to the British blockade. Haitian rulers, from the negro King Henry Christophe in the early nineteenth century to the mulatto Stenio Vincente and the negro François Duvalier in the twentieth, almost invariably developed into dictators after a short period of power.

I was delighted to find my old friend Guy Boulton installed as Vice-Consul in the British Legation in Port-au-Prince. At one time he had been a member of the Consular Service which he had left to follow another career, but had recently rejoined the service, having previously been acting in charge of the Travellers' Censorship in Bermuda. I immediately recommended to Stephenson that he should appoint Boulton as MI6 representative in Haiti in addition to his consular duties, an action which Stephenson took with characteristic promptitude – letting London know afterwards – since there was abundant evidence of anti-Allied activities among the German colony in Haiti. There was obviously plenty of SIS work for Boulton to do which it would not have been proper for the Minister-Resident Mr R. A. N. Hillyer to undertake, although the latter was to prove most co-operative once we had taken him into our confidence.

Boulton and I decided to explore the island and to spend

several days doing this. Our first objective was an hotel at Pétionville, a small town in the hills about five miles above Port-au-Prince, where the hotel proprietor was a German Nazi named Wilhelm Kahl. Boulton and I dropped in 'by accident' on a Saturday evening, when we found about a hundred members of the German colony at a social gathering. On our arrival there was a raffle in progress allegedly to raise money for the German Red Cross, one of the articles raffled being a picture of Hitler, for which, needless to say, neither Boulton nor I took tickets. We stayed for an hour and fortunately neither our identity nor nationality was detected, although four Americans were recognized the same evening and were escorted off the premises by the German Chargé d'Affaires in person.

Our 500-mile tour took us to various places where we were able to make useful local contacts, including Cap-Haïtien in the north where we saw the ruins of the pretentious palace, Sans-Souci, and the mighty fortress, La Ferrière, built by the power-crazed Christophe at enormous cost of human life while the monarch rewarded his intimates with such bizarre titles as Duke of Marmalade and Count of Lemonade, which still persist as place names. In Cap-Haïtien we encountered a British Baptist minister whose religious duties were combined with that of Admiralty Reporting Officer. 'He is most anxious to furnish intelligence,' I noted at the time.

Back in Port-au-Prince I found the various local authorities ready to co-operate for a suitable monetary consideration. The Post Office officials, for instance, were quite ready to hand over the correspondence of prominent Germans when suitably rewarded, while the Immigration officers were equally willing to provide information about suspicious individuals entering and leaving the country. Accordingly I arranged that Boulton should be furnished with a sufficient imprest of money to enable him to act appropriately and without delay. Any possibility that President Vincente would thwart these arrangements was fortunately nullified a few weeks later when he failed to get re-elected for a third term, owing to opposition from the State Department in Washington. He was succeeded, with American support, by the

Haitian Ambassador in Washington, Elie Lescot, who like other occupants of the Presidential Palace lost no time in assuming the trappings of dictatorship, though he proved to be staunchly pro-American and after the Japanese attack on Pearl Harbor obediently declared war on Germany, Italy, Japan and the other enemy allies.

A short flight took me on to Kingston, Jamaica. I landed at the Palisades airport, where I was agreeably impressed by the local custom, long since discontinued, whereby all disembarking passengers were given a large glass of rum punch, a gesture designed to advertise one of the colony's staple products. Commander Harington had not yet arrived to take up his duties as local MI5/MI6 representative, specifically to act as the opposite number to Freckles Wren in Trinidad. I immediately made for the Myrtle Bank Hotel which housed the Naval Intelligence Centre besides transient guests. The Myrtle Bank was an old-fashioned establishment with primitive air-conditioning, and I was glad to learn some years afterwards, when I paid a second visit to Jamaica, that it had been demolished.

The main object of my visit was to make arrangements for the establishment of a censorship station for the examination of transit mails, which duly came into being, although it was never to achieve the importance or results of Bermuda or Trinidad. In this I had the full support of the Naval Intelligence people as well as of the Governor Sir Arthur Richards, later Lord Milverton, who had been on leave in England when Wren and I had passed through Kingston a fortnight previously. Richards, who was then fifty-six, was unquestionably the ablest member of the senior branch of the British Colonial Service, while his Colonial Secretary, Alexander Grantham, later Governor of Hong Kong, was barely forty and easily the most brilliant member of the younger intake of the service. Richards was a tough and determined administrator and shortly afterwards he had no hesitation in interning the foremost trade unionist and leader of the Jamaica Labour Party, Alexander Bustamente ('Call me Busta!'), on security grounds. Yet Busta, whom I recall meeting, was eventually to become a knight, Privy Councillor, and Prime

Minister, as well as Minister for External Affairs, when Jamaica received constitutional government. He enjoyed enormous popularity with all classes and had an immense capacity for consuming rum punches.

There used to be a thriving call-girl business in Kingston, but this had been badly hit by the war and the consequent lack of tourists. I was not troubled by any of their invitations, but shortly after I left I heard that Edwin Herbert, the Director of Censorship, who had arrived from London to approve my preliminary censorship arrangements, was stopped by a personable dusky lady in Kingston's main street and handed a card with her name, address, and telephone number, and also the following legend in large letters at the bottom of the card: 'Particularly patient with elderly gentlemen!' Since Herbert was barely forty years old at the time, he thought this additional information might have been omitted in his case.

From Kingston I flew on, in a Pan American Sikorsky flying-boat, to Santiago in Cuba and thence in a Lockheed Electra land-plane to Havana. I did not expect to have much to do in Cuba, since Stephenson already had a representative on the island. As it happened I did not even see him, since I was told that he was touring the island with the British Minister Sir George Ogilvie Forbes, and I was unable to wait until he returned since I had promised to be in the Bahamas not later than 18 March, which was two days ahead. I was met at the Havana airport by the Vice-Consul, Mr J. H. Wright, a congenial and helpful young man who subsequently attained ambassadorial rank when he became our man in Honduras. He arranged for my accommodation in the Hotel Nacional, Havana's largest hotel, still in existence though I imagine in a somewhat run-down condition under the Castro regime. But there were still twenty years to go before the Marxist leader took over and Cuba became the Soviet Union's strongest bastion in the Caribbean. When I was there, there was a military dictatorship in being under General Fulgencia Batista, a pro-American who was to follow the example of his Haitian counterpart by declaring war against the United States's enemies after Pearl Harbor.

The MI6 man whom I did not meet was of somewhat unorthodox habits, and, recalling the first telegram which he had sent Stephenson after his appointment, I hoped that he was behaving himself and not shocking the somewhat strict moral outlook of the Catholic Minister Ogilvie Forbes. The telegram was brief and to the point: *Please send one blonde repeat blonde who can speak Spanish, dance the samba, and ——.* The figures of the last group in the cipher telegram were incomprehensible, and the people in Stephenson's cipher room in New York never understood what they meant, although no doubt they made a shrewd guess.

Although more than forty years had passed since Winston Churchill was in Cuba as a special correspondent covering the Spanish-American war for the London *Daily Graphic* (when he heard shots fired in anger for the first time on his twenty-first birthday and was awarded a Spanish medal which he was not allowed to wear), there were still some good stories being told about him. One concerned an incident which happened when he was riding along a country road and saw a number of girls picking tobacco leaf in the fields for cigars. One of the girls approached him and offered to roll him a cigar, an offer which he gratefully accepted. The girl immediately pulled up her skirt and rolled the leaf on her thigh, presenting him with the result of her efforts. 'Ah, what a wonderful smoke!' Churchill was said to have remarked afterwards, when he had taken a few puffs. 'And what a superb aroma!'

3

British Security Co-ordination

BY THE TIME I arrived in the Bahamas on 18 March 1941, the Governor, the Duke of Windsor, formerly King Edward VIII, was comfortably installed with his Duchess and staff in Government House, Nassau, which had apparently been in such shabby condition when they arrived in the previous August that they were not able to move in for about two months. By this time the mansion, a handsome building in old colonial style, had been decorated in fairly lavish style to the Duchess's taste, the consequent expense being a source of dispute between the new Governor, the British Treasury, and the Bahamian Legislative Assembly which was called upon to meet £1,500 of the cost. The Duke's study, where he received me, clearly bore the stamp of the Duchess's personality in the matter of interior decoration, besides being filled with portraits and photographs of her. It seemed to me – and I had other opportunities of observing this – that the Duke was still quite infatuated with her. While Government House was being got ready for them, they had stayed for part of the time at Westbourne House, later the Bahamas Country Club, which had been put at their disposal by the American-born self-made millionaire, Sir Harry Oakes, a rough and overbearing man who had made a fortune in Canada from gold-mining, subsequently becoming a naturalized British subject and being created a baronet for his philanthropic benefactions.

The peculiar physical condition of the Bahamas posed considerable difficulties in the field of security, as I stressed to the Governor when we met. The Bahamas were composed of a scattered series of coral islands and cays, of which about thirty were uninhabited, extending from the Florida coast to Santo Domingo and the eastern end of Cuba. Thus it was extremely

The Duke and Duchess of Windsor in the summer of 1940, shortly after their arrival in the Bahamas on his appointment as Governor of the Colony.

difficult to control the movements of individuals within a territory of more than 4,000 square miles. I noticed, too, a general lack of war-consciousness; the development of the tourist trade on which the colony largely depended was of obviously greater importance to many local eyes, as well as local pockets, than any defence or security measures, however desirable these might be for Britain and the conduct of the war. There was plenty of capital in the Bahamas, owing to the large profits made from dealings in land and property by the so-called Bay Street boys, the street with their offices being the chief thoroughfare in Nassau and running the entire length of the town parallel with the sea-front. The principal dealer in real estate, whom I met during my visit, was the Hon (later Sir) Harold Christie, a member of the Legislative Council, later accused of murdering Sir Harry Oakes.[1] Because of the numbers of American visitors and the proximity of the United States mainland, the wartime exchange – control regulations were being flagrantly infringed.

My host in Nassau was Captain R. M. Millar, who combined the duties of Naval Reporting Officer with those of Super-intendent of the local prison. I stayed with him in his quarters in the prison, the only time in my life when I have slept in jail. Millar immediately took me to see the Colonial Secretary, Leslie Heape, who duly introduced me to those local officials whom he thought I should see, such as the Attorney General, Chief of Police, Postal, Cable and Telephone Censors, and the controllers of Customs and Immigration. They all proved most co-operative, particularly the Attorney General, Mr (later Sir) Eric Hallinan, a cheerful and hospitable Irishman who was later Chief Justice of the West Indies and an appeal judge in the Bahamas and Bermuda. Finally, the Colonial Secretary told me that the Governor would be pleased to see me the following afternoon.

Meanwhile I learned some interesting facts about the local government, one of which was most unusual and, in my view, un-constitutional. But this was not the Duke's fault. His predecessor in Government House, Sir Charles Dundas, who reluctantly retired to make way for His Royal Highness although in the normal course he had two more years of office to run, had held Heape's job of Colonial Secretary in the Bahamas from 1929 to 1934, and at various times during this period was Acting-Governor. When he returned to Nassau as Governor in 1937, being naturally familiar with the conditions and problems of Bahamian administration, Dundas found it more convenient that the confidential business of the colonial secretariat should be transacted in Government House, and he issued instructions that all the confidential and secret files should be brought up from the

Colonial Secretary's office to Government House. These instructions were carried out, and when the Duke of Windsor
arrived as Governor in August 1940, he accepted this practice as
a normal feature of colonial administration, and even enlarged
upon it to the extent of giving orders that certain files, including
that relating to Marshal Goering's friend and relative the Swedish
industrialist and suspected pro-German, Axel Wenner Gren, as
well as files on other individuals of security interest, should not be
shown to anyone, not even the Colonial Secretary, without his
express permission. Since the official code and cipher books had
also been transferred to Government House, Leslie Heape had to
go there whenever he wished to send a telegram, whether on a
simple routine matter or a serious matter of security. Fortunately,
for my own part I was able to establish friendly relations with the
Chief Clerk in charge of the confidential registry, whose name
was Mrs Chipman, and I do not think that any security information in which I expressed interest was withheld from me.

I had two interviews with the Duke, each lasting for about an
hour, and on both occasions I must say that I was received with
characteristic graciousness, and the atmosphere throughout was
both friendly and frank. On the second occasion I suggested that
Leslie Heape should also be present, as I wished to make sure that
any security, and other, suggestions of mine to which the Duke
assented would be acted upon by the Colonial Secretary. To this
the Duke was agreeable and Heape's presence proved most
helpful. Both meetings took place in the Governor's newly decorated office-study, with its plethora of pictures of the Duchess.

I thought the Duke looked considerably younger and more
relaxed since I had last seen him with Mrs Simpson (as she then
was) at a Londonderry House reception in London shortly before
the abdication crisis. 'Ah!' was his opening remark as we shook
hands and he beckoned me to a chair, 'I see you're wearing my
old Oxford college tie.' After a few questions from him about
Magdalen and when I had last been there, I immediately raised
the question of the security of the islands.

I began by pointing out that New Providence Island, which
contained Nassau and was the seat of the colonial government,

The Duke of Windsor's study in Government House, Nassau.

possessed no coastal defences of more recent construction than a few eighteenth-century forts, which had no current military value. 'You know, Sir,' I said, 'a U-boat appearing suddenly off this island could shell the Cable and Wireless station, and carry off Your Royal Highness and the Duchess and the rest of the occupants of Government House, before the Bahamians realized that the island was being attacked.' The Duke nodded, as if in agreement, adding that there were 'coastal watchers'. I agreed that the measures passed by the House of Assembly in Nassau provided for about thirty such watchers, but they were only stationed on New Providence, whereas the Bahamas consisted of about 700 smaller islands. Even in New Providence the exact locations of the watchers did not appear to be governed by strategic considerations, since at one point the watcher's vision only embraced water to a depth of a few fathoms.

I then passed to the touchy question of Immigration, and went on:

So far as I can see, the Immigration regulations and the

methods by which they are enforced are conspicuous for their laxity. United States visitors are not required to be in possession of valid passports or indeed to provide any proofs of identity whatsoever. It is extremely unlikely that anyone representing himself to be a United States citizen would be challenged by the Immigration officials on landing. All that the visitor is obliged to do is to fill up a landing card prior to dis-embarkation, purporting to state his or her nationality and country of birth. These cards are taken to the Immigration Office, but no attempt is seemingly made to check the veracity of their statements. But even this limited information is only obtained from alleged United States passengers arriving by the recognized sea and air routes. Other passengers are in the habit of visiting the islands in privately owned craft, and no official record exists of their movements.

As an example, I added that earlier that day, while looking through copies of some of the recent outward telegrams in the Cable Censor's office, I noticed a telegram to an address in Dublin signed 'Byers', which interested me as I thought I knew the sender. However inquiries at the Immigration Office failed to reveal the entry into the colony of any person of that name at the date in question, and there was no doubt that he or she had entered and left the island unobserved by any Immigration official.

The Duke replied that he had taken note of what I said and suggested that we should bring up the question at our next meeting, when the Colonial Secretary would be present.

At this moment the house telephone rang on the Duke's desk. He answered it and after listening for a few moments to the voice at the other end of the line, he replied: 'Send them in.' He then turned to me and said: 'Don't go. It's only Harry Oakes. He has arrived with some Mexicans whom he wants me to meet.'

Oakes and the Mexicans were then shown in, and Oakes presented the leading Mexican who turned out to be General Maximinio Camacho, governor of Puebla province and brother of the Mexican President Avila Camacho. There were about sixteen other Mexicans in the General's entourage, and I subsequently gathered that they were all being put up as Oakes's guests in the luxurious British Colonial Hotel in Bay Street. In the circumstances I could not avoid being introduced to both Oakes and Camacho, although I felt considerably embarrassed, particularly when I heard the Duke speaking to Camacho in Spanish and inviting him to come and see him for a talk next day.

As the Governor must have known, Mexico had recently broken off diplomatic relations with Britain after expropriating all the British oil companies in the country without making any offer of compensation. It was therefore highly irregular for the Duke, as the official representative of King George VI and the British Government, to receive a Mexican provincial governor so closely related to the President of a country with which Britain had no diplomatic relations.[2] Of course, the Mexicans should not have been allowed to visit the Bahamas at all, since as aliens they were expected to be in possession of valid passports with British consular visas. Naturally it had been impossible to fulfil the latter requirement, since all the British consulates in Mexico had been closed down, but neither Camacho nor any of his companions had been asked to produce their passports on arrival in Nassau. When I left Government House, I went straight to Heape's office and persuaded the Colonial Secretary to send an Immigration official to the British Colonial Hotel to examine the passports. This was done, and one of the party, a man named Ordoñez, turned out to be on the FBI's black-list and wanted by the Bureau for 'un-American activities'.

The object of Oakes's Mexican introductions soon became clear. Oakes, although an extremely rich man, was subject to the stringent foreign-exchange controls which applied to all Bahamian residents, while the Duke was similarly restricted by the British Treasury. Somehow, Oakes illegally succeeded in transferring a substantial part of his capital to Mexico, where he emerged shortly afterwards as a considerable shareholder in the newly formed bank, the Banco Continental, in Mexico City, and in this capacity he was able to make available to the Duke all the foreign currency he needed.

At my second meeting, at which the Colonial Secretary was present, I represented to the Governor the desirability of United States visitors being in possession of some kind of identity card, such as was at present required by cruise passengers disembarking at Bermuda when their ship was in port. Since about 300 tourists visited the Bahamas every week, the Duke suggested I should take up the question with the British Embassy in Washington with a view to getting the assent of the US Department of Immigration. He himself undertook to write to the Embassy on the point and no doubt he did so. However, since the Bahamas were included in the British possessions in which the Americans were getting bases, I remarked that anything in the way of an identity card would only be a temporary measure, since the Americans were sure to insist on their nationals being in possession of passports when they came to the islands, just as they were to do in Bermuda. Eventually this happened. But like everything else it took time. Besides this, there were practically no transit mails, but there were plenty of terminal mails and correspondents in the outer islands were having their letters routed so as to avoid the small terminal censorship in Nassau. Because of the large number of foreigners, particularly at Cat Cay near the Florida coast, I felt a lot of interesting incoming letters were being missed, judging by the few which had been misdirected to Bermuda and which had contained much useful information about conditions in Germany and other enemy countries.

Incidentally, the terminal censorship was extremely unsatisfactory. The Chief Postal Censor only had the help of a few voluntary assistants, whose attendance was irregular and spasmodic, with the result that he was left virtually single-handed to deal with the heavy terminal mail by air and sea. His work was carried out in a small room in the House of Assembly building which also housed the Post Office. This room was required from time to time for meetings of the Legislative Council Committees, and on such occasions censorship work had to be abandoned at the shortest notice and the room vacated. Naturally I reported this to Herbert and des Graz and some improvements were eventually made, although the terminal censorship in Nassau continued to be exercised as a purely defensive weapon and no effort was seemingly made to 'submit' letters which might be of value to authorities outside the colony, particularly as there were so many enemy aliens, refugees, and others with international associations resident in the islands.

I parted from the Duke after he had agreed to have a security officer if MI5/MI6 could provide one, and I suggested that for the time being the Bahamas could be covered by the officer in Jamaica. This was the best I could do, but I felt it was not very satisfactory.

'By the way, Hyde,' the Duke said to me as I was leaving, 'what were you doing before the war?' I said that I had been Private Secretary to the Air Minister Lord Londonderry.

'Wasn't it his wife who gave those dreadful receptions at Londonderry House?' he went on. I replied that Lady Londonderry did occasionally give large receptions, but it was in her capacity as leading Conservative Party hostess, usually on the eve of the opening of Parliament.

'Well,' he remarked. 'Thank goodness, one thing the war has done is to put an end to *that* kind of entertaining!' He had evidently forgotten that both the Londonderrys had written him sympathetic letters at the time of the abdication. He only remembered his animosity to Mr Baldwin and the majority of Conservatives, with the exception of Churchill.

A curious thing happened before I departed for New York; apparently the Duke had taken a fancy to me, since I was sounded out as to whether I would be interested in joining his staff. I replied that, while I appreciated the honour reflected by this invitation, I felt that I could not abandon my security work.

On reaching New York I wrote a detailed account of my tour and my recommendations for the improvement of local security and censorship. Many of these recommendations were implemented, although the one about the Duke of Windsor and the possibility of an attack on Government House apparently did not attract the Prime Minister's attention for eighteen months, when there was still a chance that Germany would win the war and try to put forward the Duke as a puppet sovereign. Lord Cranborne (later Marquess of Salisbury), the Secretary of State for the Colonies, wrote a memorandum to the Prime Minister to which Churchill replied:

> 31 August 1942. Am I not right in thinking that the only attack against the Bahamas is by a party landed from a U-boat? If so, Government House seems to be the obvious quarry. A U-boat would not have the facilities for finding out where the Duke of Windsor was if he were not there or were moving about. The right rule is, one may always take a chance but not offer a 'sitter'. I am therefore in favour of putting an electrified fence round Government House and the other places mentioned, but not interfering with H.R.H.'s liberty of movement otherwise than by informing him of the dangers. It is essential that the seat of Government should be protected against a U-boat raiding force, and for this purpose additional platoons should be sent.[3]

The platoons already in the colony belonged to the Cameron Highlanders who had helped to suppress the riots which had broken out in Nassau in June 1942 consequent upon the disparity in wages paid to the Bahamian workers and the Americans employed on the construction of the new bases on two of the outer islands, Great Exuma and Abaco. The additional platoons came from the same regiment, and their presence, together with the other measures recommended by the Prime Minister, no doubt gave the Duke an additional sense of security. But until the issue of the war was beyond doubt, following the European landings in June 1944, the Duke was always apprehensive that he might be kidnapped when he was living in Government House in the Bahamas.

I got back to Bermuda early in April, 1941, to find Censorship and Contraband Control in full swing. The Censorship department had been increased to nearly 900 examiners under the benevolent and experienced direction of a retired member of the

Indian Civil Service, Charles Watkins-Mence, who had been the Trade Censor at Liverpool. Room 99 was producing remarkable results and the team of Special Examiners was reinforced by several experts, including a very determined young lady named Nadya Gardner who was to play a highly important part in uncovering enemy espionage and propaganda activities in the United States. The Bermuda Customs, under the vigorous leadership of Rowe Spurling, continued to co-operate enthusiastically with the Censorship in the seizure of contraband, although his hauls occasionally caused a rumpus in higher quarters. For instance, acting on prior information that the *haute couture* dress designer Elsa Schiaparelli was carrying a large sum of money in dollars in a ship to Lisbon, he asked her to hand over the money. She did, but it turned out to amount to only $2,360. However, she was also carrying a large amount of vitamin pills intended, so she said, for a Quaker organization for famine relief in occupied France. Her story turned out to be true and the vitamin supplies were allowed through even though they were consigned to an enemy-occupied country. Similar consignments to individuals from their relatives or friends in the United States were of necessity seized, despite the fact that for the most part they were pathetic packages of commodities such as coffee, sugar, edible oils and powdered milk.

Three times a week there was a sale of the confiscated contraband at No 1 shed on the Hamilton waterfront, which usually began at 11 a.m.

One particular consignment I recall was a large parcel of rare cyclamen seeds worth between $5,000 and $15,000, consigned from Holland to a Dutch firm in New York, which we condemned on the pretext that it was a Nazi method of obtaining foreign currency. The worried consignees in New York sent a Dutchman with instructions to buy it when it was auctioned. However, we got wind of this plan when the Dutchman arrived and turned up at each auction day punctually. On the day of the sale we changed the opening of the auction to 10.30, so that when the Dutchman appeared he discovered to his consternation that the cyclamen seeds had been knocked down to a Bermudian for $5. The Bermudian then went up to New York where he sold the seeds for $4,000 to a reliable purchaser, and on his return to Hamilton patriotically turned over the money to the Bermuda War Fund – although the Dutchman, acting for the Germans, would have been prepared to go considerably beyond that figure had he been able to bid at the auction.[4]

It will be recalled that when Stephenson and Donovan stopped off in Bermuda on their way to London in December, 1940, I drew their attention to a typewritten letter with a New York postmark, addressed to a certain Mr Lothar Frederick in Berlin, which the censors had intercepted and which gave a list of Allied shipping in New York harbour with details of their movements and armaments. The letter was signed 'Joe K', and, although written in English, its style and wording gave the impression that the writer was a German, possibly a Nazi spy, who was reporting to his chief in Berlin in plain-language code. When I showed it to him, Stephenson had expressed the view that it might turn out to be a most important letter and urged me to 'keep a look-out for any more like it'. I promised to do this and showed the mail sorters how to recognize the mysterious Joe K's handwriting on the back of the envelope which he had typed and which appeared to indicate the name and address of the sender in New York. On inquiry through the FBI, these names and addresses turned out to be fictitious. I asked the industrious and perceptive Nadya Gardner to work on the secondary meaning of the letters. The various names on the back of the replies, as Miss Gardner was quick to note, although bearing different New York addresses, always began with the letter J. The correspondence on the face of it purported to be from an ordinary commercial agent dealing in various commodities, but the secondary meaning was not difficult to determine. The names of the addressees in Europe, such as Lothar Frederick in Berlin, were later established to be cover names for the Nazi Secret Service and Gestapo Chief Heinrich Himmler. More than thirty such letters were intercepted, and copies were sent to the FBI in Washington.

Here, for example, is a letter from Joe K to a Spanish intermediary, Manuel Alonso, at an address in Madrid:

Your order No 5 is rather large – and I with my limited facilities and funds shall never be able to fill such a large order completely. But I already have many numbers in stock, and shall ship whatever and whenever I can. I hope you have no objections to part shipments . . .

The Nos 852, 853, 854 and 857 are not so very easy to obtain now . . .

Please give me more details about the merchandise to which our customers have any objections. Since they are paying for it, they are entitled to ask for the best. From the paying customers I take any time criticism – and I should also appreciate your suggestions for improving the quality and delivery.

In plain language this meant that the German Intelligence Chief's letter marked No 5 called for a lot of work on the part of the writer, which with the relatively small organization and little money at his disposal it would take him some time to accomplish. The numbers referred to specific items in which German Intelligence was particularly interested. The writer went on to ask where his reports had fallen short or were otherwise unsatisfactory. He concluded by asking for suggestions as to how his work could be improved and how best his reports could escape detection by the authorities such as the Censorship.[5]

I noted that in every case the letters were typed on one side only, the reverse being blank. I thought that the blank side might contain secret writing, and before leaving on my Caribbean tour asked Nadya Gardner to send the letters to the laboratory with which Censorship headquarters in Bermuda was now equipped and have them tested accordingly. This she did, but to her intense disappointment the initial tests revealed nothing, so that eventually the laboratory chemists did not consider it worth their while continuing. But Miss Gardner was not the kind of girl to take no for an answer, and she persevered on her own. She possessed a slight knowledge of inorganic chemistry and she suggested that the old-fashioned iodine reagent, which was used by the Germans in the First World War, should be tried. At first her suggestion was pooh-poohed as being hopelessly out of date. Nevertheless she persisted, and to satisfy her this test was eventually made, although the experts said it would be a waste of time. But the results were astonishing – secret writing was brought out by this test on each letter. In every case it was seen to contain the latest information on aircraft production and shipping movements in the mainland ports and factories. Moreover the secret ink used was revealed as a solution of pyramidon, a powdered substance often used as a cure for headaches and readily obtainable at any pharmacy or drug-store. It could be used with a toothpick and as it dried it became invisible.

Meanwhile a letter in German to a suspected agent at a cover address in Portugal was intercepted in Bermuda. It contained elaborate details of aircraft supplied to Britain by the United States and also of the US Army training programme. It was signed 'Konrad' and was evidently the work of a trained military observer. This letter was also tested for secret writing in a pyramidon solution, and the result showed that the writer's address in the United States was 'c/o Joe', and also that he was mailing duplicate reports to Germany via China and Japan. The writer added: 'If further information on Puerto Rico is desired (see my report sent through Smith, China), please send Joe a telegram of good wishes.'

At the same time Joe's letters indicated that he was in touch with Konrad, whom he sometimes called 'Phil' or alternatively 'Junio'. Thanks to this lead given by the Bermuda Censorship, the FBI succeeded in intercepting a report from Konrad to 'Mr Smith of China', giving exact details of the defences of Hawaii, with maps and photographs, notably of Pearl Harbor. 'This will be of interest mostly to our yellow allies,' Konrad's report concluded. Nevertheless the FBI was still no nearer discovering the identity of either Konrad or Joe.

It was the Bermuda Censorship that provided the vital clue. On 20 March 1941, a letter addressed by Joe to Manuel Alonso in Madrid and intercepted in Bermuda contained a most important piece of news. Two evenings previously, while attempting to cross Broadway near Times Square, New York, Phil had been knocked down by a taxi and struck by another car as he lay on the ground. He had been taken to hospital, where he had died the next day without recovering consciousness. 'I was with him all evening,' Joe continued, 'but I did not try to cross the street with him as I thought it too risky.'

As his condition was, according to information received by telephone, very critical and as I myself could not do anything, I notified 'his' consulate (through an old friend) which acted at once but it was impossible to save his life – his injuries were too serious.

This letter also contained secret writing on the reverse side which gave further particulars of the accident, including the number of the car which had caused the fatal injury, and the name of the hospital to which Phil had been taken, St Vincent's. 'The Consulate mentioned is the Spanish,' this part of the letter stated. Joe added the text of several short cables he had sent after the accident. 'Phil's things are still at the Hotel Taft,' he concluded.

This information was immediately sent by my Bermuda office to Stephenson, who passed it on to the FBI. In fact, Hoover's men were already working on the accident from a different angle and had easily traced the victim from the Spanish passport he was carrying in the name of Junio Lopez Lido. They had been called in following the prompt action of the manager of the Hotel Taft, where Lido had been staying. After the accident Joe had managed to grab Lido's briefcase but was worried about his luggage. The same evening he had telephoned the hotel and said that his friend had met with an accident and asked that his luggage should be taken good care of. When the voice at the other end of the line, presumably that of the hotel manager, began to ask questions, Joe became uneasy and hung up without giving his name.

It was this incident that aroused the hotel manager's suspicions. In the hotel register Lido had signed the register as Junio Lopez, adding that his nationality was Spanish and that he had come from Shanghai. This seemed innocent enough, but the manager thought the anonymous telephone call was rather

Secret writing on the back of the 'Joe K' letter, giving further details of Von der Osten's accident and death, 20 March 1941.

suspicious. Anyhow he informed the police, who in turn informed the Public Administrator, the official responsible for dealing with the affairs of intestates. The Public Administrator took possession of the dead man's luggage and other personal effects, including his passport showing his surname as Lido, and afterwards turned them over to the FBI. Some letters were found amongst his effects addressed to a certain Carl Wilhelm Von der Osten in Denver, Colorado. It so happened that the FBI already suspected this man of being a German agent and proceeded to interrogate him. Under interrogation he admitted that the dead man was his brother, Captain Ulrich Von der Osten, who was attached to German military intelligence, that is the *Abwehr*. But he could throw no light on any of his brother's associates or acquaintances.

In his letters Joe had often referred to his Uncle Dave and Aunt Loni, who had a shop in New York which they intended to sell. Later Joe wrote: 'Mr H. sold his store,' and in the letter of 20 March to Manuel Alonso, giving the details of Ulrich Von der Osten's fatal accident, Joe stated:

As mentioned in one of my cables my aunt sold her store recently, and so it is not advisable to send her any more mail, but my other friends and relatives are still in business.

Among the effects of the dead Von der Osten the FBI found a telephone number which the Bureau traced to a delicatessen shop in Brooklyn. It now appeared that the owner had recently bought it from a couple named David and Loni Harris. Further enquiries by the Bureau revealed that this couple had a nephew named Fred Ludwig living somewhere in New York. The next problem was to find him among the city's millions of inhabitants.

It was Stephenson's organization, BSC, which provided the missing link in the chain of investigation. London headquarters of MI6 had recently advised Stephenson that a known German agent in Lisbon had telephoned a coded message to 'Fozie' in New York, and they asked Stephenson to ascertain the identity of Fozie. The FBI was requested to help, but replied that, since 10,000 cablegrams were filed every day in New York, identification was impossible. This reply was somewhat disingenuous because there was a Central Bureau for Registered Cable Addresses in New York, and although its records were confidential there is no reason to suppose that the FBI, in its official capacity, could not have obtained access to it. Possibly the Bureau's New York office thought they did not have the authority to obtain this information, or it may have been owing to jealousy. In any event, it is difficult to see why they should not have responded to Stephenson's request, in view of the valuable information and other assistance the Bureau had received from BSC. Stephenson now took the matter into his own hands and, having discovered the name of the cable company, he was able to use a contact he had in the company's New York office. This contact informed him that Fozie was the code name used as a cable address by one Kurt Frederick Ludwig, whose address was in Brooklyn. Stephenson duly conveyed this information to the FBI, which replied two days later: 'Investigation has disclosed that Joe K is identical with one Fred Ludwig.'

Further investigation revealed that the spy, whose age was forty-eight, had been born in Freemont, Ohio, and, as a child, had been taken to Germany where he grew up, married, and now had a wife and three children living in Munich. He had visited the United States several times in the 1920s and 1930s, and when he finally returned to organize a spy ring in March 1940, he had entered the country on an American passport (which as an American-born citizen he was entitled to do), posing as a salesman of leather goods. He then proceeded to gather a number of willing helpers, mostly from the ranks of the pro-Nazi German-American Bund. It must have been love of his work and devotion to the Nazi cause which kept him at it, as he was certainly not overpaid, his remuneration consisting of sums ranging from $50 to $500 which from time to time would be passed to him surreptitiously in an envelope by a member of the German Consulate-General in New York at some pre-arranged meeting place, such as Child's Restaurant on 34th Street. After Ulrich Von der Osten arrived in the United States early in March 1941, and registered at the Hotel Taft in New York under the name of Junio Lopez, Ludwig acted under his orders; but it was only for a very short time, since Ulrich was killed in the car accident on 20 March, which led to the discovery of Joe's identity.

Ludwig was not arrested immediately, as the FBI wished to get on the trail of as many of his confederates as possible. Instead he was kept under careful surveillance, while his acquaintances were investigated at the same time. Towards the end of June 1941, the FBI uncovered another spy ring which was acting independently of the Ludwig ring, and made a number of arrests. This was effected through the co-operation of a double agent named William Sebold, a naturalized American citizen of German birth who ostensibly ran a secret radio-transmitting station for the Germans while really working for the FBI, which fed him with appropriate information. (The story of this operation, which was an exclusively American one, was later recorded in the movie *The House on 92nd Street*.) Although the two rings were independent of each other, Ludwig knew several members of the Sebold ring, including a man named Scholz. In this context Ludwig had a narrow escape. He had arranged to meet Scholz in a bookshop in Yorkville, the largely German-inhabited district of Manhattan, and as he arrived he saw two strange men preceding him into the shop. Ludwig entered cautiously and went to the back of the store, where he pretended to be looking at some books. The two strangers were FBI agents and before his eyes Ludwig saw them arrest the very man he had come to meet. The 'competition' and 'our competitors' (as Ludwig referred to the FBI or US Military Intelligence in his reports to the Gestapo) were getting hot, like the New York weather in July. Consequently he wrote to Germany that he was going to a summer camp called Lutherland in the Pocono Mountains in Pennsylvania for a rest. From the camp he kept in touch with his secretary, an eighteen-year-old German blonde named Lucy Boehmler, to whom he had been in the habit of giving or sending reports, asking her to 'inform Marion Pon', Marion being the code name for Himmler and Pon the code word for secret writing, in the use of which Lucy had been instructed.

While he was in the Lutherland camp Ludwig also kept in touch with other confederates, including a man named Froehlich, whom Ludwig asked about Scholz. 'I am sorry for our friend,' Froehlich replied, 'and I hope he will be able to go through the ordeal without cracking up.' However, Ludwig also learned that several members of the Brooklyn spy ring were 'cracking up' and telling the FBI agents what they knew, and what they and others had been doing. In the result, Ludwig wrote several letters to Himmler reporting which ones were making 'unpleasant statements', in order that the Gestapo might take reprisals against their families.

Although he was not yet aware that he was under surveillance, Ludwig had a feeling that the time had come for him to get out of America and return to Germany. Consequently he returned to

New York for a few days to wind up his affairs and then headed west in his car, with the object of picking up a Japanese ship on the Pacific coast and making his way home via the Far East. It was not until he reached Chicago that he realized that he was being followed. He then panicked and drove at eighty miles an hour, hoping to escape his pursuers. But the FBI had plenty of agents along the route and one or other of them always kept Ludwig in his sight. By the time Ludwig reached the Rockies his money was running short and he appealed to Lucy for help, writing that 'the competition is very bad'. She sent him $20, saying that was all she could do, although he had never paid her much, if anything, in the way of the salary he had promised her. He spent the night of 21 August in the Yellowstone National Park, where he took a cabin in which he burned all the incriminating papers he had with him. The charred remains were subsequently recovered by FBI agents who sent them to Washington for analysis, which revealed, with the help of an infra-red ray lamp, that they were full of military information.

After leaving Yellowstone Ludwig made a final effort to shake off his pursuers. When he reached Missoula, Montana, he forwarded his suitcase and a portable typewriter by express to Seattle, left his car in a local garage, and just caught a bus which was leaving for the Coast. An FBI agent, who had been watching his movements, took possession of his car in which he found a short-wave radio-receiving set, and he telegraphed ahead to colleagues in Washington State after he had seen Ludwig board the bus. Another Federal agent was waiting when the bus stopped at Cle Elum, a small coal-mining and lumber town about a hundred miles east of Seattle, and Ludwig was immediately placed under arrest. He was formally charged with attempting as a foreign agent to furnish precise information on the strength and location of United States Army units to a foreign government. Bail was fixed at $50,000, and since he could not raise this sum he was lodged in the county jail in Spokane, pending his transfer to New York. Meanwhile the special agent in charge of the district FBI office recovered Ludwig's suitcase and typewriter from the express office in Seattle. The suitcase was found to contain several bottles of pyramidon tablets, a packet of stained toothpicks, and a broken eye-cup. Asked about the pyramidon, Ludwig replied that he had the tablets to relieve the headaches from which he suffered.

In Spokane jail the local deputy sheriff was asked to keep a watchful eye on the prisoner. Ludwig subsequently suggested that, if the American Government valued him at $50,000, he was sure he would be worth as much to the Germans, and asked his jailer would he like to earn that much money? The deputy sheriff reported this to the Federal agent, who instructed him to 'play along with the prisoner and see what might come out of it'. The deputy sheriff thereupon told Ludwig that he had thought it out and believed he could 'arrange things', but that first he needed some guarantee that the $50,000 would be paid over to him when they both reached South America, to which Ludwig had proposed that they should go. Was there not someone in the country who could make a deposit on account? Yes, there was, said Ludwig, and he told the jailer to make a long-distance call to a certain number and address in New York and ask for $200 for Joe. The call was duly made, and its recipient turned out to be a certain Paul Borchardt, the most interesting spy in the ring, since he was a major in the German army, a former professor of military geography in Munich, and an intimate associate of General Haushofer who invented the science of geopolitics, who created a technical school for the training of Nazi spies and fifth columnists, and who was perhaps more than anyone else responsible for formulating Hitler's plans for conquest.

With Borchardt and Ludwig in custody, it was a simple matter to round up the rest of the spy ring, six men and one woman in all. They were duly indicted as spies by the US Attorney for the Southern District of New York, Mr Mathias F. Correa, and the Grand Jury returned a true bill against all seven.

After I had returned from the Caribbean and made my reports to Boyle in London and Stephenson and des Graz in New York, Stephenson considered that, on account of my connection with and knowledge of the secret aspects of censorship, I would be more useful if I joined his office in New York. Neither Boyle nor Menzies, the MI6 chief in London, raised any objection, and I was instructed to wind up my affairs in Bermuda and report to Stephenson, under whose orders I should regard myself in future as being. It was also agreed that Dorothy and her assistant Betty Raymond, would be similarly transferred, so that they could be immediately available for instructing the FBI in their specialized techniques, as Stephenson had promised Hoover. I came up ahead of the other two in May, leaving Dorothy to settle our affairs in Bermuda and arrange for the continuance of my liaison with Rowe Spurling, Hamish Mitchell, and other key people such as Nadya Gardner. At first, we stayed in the New Weston Hotel at the corner of 52nd Street and Fifth Avenue in Manhattan, a most comfortable establishment which I was sorry to see disappear some years later. Eventually we found a very satisfactory apartment in a new block at 400 East 52nd Street, opposite the River Club, where we remained until our departure from New York early in 1944.

'You were a senior officer of the organization from May 1941 to February 1944 – a lengthy and at times difficult period in the history of our affairs,' Stephenson wrote to me afterwards from his New York office. 'Before that you were employed on special censorship duties in Bermuda, and in that capacity achieved results which were of considerable assistance to our work here. There was accordingly obligation already owed to you before you joined us, and it increased thereafter. You were entrusted with numerous tasks, and as a result of the hard work, good judgment and lively intellect which you devoted to them, carried them out with invariable success.' This was a tribute from Intrepid which I greatly appreciated.[6]

By this time Stephenson was established in a suite of offices on the thirty-sixth and thirty-seventh floors of the International Building in Rockefeller Center, which one entered from 630 Fifth Avenue. He also had a down-town office which was under the direction of the shipping expert Sir Connop Guthrie, who was primarily responsible for the security of British shipping in

American ports. He was a shrewd and genial baronet, whom I liked and also respected immensely, since he was as popular on the New York waterfront as he was in Manhattan café society. Another and younger business associate of Stephenson's was John Pepper, an expert in economic intelligence. Then, as I have already mentioned, there was Walter Bell; and finally there was a more senior member of the service, Colonel C. H. Ellis an Australian, aged forty-six at this time. Stephenson had deliberately chosen Ellis to accompany him to New York, as Stephenson considered him to be the best member of MI6 he had met in London.

Ellis (familiarly known to his friends as Dick) I got to know intimately, particularly since we had a common interest in Russian history and Soviet affairs generally. He died on 5 July 1975 after a long service career marked by numerous orders and decorations. Fortunately I was allowed to supplement his formal obituary in *The Times* of London with a less formal piece which appeared under my initials and in which I tried to show how his official appointments served as 'a convenient cloak for his work for British Secret Intelligence, which was his forte and at which he excelled'.

Friendly and unassuming, he was a man of proven loyalty and outstanding integrity of character. He disliked intrigue of all kinds and he deplored the personal and inter-departmental rivalries which sometimes marred the atmosphere of SIS head-quarters in London. Consequently he preferred working quietly and unostentatiously in the field with secret agents whose intelligence reports he was an expert at evaluating, and where his knowledge of languages, particularly Russian in which he was virtually bilingual, proved invaluable to his country.

He had an initially difficult task during the war when he acted as deputy to the 'Quiet Canadian' Sir William Stephenson, who was the chief representative of both SIS and SOE in the Western Hemisphere, since he found himself involved through no fault of his own in the running warfare between

Colonel Charles Howard ('Dick') Ellis, CBE, CMG, in Washington in 1941. A professional member of MI6, and Sir William Stephenson's principal SIS assistant in the US, he was accused after his death of being a German and also a Russian agent.

'Broadway' and 'Baker Street'. His task was rendered no easier by the fact that while he was the appointee of the former organization with which his loyalties primarily lay, his Canadian chief in New York inclined to favour the latter as the more enterprising organization which had been created expressly to meet the necessities of war . . .

In the period before Pearl Harbor when German agents were

operating freely in the United States, Ellis gave the late J. Edgar Hoover and the FBI some useful lessons in counter-espionage techniques as well as passing on important domestic security intelligence which they could not otherwise have obtained. Also, without Ellis's help General William Donovan could not have laid the foundations of the Office of Strategic Services. Indeed Ellis produced the original blueprint for OSS and for this he was deservedly awarded the American Legion of Merit.[7]

I have mentioned Ellis's wartime services in some detail here, since it will be necessary to return to them later in this narrative in the context of the charge of betraying secrets to the Germans and the Russians brought against him after his death by Chapman Pincher, the writer and former Chief Defence Correspondent of the London *Daily Express* and Beaverbrook Newspapers, in his book *Their Trade is Treachery*.

Other members of the BSC staff, who spent longer or shorter periods in New York, had already achieved prominence in their respective fields or were to do so later. I have already mentioned David Ogilvy, Eric Maschwitz, Benn Levy, and Freckles Wren – the latter never lost an opportunity of getting away from Trinidad so that he could come up to New York and report progress. Then there was Alexander Halpern, a naturalized British subject born a Russian, who had been legal adviser to the Kerensky Government in Petrograd in 1917 and had managed to escape the Bolshevik clutches. There were also several university teachers. They included Freddie Ayer (later Sir Alfred and Professor of Logic at Oxford), Gilbert Highet, Professor of Latin Languages and Literature at Columbia (who was married to the best-selling novelist Helen MacInnes), and William Deakin (later Sir William), who was later to be parachuted into Yugoslavia and to win the DSO for his exploits with Tito's partisans, afterwards becoming the first Warden of St Antony's College, Oxford.

Finally there was A.M. ('Bill') Ross-Smith, a London-based Australian business man and one of the first to join the Stephenson organization, having been brought in by his fellow Australian

Dick Ellis. Bill Ross-Smith's great achievement was to recruit and operate the activities of several hundred secret agents on neutral ships trading between America, north and south, and other parts of the world, notably Spain, Portugal and Japan. These agents were known as ships' observers and their activities provided the British SIS with a wealth of secret information, from the locating of Axis shipping and essential commodities such as industrial diamonds and platinum covertly destined for Germany, to the prevention of the repatriation of German technicians on Japanese vessels via the Panama Canal. Ross-Smith became friendly with the leading Basques and Spanish Republicans in exile and also with the wealthy Portuguese shipowner, José Bensaude, who arranged for two million escudos to be paid through his Lisbon office to British secret agents in occupied Europe.

I was familiar with some of the details of these operations as I had, where necessary, to make available my wife Dorothy's expertise and that of her assistant Betty Raymond in the secret opening of sealed documents which Ross-Smith was able to procure, particularly with the Basque help – documents such as the top secret instructions to Spanish ships' captains to be followed in case of certain eventualities.

In particular I remember the telephone in our apartment ringing around midnight, after we had gone to bed, with an urgent message from Ross-Smith asking Dorothy to meet him in her Room 99 office in Rockefeller Centre. 'It's that menace Ross-Smith,' she said as she put down the receiver, 'but I suppose I had better go.' Naturally I agreed, as I sensed it must be something important at that time of night and at such short notice.

It turned out that Bill Ross-Smith and the Basque Government leader in exile had been dining with a Spanish ship's captain who also happened to be a Basque, and they had plied him with so much strong liquor that he had fallen asleep. Ross-Smith then succeeded in taking the wallet, only to be opened in a certain emergency and containing specific secret instructions, out of the captain's inside breast pocket. He rushed off to Rockefeller Centre, where Dorothy and the office photographer, who had also been alerted, were waiting for him. Dorothy opened the sealed envelope, abstracted the contents which were photographed, and resealed the envelope, leaving no trace that the seal had been melted down and then reconstituted with a plaster of Paris impression which she had taken before opening the envelope. Two hours later, while the Captain was still asleep, Ross-Smith was able to return the wallet, unnoticed by its owner, to his breast pocket.

The secret instructions were prefixed by the code word which was already known to the Captains and was intended to be broadcast as a warning to them to open their envelopes immediately. The instructions indicated in detail the various routes by which the 600 ships of Spain's merchant navy were to proceed to German or German allies' ports in the eventuality of Spain's coming into the war against Britain and her allies. The instructions clearly established that Spain's dictator General Franco anticipated this eventuality, although he preferred to remain neutral, and in the event succeeded in doing so.

Some months later Ross-Smith learned from his Basque contacts that the code word had been changed. The Basques added that there was a Spanish ship lying in Buenos Aires harbour for a fortnight and that the new code word might be surreptitiously obtained there with a little ingenuity. Ross-Smith immediately flew to Buenos Aires, taking with him my wife's assistant Betty Raymond, since Dorothy was busy on another job in Trinidad; he also took along a replica of the wallet in case it might come in useful. The friendly local Basques immediately cultivated the Captain, who also happened to be a Basque, and they would lunch every day together in the Odeon restaurant. Ross-Smith brushed against the Captain as if by accident and clearly felt that the Captain's wallet was in his breast pocket. Before the meal the Captain used to visit the washroom and hang up his coat on a peg before entering one of the lavatory cubicles. One day as he did so, Ross-Smith, who had stationed himself in an adjacent cubicle, slipped out, substituted the replica wallet for the original in the Captain's coat, hurried off with it to the local British SOE agent's office, where Betty opened the envelope with considerable difficulty, since the seal contained white of egg. However, she succeeded, and next day when the Captain went through his usual routine preparatory to having lunch, Ross-Smith was able to replace the original wallet in place of the replica, without the Captain being any the wiser.

Altogether Bill Ross-Smith was a most remarkable character, genial and vivacious, who did not know the meaning of the word fear. However some of his more daring exploits on the waterfront and elsewhere alarmed his immediate superiors, notably Ellis and Stephenson himself, who were afraid that he might cause serious trouble for BSC with the American authorities. But somehow or other Bill always managed to get away with it, and he was never caught by either the Americans or the enemy. But he was often in 'the doghouse' in the BSC offices. Once after Stephenson had ignored him or refused to see him for several weeks, Bill put a photograph in an envelope and gave it to one of Stephenson's secretaries to deliver to Intrepid. When Stephenson opened the envelope and removed the photograph, he saw that the picture was one of Ross-Smith himself, characteristically inscribed by its subject, *Remember me?* He is still remembered with admiration and affection, not least by the author of this book.

In 1942, after Pearl Harbor, the ships' observers organization was handed over to US Naval Intelligence. When Frank Knox, the US Secretary of the Navy, looked through the long lists of observers on American ships, he asked: 'How the hell did the Limeys recruit all these Americans without the US Naval Intelligence knowing about it?'

Precautions taken by the various London headquarters in sending out specialist officers were sometimes wrapped in unnecessary mystery. Benn Levy, for example, was not given the address of the BSC offices in Rockefeller Center, although this was undoubtedly known to the Germans. Instead, he was told to memorize a certain telephone number, which he was to call as soon as he arrived in New York, saying 'This is Mortimer'. He remembered the number correctly, but he forgot his cover name. 'This is . . .', 'This is . . .', he kept saying after he had dialled the number. Finally he blurted out, 'This is Benn Levy.' 'That's quite all right,' answered the voice at the other end of the line.

'We've been expecting you. Come right on up.' He was then directed to Room 3603 in the International Building at 630 Fifth Avenue.

Eric Maschwitz had a slightly different experience. Although he held the army rank of major he was sent out as a civilian, a necessary precaution since the United States were not yet at war with the Axis powers. His occupation was given in his passport as 'Ministry of Supply'. At New York Immigration he was questioned at some length by two crew-cut young men, who turned out to be FBI agents.

'Great to see you, Mr Maschwitz,' said one, after inspecting his passport. 'Guess you fellows over the other side must be getting pretty short of supplies, huh?'

Maschwitz nodded gravely, feeling none too comfortable.

'So you're with the Ministry, huh?'

Maschwitz replied that this was indeed the case.

'Could we know what line of supplies you're particularly interested in?'

Maschwitz was completely nonplussed. He had no answer ready. What should he say? Corn flakes? Heavy artillery? Nuts and bolts? He had now begun to perspire. Luckily, however, he eventually recalled the formula he could use if he found himself in difficulty. 'If you will get in touch with Washington,' he answered with as much dignity as he could muster, '*they* will tell you what my business is!'

This reply seemed to satisfy his interrogators and he was allowed to go. But as he did so, he could not help noticing the two G-men exchanging grins. Apparently one of their favourite pastimes was taking the mickey out of Limeys of whose credentials they were perfectly well aware! [8]

Eric had not been given a mysterious telephone number to call, but had been told to go to a certain hotel in mid-town Manhattan and wait there to be collected. He was agreeably surprised to find that the emissary for this purpose was Freckles Wren, who had arrived on one of his frequent visits and had to be given something to do after he had made his progress report on the Caribbean situation.

Eric's marriage to the actress Hermione Gingold had broken down – and he had not yet fallen in love with his second wife, the charming Phyllis Gordon whom he was to marry after the war. Hence while in New York he was 'heart-whole and fancy-free'. He was also extremely busy in his job with BSC and he had no time to look for the kind of apartment he wanted. However, he asked my wife Dorothy, whom he knew from Liverpool days, if she would undertake this task for him. He explained that what he wanted was not an apartment in a modern block with the usual amenities, such as porters who would be sure to note whom he brought in and out. In fact, he would like a walk-up in an old brownstone house with an apartment on an upper floor connected by a speaking-tube to the front door, by means of which he could satisfy himself that his caller, usually female, was the person whom he was expecting and then press a button which opened the front door by remote control.

Dorothy, who liked Eric, gladly accepted this chore and after a relatively short time found something she knew would suit him, in the mid-Fifties. She explained to the house manager that she was taking the apartment for a friend who was connected, as she herself had once been, with the theatre, and who needed a quiet apartment in which to write a musical play.

'What is your friend's name?' the manager asked.

'Mr Eric Maschwitz,' replied Dorothy.

'But this is a restricted house,' said the manager, by which he meant that Jews and blacks were not acceptable tenants.

Dorothy did not understand what the manager meant by 'a restricted house' and thought it must have something to do with having liquor on the premises. 'That's no problem,' she said, 'he can bring it in with him!'

When the manager explained the meaning of the term, Dorothy assured him that her friend was not Jewish but had a Polish grandfather. This explanation was accepted, and Eric duly moved in to premises where he could enjoy female company undisturbed and undetected. The unfinished draft of his play *Waltz Without End*, which he had brought with him, was still on his desk when he left. It was eventually completed and produced at the Lyric theatre in London in 1942, where it ran into the following year.

I always thought that Eric was more interested in the theatre than in Intelligence and Special Operations. Certainly he was able in New York to exploit his theatrical expertise, for example, when the American impresario Gilbert Miller produced Lesley Storm's play *Heart of a City*, in which the authoress had dramatized the story of London's famous Windmill Theatre. 'We never closed' was the theatre's proud boast during the worst period of the German bombing of London, although the wits changed this to 'We never clothed' in reference to the scantiness of the women players' apparel and their almost naked appearance on the stage at the Windmill. Eric supervised the air-raid details for the Broadway production, based on a real-life recording made on the roof of Broadcasting House at the height of the Blitz. Indeed the effects were so noisy that they could be heard in the adjoining theatre where Ethel Barrymore was playing in *The Corn is Green* and she asked if they could be turned down a little. The two stars in *Heart of a City* were the glamorous redhead Margot Grahame and the child-like Gertrude Musgrove, then married to Alexander Korda's brother Vincent, the artistic director.[9]

Just about the whole of the staff of BSC turned up for the first night of *Heart of a City*, which they applauded vociferously. Several of the male members fell in love with the ladies in the cast, Eric himself falling for Margot Grahame. However, the play was not a commercial success and Gilbert Miller lost money over it. But it was good propaganda for Britain when she direly needed it, as also was the film *Mrs Miniver*, with Greer Garson in the name part, and above all *That Hamilton Woman* made by Korda in Hollywood on a shoe-string budget in six weeks, with Vivien Leigh and Laurence Olivier as the principal stars. The story of the romance between Emma Hamilton and England's foremost sailor Horatio Lord Nelson proved a smash hit in America, and also in England, where Winston Churchill was reputed to have seen it eleven times and to have wept on each occasion.

Of course, it was sometimes difficult for the senior members of Stephenson's staff, who had come out from England, to conceal the true nature of their activities, particularly when they encountered friends from former civilian life. For example, I had been on terms of intimacy in Dublin with the witty Irish poet and autobiographer, Dr Oliver St John Gogarty, and after Gogarty came to live in New York, shortly after the outbreak of war, it was inevitable that sooner or later our paths would cross. So it happened and our former close friendly relations were resumed. For a long time Gogarty never showed by the slightest hint that he was aware of the nature of the secret work upon which I was engaged. Then one night Dorothy and I invited him to a small dinner party which we gave in our apartment on 52nd Street overlooking the East River. Besides Gogarty, the only other guests were from BSC.

In the course of the evening Gogarty asked for a sheet of writing paper. He scribbled away for a minute or two, and then handed me the result, saying to the assembled company, 'I think you will like this!' It was a limerick which read as follows:

> A lady of doubtful nativity
> Had a fanny of great sensitivity
> When she sat on the lap
> Of a Nazi or Jap
> She could detect fifth column activity.

Needless to say we were all highly amused, as also was Bill Stephenson, to whom the original manuscript was subsequently presented.[10]

Unhappily for his posthumous reputation, Dick Ellis was to achieve an unenviable notoriety when Mr Chapman Pincher, in his book *Their Trade is Treachery* (1981), accused him of having 'confessed' during his retirement to having spied first for the Germans and later for the Russians, thereby causing considerable distress to the surviving members of his family. Mr Pincher did not specify his sources beyond indicating that they belonged to the security service (MI5) and preferred to remain anonymous.[11]

Because of this very serious accusation against a man who is no longer alive and is consequently unable to defend himself, this is perhaps a convenient point at which to recount briefly the story of his life and professional career as I knew it.

Charles Howard Ellis was born in Annandale, a suburb of Sydney, New South Wales, on 13 February 1895, the son of William Edward and Lillian Ellis, *née* Hobday.[12] His parents were both English, from Devonshire, his father and several sisters having emigrated to Australia in the 1850s during the early days of the gold discoveries and the rapid growth of New South Wales and Victoria. William Ellis, who was in business as a clothing manufacturer, was a near kinsman of William Webb Ellis, legendary inventor of Rugby football as a boy at the school in 1823, who, it has been said, 'with a fine disregard for the rules of football as played in his time, first took the ball in his arms and ran with it, thus originating the distinctive feature of the Rugby game'[13]. Dick Ellis's mother's people, the Hobdays, who also emigrated from England, settled in Christchurch, New Zealand, but he cannot have remembered much about his mother since she died when he was only three; his father lived to be ninety-one, dying in 1920. Consequently Dick was largely brought up by his maternal grandparents in Christchurch until the time came for him to go to school in Melbourne, to which his father had moved. His schooling was somewhat desultory, but after a few years, when he would normally have left, he was kept on as an usher or under-master, when, so he told me, he learned much more than as an ordinary pupil. He also became interested in music and by the time he was seventeen was an accomplished cellist.

Two years later, on the outbreak of war in 1914, after spending a short time at Melbourne University, he joined an Australian troop-contingent bound for England, and in the following year he enlisted in the Royal Fusiliers as a private. He was later commissioned in the Middlesex Regiment, and, after serving for two years at the front in France, where his favourite cousin and many of his comrades were killed, he was posted successively to Egypt and India, being eventually attached to a battalion of the South Lancashire Regiment at Quetta in the autumn of 1917. This was largely garrison soldiering, but in his spare time he succeeded in picking up a working knowledge of Persian and Russian. Consequently, following the developments in Russian Turkestan and the Caucasus owing to the collapse of the Tsarist armies in that region, the British planned to send a military mission to Meshed in north-east Persia to co-operate with the White Russians and other anti-Bolshevik elements such as the Mensheviks. Ellis volunteered to serve with the mission, which was commanded by Major-General Sir Wilfrid Malleson, and he was accepted. He arrived in Meshed in July 1918 to find the small mission, consisting besides Malleson of three or four officers, a field-wireless unit, and a small guard of Indian cavalry, installed in the old British Consulate building.

The mission's first task in Meshed was to open negotiations with the dissident group of Mensheviks, which had set up a government at Ashkhabad on the Central Asian Railway and was consequently in a position to block communications by that route with the Bolsheviks in Samarkand and Tashkent. Since the Mensheviks favoured continuing the war against Germany and Turkey, they agreed to help Malleson oppose any projected enemy advance from the west. How difficult and unreliable were the Malleson mission's new-found allies, was quickly demonstrated by the unhappy incident of the twenty-six Bolshevik commissars.

The commissars, who had taken over the administration of Baku on the west coast of the Caspian Sea, escaped by ship on the eve of the capture of the town by Turkish forces in September 1918. Their vessel was ostensibly bound for the northern port of Astrakhan, which was in Bolshevik hands, but for some reason it was unexpectedly diverted to Krasnovodsk, the east coast port and terminus of the Central Asian Railway. The Mensheviks promptly arrested the commissars, although Malleson, who feared for their future, wished them to be handed over to him for safe conduct to India where they would be sureties for the safety of British prisoners held by the Bolsheviks. While seemingly agreeing to this course, the Ashkhabad government allowed all the detained commissars to be shot by the Menshevik authorities in Krasnovodsk. In spite of Malleson's strong protest to the Ash-khabad government, Soviet propaganda has persistently attri-buted responsibility for the executions to the British, and the legend has been embodied in the *Great Soviet Encyclopedia*. An inscription on the memorial to them in Baku records that they were 'slain by the British'. It is also the subject of a graphic picture painted by the Soviet artist Isaak Brodsky, which I saw many years later in the State Museum in Samarkand, noting that two British officers were looking on, if not actually directing the executions, and that one of them bore a striking resemblance to Ellis, who was known by the Bolsheviks to be operating in Transcaspia at this time. Ellis later convincingly refuted the story in his excellent account of the Malleson mission's activities, *Transcaspian Episode* (1963), in which he included a reproduc-tion of Brodsky's picture, after I had drawn his attention to the location of the original. This is only one of Ellis's many exposures of Soviet distortions of history, and hardly accords with Chapman Pincher's charge that he was a Soviet spy.

During 1919 and the early part of 1920, Ellis (by now a Captain) was involved in the British-Afghan war, since the Emir of Afghanistan was being supported by the Reds in Moscow, and also with operations in the Caucasus. With the winding up of the Malleson mission he was awarded the OBE (Military Division), and with the end of Allied intervention and the final defeat of the Whites he returned to England, where he matriculated at Oxford and was enrolled as an undergraduate at St Edmund's Hall in the Michaelmas term, 1920. It had always been his ambition to go up to Oxford, and it was only the War which had prevented this. However, he left without taking a degree in order to continue his language studies at the Sorbonne in Paris.

At this period there was a considerable White Russian colony in Paris. It included a family named Zelensky, with two of whom, Alexander (Sasha) and Lilia, Dick Ellis became friendly. He sub-sequently married Lilia, by whom he had a son, Oleg, generally known as Pete. This was in 1923, when for a time Ellis was attached to the British High Commission in Constantinople, moving on towards the end of the same year to Berlin where he was appointed Acting Vice-Consul. Lilia was certainly with him in Constantinople, where he had a fine house in Pera, the European quarter of what was then the Turkish capital; and she followed him to Berlin. It was about this time that they got married and that Dick Ellis joined the British Secret Intelligence Service on what was apparently a part-time basis, since he also acted as foreign correspondent for the London *Morning Post* and a number of other journals.

He remained based in Berlin on and off for the next fourteen years or so, frequently visiting Geneva, where he covered the League of Nations Assembly meetings and conferences, including the abortive conference on naval disarmament in 1927. He also recruited his brother-in-law Alexander Zelensky as a British agent, and Zelensky succeeded in providing some useful information for the British SIS, although Chapman Pincher has suggested that he was 'only in the game for the money' and with characteristic fecklessness sold secrets both to the Soviets and the Germans. Pincher has also accused Ellis, acting as the result of pressure from his brother-in-law from whom he had borrowed money, of spying for both the Nazis and the Russians – in other words of being a double, or even a triple, agent. But without cogent proof, this charge can be dismissed as pure speculation.

What is certain is that Ellis did produce valuable data on German rearmament, and this has been endorsed by Stephenson, who was aware of his work since he himself was supplying Churchill with similar information as the result of his own industrial activities in Europe. At all events it would appear that Ellis did not become a full-time MI6 officer until 1938, when the Nazi threat caused serious alarm at the time of the Munich crisis. Meanwhile he had divorced his Russian wife, and in 1933 had married an Englishwoman, Barbara Burgess-Smith, by whom he had one daughter, Ann.

After the sudden death of Leopold von Hoesch, the German Ambassador in London, in April 1936, his successor, the notorious Joachim von Ribbentrop, gave instructions, before his arrival in the autumn of the same year, that the Embassy at No. 9 Carlton House Terrace should be completely renovated and redecorated. The two adjoining houses, Nos. 7 and 8, were to be joined to it, so as to make one enormous building which Ribbentrop planned to use for luxurious entertaining when he took up his new post, with the object of promoting better Anglo-German relations. The relevant British department, the Office of Works, would not allow him to make any structural changes to the outside of the houses or to alter the original interior Regency decorations. Although he could not do anything about the former, inside the Embassy he installed new lower ceilings and covered the ornamental walls with plain substitutes in the severe style then favoured by Hitler's architect, Albert Speer. The horde of workmen necessary to carry out this operation were imported from Germany, and they installed a number of listening devices, burglar alarms, and a special direct telephone line to the Chancellery in Berlin so that Ribbentrop could speak to Hitler without going through the normal telephone exchange. The most valuable painting, so I gathered from Ellis, was a picture of the Madonna by Fra Angelico, which belonged to Frau Annelies von Ribbentrop, and it was protected by a special alarm which would go off at the slightest touch, even when the frame was being dusted. As Frau von Ribbentrop was the only one who had the key to stop it, it would continue indefinitely when the ambassadress was out or away, emitting an excruciating sound which the staff customarily described as 'Fra Angelico in distress'.[14]

English workmen were necessarily employed to supplement the work of their German counterparts, and some of these succeeded, so Ellis told me, in installing counter devices.

In this way the direct London-Berlin telephone line was tapped, and the Embassy was bugged for the benefit of the British SIS. The telephone calls between Ribbentrop and Hitler were intercepted in the secret Security Division of the Post Office, where trustworthy British Intelligence agents such as Ellis would translate them. The fact that the Germans suddenly abandoned the telephone link Chapman Pincher suggests was due to the fact that Ellis had alerted them to the leak, but a more likely explanation is that Ribbentrop left London to become Reich Foreign Minister in March 1938 and the link was no longer required.

Pincher states contradictorily that the telephone was being tapped 'almost up to the outbreak of the war'.

I have already described the general tenor of Ellis's work with Stephenson in the United States. To this I will only add here what President Truman stated in 1946 when making him an officer of the Legion of Merit, an honour awarded to Stephenson at the same time.

He gave unreservedly of his talent and wealth of information toward the development of certain of our intelligence organizations and methods. His enthusiastic interest, superior foresight and diplomacy were responsible in large measure for the success of highly important operations.

Ellis had previously been created a Commander of the British Empire (CBE) by King George VI in England.

In 1946 Ellis, who had returned to SIS headquarters in London, was appointed field officer in charge of South-East Asia and the Far East, being based on Singapore. I stayed with him in his house there in December 1951 on my way to Korea, where, as an MP who had constituents fighting with the Commonwealth Division, I went to the front above the 38th parallel to see the troops in action. I also stayed with Ellis on my way back and saw Mr Malcolm Macdonald, the British Commissioner for South-East Asia, who spoke very highly of the valuable quality of Ellis's work, with which he was familiar.

Ellis retired from the service in 1953, and afterwards paid a short visit to his native Australia, where he was in touch with the Australian intelligence authorities, who, in exchange for information about the suspected English spy Philby, briefed him on the activities of Vladimir Petrov, the KGB chief in the Soviet Embassy in Canberra. A little later this became a sensational spy scandal, when Petrov's wife defected after she had been ordered back to Moscow with her husband. Meanwhile Ellis, who had obtained a divorce from his second wife a few years previously, returned to England where he married again, his third wife being a retired school-teacher and widow named Alexandra Wood, with whom he lived in the salubrious Hampden Park district of East-bourne. At the same time, besides keeping up his journalistic interests, he wrote two anti-Soviet books, *The Expansion of Russia* (1965) and *Soviet Imperialism* (1970). After his third wife's death, he married for a fourth time, and continued to live in Eastbourne until he died.

During the period of his third marriage, when (according to Chapman Pincher) his loyalty came under suspicion in MI5, he went back to part-time work with SIS. This work was highly confidential and it is inconceivable that he should have been entrusted with it if he were officially regarded as being, or as having been, a traitor to his country. It was nothing less than going through the SIS files and weeding out those which he did not consider worth preserving. On the other hand, Chapman Pincher puts the case against him in these words:

> If he was an active spy or keen to cover up past evidence of his own operations and those of his pro-Soviet colleagues, the damage he may have caused in destroying leads to KGB activities is incalculable. Fortunately there were documents concerning himself and Philby which did not come his way.
>
> The disquiet among those senior Secret Service men who had not been able to bring themselves to believe that Dick Ellis could possibly have been a spy was intense. After their recent failure to smother Philby's treachery, because he defected rather than accept immunity, they decided that 'in the interests of the Service' the Ellis case should be completely suppressed. It has been until now.[15]

Shortly after Chapman Pincher's book appeared, Ellis's daughter appealed to the British Prime Minister, asking her if she could allay the distress of the family which the publication of Chapman Pincher's allegations had caused. 'I am very sorry for the distress that you are suffering on account of the reference to your father in Chapman Pincher's book,' Mrs Thatcher replied, 'and I deplore as strongly as you do his attacks on the memories of those who are no longer living and cannot defend themselves.' However, she went on to repeat what she had already said in the House of Commons – that she could not comment on any allegations or insinuations apart from those relating to Sir Roger Hollis, the late head of MI5, whom Chapman Pincher had also attacked, suggesting that he too might have spied for the Russians. 'I cannot make an exception in one case without being pressed to make it in others as well,' Mrs Thatcher added: 'and that, I fear, would do more harm than good.'

My own feelings about the matter were expressed in a letter which I wrote to *The Times*, from which it is sufficient to repeat the penultimate paragraph:

Throughout my long correspondence with Ellis and my many conversations with him continuously over the years, he never betrayed the slightest hint that his sympathies and actions were other than altogether loyal to the British cause and the service which he served devotedly for 30 years, as evidenced by his many decorations including the American Legion of Merit.[16]

My first important assignment from Stephenson, besides continuing my liaison duties with the Censorship stations in Bermuda and the Caribbean, was the result of an urgent message which Stephenson received from Hoover in May 1941 and which called for immediate action in a field in which the FBI was precluded from operating by the terms of its presidential directive. The message was to the effect that Major Elias Belmonte, the fervent pro-Nazi Bolivian Military Attaché in Berlin, was in close communication with Nazi elements in Bolivia and was understood to be planning a *coup* with the object of overthrowing the existing pro-American and pro-British Bolivian Government of President Enrique Peñaranda and establishing a pro-German military dictatorship. Although Peñaranda had been democratically elected, his constitutional position was far from secure and, like his immediate predecessors, he faced constant domestic unrest and revolutionary threats, of which he was well aware. Hoover added that the US President was most anxious that evidence confirming the report about Major Belmonte and his planned *coup* should be conveyed to the White House as quickly as possible. Franklin Roosevelt's anxiety was owing to the fact that Bolivia was the main source of supply to the United States of wolfram, the ore from which was derived the ferro-alloy tungsten used in the manufacture of steel and arms, particularly aircraft. No doubt he feared that such a *coup* as Belmonte was plotting would, if successful, stop the flow of this essential commodity to American factories.[17]

This development seemed a logical follow-on from the diplomatic pressure exerted by Germany on the Latin American states at the time of the Pan-American Conference at Havana in the previous year, when Germany advised these states, particularly the smaller ones, not to take part in any Pan-American economic arrangements because these 'would be against the economic interests of the majority of the Latin American states, since only European suppliers, *and especially German ones*, are in a position to receive in payment the products of the Latin American states'. In this context Bolivia had been singled out for an ominous warning, when the German Minister in La Paz 'advised' an official of the Bolivian Foreign Office that Bolivia had no interest in the Havana Conference and should take no interest in it. This happened only a few months after Peñaranda's election as President.[18]

Stephenson explained the position to me briefly – he was always a man of few words – and sent me off to Bolivia to 'investigate and plan a counter-offensive'. As a matter of courtesy – and also as a precaution in case I should become embarrassingly involved with local authorities – the British missions in the various countries I was to traverse (Colombia, Ecuador, and Peru as well as Bolivia) were officially informed of my visit, though not of its precise purpose. Owing to engine trouble I was obliged to spend twenty-four hours in Peru, where curiosity prompted the British Minister Sir Courtenay Forbes to invite me to lunch.[19] On arriving at the Minister's house in a suburb of Lima, I discovered that I was by no means the only guest, and that the lunch party was a large mixed one, consisting mainly of prominent Peruvians and their wives. Unfortunately the Minister was neither so tactful nor so discreet as his colleague in the Bolivian capital turned out to be. No sooner was the assembled company seated at table than His Britannic Majesty's representative addressed me in tones which reverberated round the dining room: 'So you've come down here to do a secret service job, have you?'

I did my best to laugh off this query, and remarked that he must be joking, adding that I was on leave and on my way to stay with an old friend in La Paz. Nevertheless I had the uncomfortable impression that my journey would be news in the German Legation by tea-time, and that I had better get on my way as quickly as possible. The Pan American Clipper was still delayed by engine trouble, but luckily I was able to get a seat on a small local aircraft which took me on to Arica in Chile without mishap, although the pilot alarmed me, as soon as we were airborne, by spreading out a copy of the local newspaper on the windscreen and reading it. From Arica I changed into a larger aircraft which flew across Lake Titicaca and eventually landed at the Alto Plano airport above La Paz – the highest airport in the world at 13,000 feet. I had arranged to stay with the manager of the British-owned Bolivia and Antifogasta railway, which had not then been nationalized, and he and his wife were most hospitable and helpful with local introductions. Through them I met a certain very pro-British Bolivian national whom I was assured was absolutely trustworthy and could be relied upon to carry out any surreptitious work I might have in mind, for a modest monetary consideration.

To my surprise and gratification, I found the Bolivian already had an inkling of Belmonte's plot when I talked to him. He confirmed that Belmonte in Berlin had been corresponding with the Bolivian Army Chief of Staff, hinting at the possibility of a *coup*; also that the Government had got wind of this and was already seriously concerned that Belmonte and his Nazi-disposed friends in the country might attempt to bring off the *coup* in the guise of a military revolt. I quickly made friends with the Bolivian and in the course of several subsequent meetings I determined to take the bull by the horns and put an important proposition to him. We agreed that it was likely that Belmonte's plans for the *coup* would in due course be dispatched by diplomatic courier to the German Legation in La Paz. Why not anticipate this development by fabricating the kind of letter Belmonte would be expected to write in the circumstances, and give it the maximum publicity? If my Bolivian friend agreed, would he be prepared to draft a letter in the Spanish language style which the Military Attaché might be expected to use? After some reflection he said he would. I then decided that I must in fairness let the British Minister into the secret, since in case anything went wrong he might be blamed. He was Mr (later Sir) James Dodds, a professional member of the diplomatic service, fifty years old, who had served in many parts of the world. Although at first he appeared rather shocked by the audacity of my plan, he thanked me for taking him into my confidence, at the same time making it clear that he would have no official knowledge of the operation if it came off. [20]

The fortnight I spent in La Paz was strenuous but rewarding. My bedroom faced Mount Ilimani, and every morning I would sniff the champagne air which reminded me of the Swiss mountains where I used to ski. But otherwise I found the high altitude of La Paz very trying and I was glad to get back to New York and report to Stephenson. He approved of the plan and I immediately set about carrying it into effect. First, I was able to obtain a genuine letter signed by Belmonte; then I succeeded in getting hold of some sheets of writing paper used by the Bolivian Legation in Berlin; finally I was supplied with a specimen of the type used by Bolivian foreign missions for their official communications. From the latter it was possible to establish the make of typewriter Belmonte was likely to use, and with assistance of various colleagues we were able to construct a suitable machine. Shortly afterwards my friend in La Paz sent me his draft of the proposed letter in Spanish which would allegedly be signed by Belmonte.

A very few others were taken into my confidence. As a result of the skills which she had learned in Room 99, Dorothy undertook to forge Belmonte's signature on the letter after it had been typed, the typing being supervised by Eric Maschwitz in Canada. I was then sent up to Ottawa with the genuine signature and two examples of Dorothy's handiwork, of which one was a reproduction of the signature on the forged letter, with instructions to obtain the opinion of the leading handwriting expert in the Royal Canadian Mounted Police. I spent several hours with this gentleman, telling him that of the three signatures one (which I indicated) was genuine, and then asking him to compare the genuine signature with the other two, whose authenticity I told him was doubtful. After the most prolonged examination of the two faked signatures, the expert eventually pronounced both to be genuine. I returned to New York, where several photocopies were made of the forged letter. Eric Maschwitz and I then took the typewriter at night to Brooklyn Bridge where we threw it over the side into the East River and where presumably it is still buried in the mud on the river bed.

Meanwhile, as a precautionary step, Stephenson informed the FBI that he had cabled one of his agents in Brazil, instructing him to watch out for any courier carrying a German diplomatic bag which was believed to contain 'incriminating documents of the highest importance', who would be arriving at Recife by the Italian airline LATI and going on to La Paz. The agent (who in fact only existed in Stephenson's imagination) was 'told' to possess himself of the documents or, if the courier should succeed in evading his attentions, to report his movements so that appropriate action could be taken elsewhere. In due course, the mythical agent 'reported' that a German named Fritz Fenthol had arrived, ostensibly representing the German Potash Syndicate, and had left by air for Buenos Aires whence it was thought he planned to go on to Bolivia. Contact was supposed to have been made with his female secretary, who for a monetary consideration allegedly supplied Stephenson's agent with particulars about Fenthol and his correspondence. Apparently, according to her, he was carrying a sealed letter addressed to the German Minister in La Paz. Shortly afterwards the local FBI representative informed his headquarters that he understood that a British agent had managed to deprive Fenthol of a letter while standing next to him in a crowded elevator in the German Bank building in Buenos Aires.

At the beginning of July Stephenson informed London that the United States authorities were aware that some document had been intercepted and were 'expressing anxiety that no time should be lost in passing it on to them if of interest'. London replied, asking for the full text of the document which was 'most urgently required here by the highest authorities'. This was followed up a few days later by another message to the effect that the Bolivian Government should be warned as soon as possible so that it might suppress the *coup* 'if and when it takes place'; the message suggested that the matter should be discussed frankly with the Americans, who should be left to take action if they so wished. ('In any case absolutely essential that warning should be conveyed with the least possible delay.')

Stephenson thereupon handed the letter to Hoover, who was as gratified as he was surprised to receive it. Hoover at once passed it to Secretary of State Cordell Hull, and Hull lost no time in sending a photostat copy to the Bolivian Government, after he had shown it to President Roosevelt.

The letter, typewritten in Spanish, and bearing what was apparently Belmonte's signature, was dated 9 June 1941, from the Bolivian Legation in Berlin, and addressed to Dr Ernst Wendler, the German Minister to Bolivia. 'Friends in the Wilhelmstrasse tell me that from information received from you, [so ran the letter] the moment is approaching to strike in order to liberate my poor country from a weak government and from completely capitalist tendencies. I go much further and believe that the *coup* (*el golpe*) should take place in the middle of July since I consider the moment to be propitious.' Cochabamba and Santa Cruz were to be the focal points of the projected rising, since they were centres which were 'most friendly to us' and 'have prepared conditions and have organized our forces with skill and energy'. The writer went on to state that he knew from some of his friends that meetings were being held without being molested by the authorities and that 'nightly exercises' were taking place. 'Further, I see that large quantities of bicycles have

CORREO AÉREO

LEGACION DE BOLIVIA
EN
ALEMANIA

BERLIN, 9 Junio de 1941

Al Excmo. Señor Doctor Ernst Wendler
Ministro de Alemania
La Paz

Estimado señor y amigo,

Tengo el agrado de acusar recibo de su interesante carta en la que me comunica de las gestiones que Ud. y su personal en la Legacion, y nuestros amigos civiles y militares bolivianos llevan a cabo en mi país con tanto exito.

Me informan los amigos de Wilhelmstrasse que por informaciones recibidos de Ud. se acerca el momento de dar nuestro golpe para librar á mi pobre país de un gobierno debil y de inclinaciones completamente capitalistas. Yo voy mas allá, y creo que el golpe debe fijarse para mediados de Julio pues considero el momento propicio, Y repito que el momento es propicio pues por sus informaciones al Ministerio de Relaciones en Berlin, veo con agrado que todos los Consules y amigos en toda la Republica de Bolivia, y especialmente en nuestros centros mas amigos, como Cochabamba, Santa Cruz y el Beni, han preparado el ambiente y han organizado nuestras fuerzas con habilidad y energia.

No cabe duda que tendremos que concentrar nuestras fuerzas en Cochabamba ya que siempre se ha prestado preferente atencion a este punto. Sé por algunos amigos mios que se siguen reuniendo sin molestia alguna de las autoridades y que se siguen haciendo los ejercicios nocturnos. Mas, veo que se han acumulado buenas cantidades de bicicletas lo que facilitara nuestros movimientos de noche ya que autos y camiones son demasiado bulliciosos. Por eso creo que durante las proximas semanas se debe obrar con muchisimo mas cuidado que anteriormente para despistar toda clase de sospecha. Deben evitarse las reuniones v las instrucciones se deben dar de persona en persona, en lugar de darlas en reuniones. Naturalmente que la entrega inicua de la LAB al imperialismo Yankee es un inconveniente ya que yo pensaba tomar control de esta organizacion inmediatamente a mi llegada a la frontera del Brazil, pero esto lo salvaré con los amigos aquí pues mi vuelo lo haré acompañado por otro avion que me seguirá todo el camino. Hemos recibido los planos detallados y mejorados de los lugares de aterrizaje mas convenientes. Este me hace ver, una vez más, que Ud. y su personal realizan un trabajo gigantesco para la realizacion de nuestro plan, todo en bien

The Belmonte letter

CORREO AÉREO

LEGACION DE BOLIVIA
EN
ALEMANIA   BERLIN

Ref.
Asunto

2.

<u>Al Excmo. Doctor Ernst Wendler</u>

de Bolivia. Tomo especial nota de lo que me escribe Ud.
referente al elemento joven de ejercito. Efectivamente
yo siempre he contado con ellos y seran ellos, sin duda,
los que mejor me cooperarán en la magna obra que llevaremos
a cabo en mi patria.

Como le digo mas arriba, es necesario que obremos
con rapidez pues el momento es oportuno. Hay que deshacer
el contrato del Wolfram con Estados Unidos y anular ó,
en ultimo caso, modificar substancialmente, los contratos
de Estaño con Inglaterra y Estados Unidos. La entrega
de nuestras lineas aereas a los intereses de Wall Street es
una traición a la patria. En cuanto a la Standard Oil que
tanta actividad demuestra para una solución "honorable" para
"restaurar el credito de Bolivia", esto es criminal. Desde mi
corte estadia en el Ministerio de Gobierno vengo combat-
iendo esto. Que afán de entregar al pais a Estados Unidos
so pretexto de ayuda financiera que nunca vendrá. Me irrita!
Estados Unidos seguirá su politica de antaño: conseguir
grandes ventajas a cambio de pequeños emprestitos ni siquiera
se nos permitira manejarlos. Bolivia no necesita de emprestitos
americanos. Con el triunfo del Reich, Bolivia necesita
trabajo y disciplina. Debemos copiar, aunque sea modestamente,
el grandioso ejemplo de Alemania desde que asumió el poder el
Nacional-Socialismo.

Ese famoso Tratado de Ostri...
un verdadero crimen. Una vez qu...
este sera uno...

<u>Al Excmo. Doctor Ernst Wendler</u>

fin, con un solo ideal y con un solo Jefe Supremo, salvaremos
el porvenir de Sud America y comenzaremos, repito, una
era de depuracion, orden y trabajo.

Hasta muy pronto, Señor Ministro.

Elías Belmonte P.

been collected which will facilitate our movement by night since motor cars and trucks are too noisy.' The writer also discussed the plans for his arrival by air to take over with the help of the younger elements in the army. 'Actually I have always counted upon them and it will be they, without doubt, who will give me the greatest co-operation in the important work which we are carrying out in my country.' The keynote was rapidity of action. The letter continued:

> We must rescind the wolfram contract with the United States, and also substantially modify the tin contracts with England and the United States. The handing over of our airlines to the interests of Wall Street is treason to our country . . . Since my short time in the government service I have been fighting this. Why hand over the country to the United States on the pretext of financial aid which will never come? This irritates me! The United States will follow their age-long policy: to obtain great advantages in exchange for small loans, and even these loans we are not allowed to administer. Bolivia does not need American loans. With the triumph of the Reich, Bolivia needs work and discipline. We must copy, though on a modest scale, the great example of Germany since National Socialism came into power . . .
>
> I hope that the last word will be my flight from here to complete the work which will save Bolivia in the first place, and afterwards the whole South American continent, from North American influence. The other countries will quickly follow our example, and then with one sole ideal and one sole supreme leader, we will save the future of South America and will begin an era of purification, order and work.*

On 19 July, which was a Saturday, Dorothy and I were cruising in Long Island Sound with Bill Ross-Smith, one of the very few other members of BSC who had been informed of the operation. In the evening one of us turned on the radio, and suddenly to our

---

*The complete text of the Belmonte letter, translated into English, was printed in the *Christian Science Monitor*, 22 August 1941.

intense surprise President Roosevelt came on the air with the astonishing news of the Belmonte letter, whose contents he proceeded to summarize. It was also announced that earlier the same day the Bolivian Government had proclaimed a nation-wide state of siege and the police had begun to round up suspect Nazi sympathizers. At the same time, Dr Wendler, the German Minister, was declared *persona non grata* and ordered to leave the country. Shortly afterwards he left for Chile. A number of prominent Germans and Bolivian civilians, including the local correspondent of the German Transocean news agency, a former Bolivian Finance Minister, and thirty officers headed by the chief of the Cochabamba military zone were arrested. Four anti-British and anti-American newspapers were suspended, while the others obediently reproduced the incriminating Belmonte letter. Belmonte himself was struck off the Bolivian Army List. The Chief of Staff identified the signature on the letter as definitely being that of the Military Attaché.

In reprisal, the Bolivian Chargé d'Affaires in Berlin Alfredo Flores, was given seventy-two hours to leave Germany. Two days later in Washington, Sumner Welles, Acting Secretary of State in Hull's absence, announced that the American Government had assured Bolivia of full assistance if her expulsion of the German Minister resulted in 'an international incident' and had informed the Government in La Paz that Dr Wendler would not be permitted to enter the United States.[21]

That the Germans were engaged in subversive activities in Bolivia at this time there can be no doubt, although the precise extent to which Major Belmonte was involved in them must remain a matter of conjecture. Two-and-a-half years later the Germans got their own back in some measure when they helped to engineer the military revolution which overthrew President Peñaranda and his Government on 20 December 1943, and installed Major Gualberto Villarroel as President. But the new Bolivian Government remained aligned with the Allies, in consequence of United States pressure.[22]

However unorthodox the affair of the Belmonte letter may be regarded, this BSC operation must be judged by its results. It probably averted a revolution in Bolivia; it certainly caused the expulsion of the German Minister and the closing of the German Legation in La Paz, as well as the arrest of a number of dangerous men; it denied Germany further exports of wolfram, while continuing them to the United States; and finally it prepared the climate for the Pan-American conference at Rio six months later, when Bolivia and eighteen other Latin American states broke with the Axis powers and banded themselves together in a common scheme of hemisphere defence – 'the decision that saved New World unity', as Sumner Welles called it.[23]*

My next assignment from Stephenson was quite different from my Bolivian mission. It was to go to Hollywood, where Alexander Korda was making films, and discuss with him various means by which Korda, with his extensive connections in the motion-picture world, could help BSC. Stephenson, who had known Korda for some time through Churchill, arranged for me to stay in Korda's luxurious villa in Bel Air, which was filled with his valuable collection of paintings.

'Are there any people here you would particularly like to meet?' Korda asked me on the day I arrived. He intimated that he knew most of the stars in the industry, and he would try to get anyone I wanted to come to dinner. It was a wonderful opportunity, and Korda clearly thought I would opt for female glamour. I replied: 'There is only one Hollywood star I would like to meet for dinner – Charlie Chaplin.' My hospitable host looked surprised. However he said, 'I think I might be able to arrange that.' I was aware that he knew Chaplin well, since they were both partners with Mary Pickford in United Artists. It was a

---

*After the war American academics and other researchers began to suspect that the Belmonte letter was a forgery. Eventually in a feature in the *Inside Yesterday* series 'Target: U.S.A.', which was broadcast over the CBS television network on 21 August 1979 and in which I participated, I was questioned in general terms about the document by the CBS correspondent Mike Wallace and I admitted responsibility for the forgery, although Belmonte and Bolivia were not specifically mentioned. The matter was then taken up by the English press, and in view of the long passage of time since the event, I gave further details: see London *Daily Telegraph*, 22 August 1979.

profitable association for Korda, because when he joined the United Artists board in 1935 he was given a substantial block of shares for nothing, so as to qualify him for this position. Twenty years later he was to sell those shares for close on a million dollars, a financial *coup* which his nephew Michael has decribed as 'almost unique in the motion-picture business'. Alex Korda was always a lavish spender both in his business and his private life; he spoke English with a strong Hungarian accent and at the age of forty-eight was as shrewd as they come. At this date he was married to his second wife, the beautiful thirty-year-old Merle Oberon, but she was away at the time of my visit and I did not meet her until later, in New York.

We picked up Charlie Chaplin at his home, and were to dine at Chasen's, a fashionable restaurant in Hollywood. I thought perhaps Chaplin would bring along his third wife, Paulette Goddard, but he explained her absence by the fact that, as he put it, he was 'having woman trouble'. He divorced her shortly afterwards to marry Eugene O'Neill's daughter Oona, whose house in Bermuda I had once considered renting but had turned down when Dorothy heard that it was supposed to be haunted.

Alex's brother Zoltan (Zoli) was directing *The Jungle Book* based on Rudyard Kipling's famous collection of animal stories, and much of the conversation at dinner turned on a title for the film which was nearing completion. Chaplin suggested *Jungle Red*, I thought *Elephant Boy* might be possible, but Alex inclined to Kipling's own title. In the event, the film appeared as *Elephant Boy*. I asked Chaplin which of all the films he had made was his favourite. I was surprised when he said *Modern Times*, but I applauded his choice of this brilliant send-up of the machine age, although the picture never approached anything like the financial success of his other films. Finally Chaplin mimicked a great womanizer whose name meant nothing to me but with whom both the others were obviously well acquainted. The amorous gentleman had been taken ill and had to go into hospital. Chaplin's portrayal of his attempt, in spite of his illness, to grab one of the nurses and undress her was quite hilarious and I have never forgotten it. How could I, when he had captivated men like

Winston Churchill with his impersonations?[24]

Next day Korda invited me to a lunch so that I could meet a number of his friends, and others, not necessarily connected with motion pictures, who were in a position to help in keeping an eye on Japanese activities on the West Coast. I also gathered that, at Churchill's suggestion endorsed by Stephenson, Korda, who had employed Churchill to write film scripts and scenarios for handsome fees before the war, had taken an office ostensibly as a motion-picture headquarters but really designed to serve as a clearing-house for British Intelligence. I took a note of the names of all these people, and passed them on to Stephenson, but I imagine that they were not able to produce much of value in this sphere owing to the Japanese attack on the United States naval base at Pearl Harbor in Hawaii, which occurred soon afterwards.

I met Zoltan in the studio where he was putting the finishing touches to *Elephant Boy*. The props were giving a lot of trouble – including the animals, both real and artificial – while a barge used on the set capsized, nearly drowning Zoli. Alex's other brother Vincent, the artistic director, was also there, and Alex told him to take me off to the Twentieth Century Fox studios and introduce me to Betty Grable who was making a film there, which Vincent dutifully did. Curiously enough, if my memory serves me right, the title of her current film was *Pin-Up Girl* which was exactly what she was, at least to the average GI. She was about twenty-five years old at this time, a petite, shapely blonde who used a lot of lipstick. She was not especially distinguished as a dancer or singer, or even as an actress, yet she was gaining enormous popularity, largely because of her greatest asset – her 'million-dollar' legs, said to be insured for this sum with Lloyds of London.[25]

She received me politely in her dressing-room, where she exhibited her legs freely for my delectation, but I did not feel drawn to her as I did to Alex's wife Merle when I eventually met her shortly afterwards in New York. As soon as I was introduced to Merle I asked her to lunch and she accepted. We met in a restaurant near Rockefeller Center and we quickly became friends, although I did not realize at first that her marriage to

Alex was already showing signs of strain. But later I was to do so.

Shortly after this I had to return to Hollywood to tidy up some loose ends left over from my previous visit. Again I was invited to stay at the house in Bel Air. But this time Alex was not there: he had been called away somewhere on urgent business. So I found myself alone in the house with Merle. She was kindness itself; she showed me her scrap book of photographs from which I gathered she had been born Estelle Merle O'Brien in Calcutta and had gone to a convent school there, and that when she had first come to Alex's attention he made her change O'Brien to Oberon and drop Estelle for Merle, the French word for the bird of which he told her she reminded him. She had leaped to stardom as Anne Boleyn in Korda's first great film success *The Private Life of Henry VIII*, in which Charles Laughton played the King. During my visit she invited two of her closest friends to meet me, Fred Astaire and Ronald Colman, I told Fred Astaire how much I admired his dancing in *Top Hat* and also told Ronald Colman that I had seen his performance in the film version of Oscar Wilde's play, *Lady Windermere's Fan*, in which he played the roué Lord Darlington. I said I thought he had one of the best lines in the play, since it was true of so many people including Wilde himself: '*We are all in the gutter, but some of us are looking at the stars.*' He agreed.

Besides the Korda brothers, Alex and Vincent, there were others connected with the theatre or the cinema who were supposed to be engaged on secret intelligence work for Stephenson – for example, Greta Garbo, Errol Flynn (he was also believed to be working for the Germans as well) and Noël Coward. But in fact, none of them were secret service agents except for the Kordas, Alex and Vincent. It is true that Stephenson, who had made Coward's acquaintance early in the war and was greatly impressed by his abilities, wished to employ him on propaganda and other secret work in the western hemisphere. Plans were made accordingly and Coward was preparing for his new job, after spending the winter of 1940–41 entertaining the troops in Australia and New Zealand, when the news was broken to him by cable, as he stopped at Bermuda on his homeward journey, that it was not to be. 'A greater power than we could contradict has thwarted our intents,' Stephenson informed him laconically. The power was Dr Dalton.

Some of Coward's friends said it was because he had made a slighting remark about the Prime Minister's son Randolph at a dinner party and the news had got back to 'the old man'. However, it is extremely unlikely that Churchill would have concerned himself in a proposed personal appointment of this kind, although he probably would have felt (if his attention had been drawn to it) that Coward would be better employed devising and acting in theatrical and variety entertainment for the benefit of the British and Commonwealth armed forces. The truth is that Coward had many enemies among the Establishment, who for one reason or another objected to his official employment. At all events, for Coward it was a bitter disappointment and, as he subsequently told me when we met and he presented me with an inscribed copy of his autobiographical *Future Indefinite*, it cost him some black hours. But things probably worked out for the best, for if the job with Stephenson had materialized, he would never have written *Blithe Spirit* and *In Which We Serve*.

By general consent Noël Coward did a wonderful job on the entertainment side during the war, which, in the fairly lavish distribution of honours and awards afterwards, did not receive the recognition it deserved. When I first met him on Stephenson's introduction, he told me that even before the war King George V had wished to knight him, but was dissuaded from doing so when whispers of Coward's homosexual inclinations reached the royal ears. As it was, Coward had to wait until 1970 before he received the coveted accolade, while Charles Chaplin did not get his 'K' until five years later, when he was eighty-six, as a kind of afterthought on the part of the then Prime Minister Harold Wilson, to whom Chaplin's left-wing politics were presumably acceptable.

There was considerable surprise on both sides of the Atlantic when a knighthood was conferred on Alexander Korda in King George VI's Birthday Honours in 1942, the honour being awarded on Churchill's personal recommendation. People could not understand it. He had been severely attacked in the English press for making pictures in Hollywood during the war instead of

Sir Alexander and Lady Korda (Merle Oberon) outside Buckingham Palace after he had been knighted by King George VI in 1942. The Kordas' marriage broke up shortly afterwards.

in an English studio. Also he was Hungarian, Jewish, and divorced, all of which militated against such an honour being conferred upon an expatriate, naturalized foreigner at such a time. Why had Churchill done it? The answer seemed to be that Churchill liked and respected Korda, he was grateful to him not only for making *That Hamilton Woman* – it was *Lady Hamilton* in England – but for reissuing his old pictures in America, thereby earning much-needed dollars for the British Treasury. Neither, no doubt, could Churchill forget his pre-war professional association with Korda, who among other things had bought the motion-picture rights in Churchill's only novel *Savrola*, although the film was never made. In short, Churchill's answer to the

British press criticisms of Alex Korda was to make him Sir Alexander.

Alex certainly enjoyed being a knight, the first in the motion-picture industry. He was staying in his suite at the St Regis Hotel in New York when I telephoned to congratulate him. Although of course he had been officially forewarned of the honour which he agreed to accept, he had not seen the announcement in the *New York Times* and other papers. He asked me about the recipients of the other honours. When I mentioned one name, adding that Alex's notice was two inches longer, he chortled like a schoolboy. Meanwhile in Hollywood, where for many years there had been a profusion of bogus titles, mostly Russian and Polish, there was some confusion as to the correct style of address for Sir Alexander and Lady Korda when they appeared. Studio guards called Merle 'Your Highness' and the head waiter at Chasen's called Alex 'Your Excellency'. Louis B. Mayer, the MGM tycoon, was heard to remark that Alex would be impossible to deal with 'now they've made the son-of-a-bitch a Lord'. But Mayer's partner Sam Goldwyn took a kindlier view of Alex's title which he declared to be '100 per cent kosher'.[26]

A few days after the announcement of her husband's knight-hood, Merle telephoned another well-known Hollywood restaurant, Romanoff's, to make a dinner reservation. 'This is Lady Korda speaking,' she said. 'I wish to make a reservation. Is that the *maître d'hôtel?*' 'No, your ladyship,' replied a male voice at the other end of the line, 'this is His Highness Prince Michael Romanoff, and I'll be glad to serve a lady!'

Alex, after he had started making films again in England, was divorced from Merle. Like her, he also remarried, this time a Canadian girl, Alexandra Boycun, much younger than himself. She remarried after Alex's death, was divorced from her second husband, and eventually committed suicide by taking an overdose of sleeping tablets. Although she inherited all the old masters and other treasures I had seen in the house at Bel Air, and sold them for close on half a million pounds at Sotheby's, she confused wealth with happiness. It was a mistake which Merle never made, although she was married four times in all.[27]

Otto Strasser, ex-Nazi and refugee: the picture was taken when the author met him in 1942 in Montreal, where he was living incognito.

An interesting German refugee and ex-Nazi whom I met at this time was Otto Strasser, younger brother of the ill-fated Gregor, who was among those murdered in Hitler's blood-bath on 30 June 1934. Both brothers had served in the First World War, and in the early years of the post-war Weimar Republic both were Socialists, as was Hitler himself. Hitler broke away from the German Socialist movement to form the National Socialist German Workers' Party (NSDAP), and with the support of Gregor Strasser, Goering, Hess and Roehm staged an unsuccessful *putsch* in a Munich beer-hall in 1923, for which Hitler spent a year in prison. Otto, who was a disillusioned Social Democrat, was persuaded by Gregor to join Hitler's party in 1925. But like Gregor, Otto sought a truly revolutionary party which would fight along with the trade unions for serious social and economic reforms and would oppose the dictatorship to which Hitler's totalitarian tendencies seemed to point the way. In 1930 Otto broke with Hitler and left the Nazi party, which he considered was becoming more 'National' than 'Socialist', while Gregor remained a discontented member, hoping to persuade Hitler to change his policies and disapproving of his relations with industrialists like Thyssen and Hugenberg, on whose backs he aimed at, and in fact succeeded in, climbing to power as Chancellor in 1933. Meanwhile Otto had found a rival movement called the Black Front which gained considerable support, particularly from the army.

At the beginning of February 1934, Hitler banned the Black Front and the publication of its newspapers. Otto Strasser consequently decided to go into hiding. While on his way by taxi to the Anhalt station in Berlin, he saw a red glow in the sky and asked the driver what it was. 'The Nazis have set fire to the Reichstag,' was the reply.

Realizing that Otto Strasser was the Nazi party's most dangerous enemy, Goering ordered the Gestapo to kill him. But Otto was always one jump ahead of the Gestapo, whether in Vienna, Prague, Zürich, or Paris, while continuing his anti-Nazi activities by secret broadcasts and by smuggling Black Front newspapers and pamphlets into Germany. Many of his friends who were caught were tortured and murdered, but none of them betrayed him. When France fell, he succeeded, in the face of the greatest difficulties which he has described in his books, in escaping through Spain to Portugal, the Gestapo always hot on his heels – they nearly captured him in a Portuguese monastery where he had taken refuge. Eventually Otto Strasser reached Lisbon where, with the help of the British SIS, he was able to obtain a passage to Bermuda on one of the American Export Line ships. He travelled under the name of Otto Bostroem on a Swedish passport, and arrived at Bermuda on 9 October 1940.

For the next six months he lived quietly, and strictly incognito, in Bermuda, where his presence was known only to the Governor, the Colonial Secretary, and one or two others including myself. During this period he planned the organization of what he styled a National Council for Free Germany, to be headed by Dr Heinrich Bruening, the former Chancellor who belonged to the Catholic Centre Party and was now living in the US as Professor of Political Science at Harvard; fortunately for him, Bruening had left Germany a fortnight before 'the night of the long knives'. Although Otto Strasser had likewise left Germany before the blood-bath I once asked him whether he had any details of how his brother Gregor had died. Yes, he had, he said, and he told me.

On 30 June 1934, Gregor was having lunch with his family in his home in Berlin, when eight Gestapo men suddenly appeared and arrested him without any explanation. He was taken to the Gestapo headquarters in Prinz Albrecht Strasse and thrown into a tiny cell. Some hours later Heydrich, the sadistic Gestapo leader, came into the cell with two others, one of whom was Eicke, later in charge of the German concentration camps. Gregor was shot from behind through the main artery, so that the blood spurted out against the cell wall. 'Isn't he dead yet?' another prisoner in an adjoining cell heard Heydrich saying some time later. 'Let the swine bleed to death!' The bloodstains on the wall remained there for several weeks, and the local SS men, who regarded them as a kind of museum piece, used to boast to the terrified inmates that it was the blood of 'a famous man', Gregor Strasser. It was only after he had received many complaints that Heydrich ordered the bloodstains to be cleaned off the wall. The man who did the cleaning afterwards escaped from Germany and joined Otto Strasser in Prague, where he gave the dead man's brother details of the shooting.

Otto Strasser left Bermuda by a Canadian National Steamship vessel on 3 April 1941 for St John, New Brunswick, under the name of Oswald Bostock. On his arrival it was arranged with the Canadian authorities that he should be registered as a Czech national, although in fact he was a Bavarian. He then moved to an apartment in Montreal where he was joined by his secretary Mme Margaret de Planellas who had come from Switzerland to be with him. She was a German who had married a Spaniard, from whom she was believed to be divorced. Here Otto eked out a somewhat

Himmler *(left)*, German police chief, and his principal assistant
Heydrich, at the height of their power in 1942. Himmler also
controlled the German Foreign Political Service.

precarious existence by writing articles and books. The National
Council for Free Germany, which he had planned in Bermuda,
did not become a reality, since Bruening and the other designated
leaders like Rauschning and Treviranus, who were ministers in
the Weimar Governments, tended to hold aloof from it. On the
other hand, the Free German Movement or FDB (*Frei Deutsch-*

land Bewegung), the foreign counterpart of the Black Front, which still had a subterranean existence within the Reich, had representatives in most of the South American countries and also in Central America and the United States. The US authorities had refused Strasser a visa since he wished to lecture there and they considered his propaganda activities suspect. The trouble with Otto Strasser and the FDB, which dogged Strasser's footsteps for the remainder of his life, was that he was more anti-Hitler than anti-Nazi, and that fundamentally his somewhat muddled political ideas reflected the ghost of Nazism. He was also a convinced anti-Semite. Nevertheless he was an interesting character and I am glad to have known him.

In particular I recall a meeting I had with him and his secretary in his Montreal apartment on the day after New Year 1942, when we talked at length over the tea to which he had invited me. His main theme, to which he continually recurred, was the possibility of an internal revolution in Germany owing to the secession of the more influential army elements from the support of Hitler's regime. Indeed he anticipated the attempted military *coup* of July 1944, though by two years. The dissatisfaction in the Reichswehr he dated from Hitler's recent dismissal of Marshal Walther von Brauchtisch from the command of the army, which Hitler himself had assumed, in addition to that of the other German armed forces.

Strasser thought that Britain was not doing enough to promote subversive elements in Germany. When I asked him for recent proofs of popular discontents there, he replied that letters and reports which reached him regularly via Switzerland were most encouraging. For instance, a well-known SA leader or former leader, who commanded 100,000 men, was already deep in a conspiracy against the present rulers. 'But that is not enough,' he went on. 'The Allies must play their part in psychological warfare – in propaganda. You must fight Hitler with his own weapons – above all with the secret weapon of which he has boasted. This weapon is simply the fifth column whose employment in the occupied countries of Europe before their fall was so conspicuously successful!' He particularly favoured short-wave

German-language broadcasts to Germany.

I replied that the British were carrying on psychological warfare, both overt and covert, including short-wave radio broadcasts, and that no doubt it would be increased as time went on.
When I questioned him about the attitude of the German police
and Gestapo, he expressed the opinion that they 'would soon
come over to the side of the revolutionaries simply out of self-
interest, since many of them, and the army, have already realized
that *Germany cannot now win the war*.'

He thought, too, that in Germany 10 per cent of the people
were pro-Nazi and 10 per cent anti-Nazi, while the remaining 80
per cent would support any government in power. In South
America, he thought from his contacts there, the Nazis were
making every effort to enlist support. Their great argument, with
which I agreed, was that Germany would always have more to
offer the countries there in the form of commercial advantages
than either Great Britain or the United States. Argentina, Brazil,
Colombia, and Peru he considered particular danger spots in view
of the arrival in Buenos Aires of a new Gestapo Intelligence chief
named Bueste. After the war, he thought, Germany would revert
to something approaching the pre-1870 confederation with
separate political entities such as Prussia, Bavaria, and Wurtem-
burg, held together on weaker federal lines than actually was to
happen, although – anti-Communist as he was – he did not envisage the political division of Germany into two separate and
ideologically opposed states, as was to happen. At the same time
he was convinced, he said, that after a general peace had been
concluded, the Soviet Union would endeavour to proselytize her
former allies politically and would not hesitate 'to take the most
drastic steps towards the achievement of her aims'.

Before we parted, he gave me a copy of the English translation
of his book *Hitler and I* which he signed and inscribed *All bests
wishes for 1942*! Originally published in France when he was
living there before that country fell, it gives a vivid account of his
relations with the Führer and the activities of the Black Front;
after forty years it still makes fascinating reading.

In a private memorandum which I dictated immediately after this meeting, I said:

> Strasser gave me the general impression of an idealist whose enthusiasm is great and who occasionally exhibits real flashes of insight but whose judgement on many matters is imperfect. He is not a political leader nor has he the makings of one, although he would very much like to be one. Above all he is by no means so much anti-Nazi as anti-Hitler and anti-present Nazi leaders. At heart he subscribes to the principles of National Socialism, although he naturally cannot endorse the manner in which those principles have been applied by the present leaders who were responsible for the murder of his brother Gregor and for the placing of a price upon his own head. He thinks in terms of *Weltpolitik* to the exclusion of ideas of the Liberal and Social Democrat school, and he believes that some form of authoritarian rule in which the elements of confidence, order, and fear appear, is best suited to the German people. There is, however, no doubt of his intense hatred of the present rulers in Germany, to whose overthrow all his energies and those of his followers are primarily directed.

I never saw Otto Strasser again, but I was later glad to learn that, unlike Trotsky, he escaped his erstwhile leader's vengeance and lived to return to his native land.[28]

4

Good-bye To All That

ALTHOUGH the American public was for many months not fully apprised of the extent of the enormous loss and damage suffered as a result of the Japanese attack on Pearl Harbor, which brought the United States into the war, the fact that America was now in the war as an ally of Britain had some significant results, not least for the British, and particularly for the British working officially in the US. Lord Halifax reported from his Embassy in Washington to the Foreign Office in London that there was a sudden and alarming decline in British popularity, which he explained by the shifting of attention from the war in Europe to that in the Pacific, and to American dis-appointment at the steady retreat of Britain before the Japanese onslaught in the Far East, where 'heroic China' led by Marshal Chiang Kai-Shek, which had been at war with Japan since 1937, appeared to be doing more to stem the Japanese advance than the British and their colonial and Indian supporters, who were operationally suspect. Britain's single-handed fight against Germany tended to be forgotten or at least overlooked, while Churchill was criticized for a defensive strategy which kept armies locked up in Britain for the defence of the British Isles.

One domestic result of America's entry into the war was the promotion of a bill in Congress by Senator Kenneth McKellar, a Democrat from Tennessee, which transferred the registration of all foreign agencies in the United States from the State Depart-ment to the Department of Justice, then headed by the Attorney General Francis Biddle; it also amended most drastically the conditions under which these agencies would be required to register, making no distinction between agencies friendly to the US and others. It was a subject with which Biddle was familiar, since aliens had been obliged to register individually since June 1940; and Biddle, who was at that time Solicitor General, was charged with the administration of the new law. It was no easy task, since there were already $3\frac{1}{2}$ million aliens in the USA and more were coming in from Nazi-occupied Europe, so that he had the double duty of protecting law-abiding aliens from public animosity, and of protecting the country from subversive elements with the help of the FBI, which was a branch of the Justice Department. As Attorney General after Pearl Harbor, he protested in vain against the evacuation of US citizens of Japanese origin from West Coast areas, since he was a liberal and a convinced defender of civil liberties as well as of national security.

Stephenson took the view, rightly, that BSC's activities were likely to come under severe scrutiny when the McKellar Bill passed Congress, which it was to do on 28 January 1942. When he heard of this, Stephenson immediately went to see Colonel Donovan in his office in Washington and told him that it would mean the end of BSC, since the measure provided that 'all records, accounts and propaganda used by foreign agents (whether allied or neutral, secret or open) would be liable to inspection by US Government authorities at any time'. If the Bill became law as it stood, Stephenson went on, Donovan's growing organization might as well fold up too.

Donovan thereupon picked up the telephone and asked to be put through to the White House. He then requested an immediate appointment with the President on a matter of extreme urgency, and hurried round to the White House. On being shown into the President's room, Donovan saw the McKellar Bill lying on Roosevelt's desk awaiting signature as soon as it had been passed. He was able to persuade the President not to sign the Bill unless and until it was modified to allow adequate safeguards for Stephenson's interests and those of BSC. A few days later the President vetoed the measure and sent it back to Congress for revision, in the light of an assurance he expected to receive from the Attorney General that British interests would not be adversely affected.

Stephenson considered that I, with my legal qualifications, was the best person in his organization available to deal with Biddle and the other Justice Department officials when BSC's status and activities were examined afresh, as they were bound to be; I was to do what I could, in co-operation with the British Embassy, to counter the internecine jealousies in Washington and the desire of certain individuals to cut Stephenson and BSC down to size. For this purpose I was seconded to the British army staff. There was indeed a proliferation of British special missions at this time, dealing with such matters as food, raw materials, shipping, finance, supply, and information, besides the British military mission and Stephenson's secret intelligence and security interests. Indeed, the size to which these missions became inflated led President Roosevelt to remark jocularly to Lord Halifax that there were more English in Washington in 1942 than there had been when they burned the White House in 1814.[1]

BSC and its chief had one influential opponent in the person of Adolf Augustus Berle, forty-seven-year-old Assistant Secretary in the State Department. A Harvard-educated lawyer – at twenty-one he had been the youngest Harvard law graduate – an expert on the law of corporation finance, and a member of an old family long resident in Stockbridge, Massachusetts, Berle owed his position in the government to his friendship with Sumner Welles, the powerful Under-Secretary of State, and also to the fact that Cordell Hull liked him because, in the Secretary of State's words, Berle 'possessed remarkable keenness, with literary capacity, and served with unusual efficiency'.[2] He had also been an active member of Roosevelt's New Deal 'Brains Trust'. As regards the McKellar Bill, Berle had openly stated that it was as much directed against British agencies as it was against Communists and subversive Axis organizations. As Stephenson informed MI6 headquarters in London, Berle admitted quite frankly that his Government would not tolerate, for instance, the continuing independent activity of an intelligence organization such as Security Co-ordination, and that its records must be available to at least one US Government Department, preferably

Adolf Berle, US Assistant Secretary of State, at his desk in the State Department.

the Justice Department and, specifically, the FBI.

On 31 December 1941, a few weeks after the Japanese attack on Pearl Harbor, a joint Anglo-American-Canadian conference to co-ordinate plans for handling security and intelligence in the western hemisphere was convened at FBI headquarters in Washington, at which Berle presided on behalf of the State Department. BSC was represented by Stephenson and Ellis, the FBI by Hoover and three of his assistant Directors, the RCMP by two of its members who had come down from Ottawa, and the British Embassy by its Head of Chancery, Mr F. R. Hoyer Millar, later Lord Inchyra. The purpose of the meeting was expressed in the following agenda, presumably drafted by Berle and Hoover:

The Government of the United States is interested in establishing a more closely correlated and official machinery for handling of investigative activities in the Western Hemi-

sphere. Matters to be considered will include the improvement of existing coverage of subversive groups, the improvement of facilities for the exchange of information, the
consideration of establishing liaison representatives at the
headquarters of various groups and the establishing of an
international body to convene from time to time for the purpose of outlining investigative and operational procedure as
joint undertakings and on a Hemisphere basis.

It was clear from the outset that Berle's principal target was BSC,
whose activities he plainly resented, although initially he veiled
his resentment in relatively conciliatory language. He began by
saying that as a result of US participation in the war and the
development of 'new problems in Intelligence activities', it was
necessary to set up machinery to cover these problems. The
President, therefore, had entrusted this task to the FBI. He went
on to say that he was aware that certain unofficial arrangements
had been in force between the FBI and BSC for some time and
the moment had now arrived when they should be placed on a
regular basis. In amplifying this theme, Hoover paid a compliment to the co-operation and assistance he had had from BSC in
the past, but he confirmed 'the desirability of establishing official
relations'.

Stephenson agreed that co-operation between his organization
and Hoover's should be placed on an official basis and he
referred to this proposal as 'a consummation of a marriage
which had been in existence for some time'. He also agreed with
the proposals for liaison and undertook to see that his staff con-
formed to the new requirements regarding the full exchange of
information and, in particular, the cessation of BSC's independent activities within US territory. A committee was also
appointed, on which BSC was invited to be represented, its
purpose being to deal with such subjects as clandestine radio
interception, Japanese espionage on the West Coast, anti-
sabotage measures in ports and factories, the joint operation of
'double agents', and the general pooling of intelligence
resources and material. The Committee, on which Ellis served

as the BSC representative, did meet from time to time, and I fed it with information from British military sources, although I gained the impression that it was never very effective.

Berle's personal animosity against Stephenson was aggravated by an incident which occurred very shortly after the Washington conference. It had its origin in a piece of information which Berle learned from Hoover's assistant Edward Tamm and which, according to Berle's official papers in the State Department archives, Berle found 'at once amusing, disturbing and irritating'. On 13 February 1942, he wrote in a private memorandum:

Tamm told me that last week their people had discovered a British Intelligence man named Paine operating in New York. His purpose was to 'get the dirt' about me and then through various channels, one of them being Pierrepoint Moffat,[3] and a couple of newspapers, to force my removal from the State Department. The FBI had watched this to a point where they had conclusive proof and then had called in the head of the British Intelligence [William Stephenson]. They told him that they wanted Paine out of the country by six o'clock 'or else'; in which case they would arrest him promptly and go right to it.

Stephenson had said first, weakly, that Paine had been a long time in the United States; to which they replied that that made it worse; and Stephenson had expressed surprise and horror that any of his men should do such a thing, and had finally put Paine on the plane for Montreal, and that was that.

It developed that the only dirt they had dug up so far was a column about having twin bath tubs in our house.

This would be amusing if it did not illustrate the danger which is run from having these foreigners operate. I plan to call the British Embassy and tell them, that I am sufficiently experienced not to be influenced by this kind of thing, and that I think they should take it up with Lord Halifax and arrange to have this kind of thing stopped.[4]

Lord Halifax, British Ambassador in Washington, outside the Embassy
with Winston Churchill in 1943.

Denis Paine, whom I remember vaguely, worked in the Ship's Observers branch of BSC, primarily concerned with the security of British shipping and their crews in American ports. I am surprised that he should have been given an assignment of the kind described by Berle, if indeed he was, which I greatly doubt; he is more likely to have done it on his own initiative, since he was in Washington fairly frequently and may have thought he was doing Stephenson a service by making enquiries about Berle. At all events, he did depart quickly for Canada. He was simply told to meet Freckles Wren, who happened to be in New York at the time, in a mid-town hotel, and, on doing so, was given a ticket for Montreal where, Wren told him, he was to wait for further instructions. According to a friend of his, Paine had no idea why he was being sent to Canada and was later puzzled to learn that he could not return to the United States. When he next met Wren, some time later, he said to him jokingly, 'You know you kidnapped me!'

The next move in the general BSC situation was an invitation from Sumner Welles to Lord Halifax to a meeting with the Attorney General in Biddle's office in the Justice Department. The meeting took place on 2 March 1942, Halifax being accompanied by the British Embassy Minister Sir Ronald Campbell. Berle also attended, representing the State Department. According to a memorandum written by Berle at the time:

> The Attorney General took up the problem of the operations of British Intelligence here. He indicated that the President and the Cabinet were both unhappy about the existing situation. He said they had come to two conclusions:
>
> First, that the activities of the British Intelligence here ought to be liaison rather than operations, and
>
> Second, that probably they needed a different type of man to head it.[5]

Halifax said that he understood from Stephenson that British Intelligence was working in the closest harmony with the FBI, that they did nothing without the approval of that organization, and that they exchanged results. He then read out a statement he had received from Stephenson about his activities, indicating that 'everything he did was submitted to, and passed upon by, and approved by Mr J. Edgar Hoover'.

Both Biddle and Berle replied that this did not correspond with the reports they had received. They thereupon telephoned to Hoover and asked him to come round to Biddle's office. Hoover arrived a few minutes later and was asked for his views. Berle's memorandum continued:

> Mr Hoover promptly said that the statement made by Stephenson did not correspond to his impression at all. They did maintain liaison and tried to work helpfully together. Not infrequently, however, Mr Stephenson reported afterwards what he was doing. But he, Hoover, did not know what was being done until afterwards, and frequently not then. When the blunt question was asked whether he thought Stephenson was the man to head the organization, Mr Hoover responded that he had no quarrel with Mr Stephenson and had pleasant personal relations with him. They did not, however, feel that they were on terms of such confidence with the organization or with Mr Stephenson as to make close working relations possible. Specifically, they were never sure whether they were getting the whole story; and they knew that in many cases they were not. Certain specific instances were discussed in which British Intelligence had tapped wires and shanghaied sailors. This matter was being reported to the Attorney General.

Halifax now remarked that his 'mental structure' had been altered on learning that there was not a close working relationship between Hoover and Stephenson, since he had previously assumed that their two agencies were 'working perfectly together'. Specifically, referring to the incident of Paine, he had understood that Stephenson had discovered Paine's activities and had promptly called him down and requested him to leave the country. He did not understand that the FBI had intervened in the matter.

Hoover then stated that the fact was that his people had found out about what Paine was doing, had called in Stephenson, and given Paine twenty-four hours to leave the country.

To this Halifax replied that he and Sir Ronald Campbell would have a further look at the Paine incident. However, the Ambassador added for the information of the others present that the British Secret Intelligence Service was headed by General Stewart Menzies in London, who was not a publicly known figure; he was nominally under the Foreign Office in the person of the Permanent Secretary Alexander Cadogan, and 'the Foreign Secretary did not usually interest himself very much in the matter of secret intelligence'.

Biddle said that he and his colleagues in the Government desired two things – first, a list of all Stephenson's men 'working here'; and secondly, a careful, detailed, statement of their activities. He concluded by saying that their own view, after careful consideration, was that the activities of BSC should be limited to liaison; and that the statement made by Stephenson that this was all that it now did 'simply did not correspond to the facts'.

'In justice to Stephenson,' Berle remarked in bringing the meeting to a close, 'it should be remembered that he came here at a time when the United States was not in the war, and probably organized on that basis. Now that we are in the war, the organization plainly ought to change its nature and resolve itself into a fully co-operative situation which now exists.'

A week later another meeting took place, at Halifax's suggestion, this time at the British Embassy in Massachusetts Avenue, the British participants being Halifax and Campbell, and the American Biddle and Berle.[6]

Halifax opened the discussion by saying that he had been considering the matter of Stephenson and British Secret Intelligence. There was a wide diversity, he said, between the statements made by Stephenson and the statements made by the American officials, but he considered that 'no good purpose would be served by trying to go into issues of fact'. Instead he had certain suggestions to make. He began by repeating that British Intelligence in the United States had done nothing except with the direct authority and co-operation of the American officials, and he said that this must be taken as established.

Biddle and Berle looked at each other a little blandly. The Attorney General observed that the Department of Justice was the competent authority in this case, working through Hoover; that he (Biddle) consequently ought to know whether there was such co-operation and approval; that he knew 'absolutely nothing about what was going on, and consequently could not be said to have approved it'.

Halifax insisted on his point. Biddle then said that he thought matters would be 'clarified' if Halifax would give them a concise picture of what was happening. 'The FBI radio is sending two or three hundred messages a week in secret code for the British Intelligence here to the British Intelligence in London, which certainly argues a considerable sub-structure, and no one knows anything about it. Perhaps Lord Halifax could tell us exactly what is going on.'

According to Berle, Halifax then stated that, quite frankly, he did not know. However, he went on, he had been told by Stephenson that instead of having a large number of employees, he had actually about 137, varying two or three either way. He said he had inquired of Stephenson whether the cipher messages going forward were kept secret because, as Stephenson had said, they reflected a correspondence between the President and Mr Churchill; but Stephenson had denied that he had ever made any such statement. The Attorney General thereupon produced a report by Hoover, dated the previous July, in which Stephenson had given this reason as an excuse for not permitting any American official to know the code.

The Ambassador then, for the first time, mentioned Colonel Donovan's name. He said he understood that a great many of these matters had been cleared with Colonel Donovan. He (Halifax) had been somewhat surprised that the State Department did not acknowledge this.

Berle replied that it had not occurred to him to consult Colonel

Donovan about espionage inside the United States, 'in view of the direct and definite presidential order that Colonel Donovan should have the overseas espionage, and that all internal intelligence should be centered through the Department of Justice. It would therefore be as unnecessary for the [State] Department to consult Colonel Donovan on this matter as it would be for us to consult the Chief of Police of Nevada City.'

'But Colonel Donovan does have internal jurisdiction,' said Halifax.

'What is it?' the Attorney General asked.

'Well,' replied the Ambassador, 'British Intelligence and Colonel Donovan do co-operate. For instance, in recruiting the Commandos for overseas, Colonel Donovan has used British Intelligence personnel. In fact, they are now on his payroll.'

'That may well be,' Biddle conceded, 'since certainly Colonel Donovan has full jurisdiction to recruit the men he needs overseas.' But, he repeated, that did not in any respect cover internal espionage operations.

Some further discussion followed on the question of jurisdicton, particularly in respect of ships and shipping, 'Lord Halifax seeking to show that the British Intelligence, which necessarily guarded British ships, naturally extended that to looking for Axis agents on shore who might connect with the crews, and so forth.'

Biddle said that this was exactly what bothered him. 'This represents actual operations on American territory, without knowledge or approval of American officials, and has led precisely to the confusion which I hoped to avoid.'

The Attorney General proceeded to shock the Ambassador with details of British Secret Service activities which, he said, unless stopped at once, would get his government into the most serious kind of trouble. It appeared that British Secret Service agents in a bar in Baltimore had picked up 'two British sailors who had deserted their battleship, handcuffed them, thrown them into a car, and driven them back to their ship in New York'.

Nice story if it got out [Biddle told Halifax] and we would of course have to arrest His Majesty's agents, and indict them for kidnapping. There were five state kidnapping laws, too; I could not remember which carried the death penalty, which only life imprisonment. I did not want any report, investigation or apology. I wanted his immediate assurance that it would not happen again . . . He knew nothing about it. His government, he pointed out, never kept its representatives informed on secret service work. But he gave me his word.[7]

Halifax agreed that the relationship between Stephenson and Hoover should be a liaison one 'pure and simple', and that no operations should be carried on in the United States except as expressly agreed between the two men. He did, however, insist that the secret radio communication should continue.

Biddle said they would reserve judgement on that but he hoped the Ambassador would let him know what went over the radio. Halifax replied that he 'probably could not do that, because these messages were none of our business'. But he undertook to furnish a statement showing by general headings the type of matter sent out. In reply to Biddle's remark, made quite courteously, that 'all this was done by American hospitality – under American licence, so to speak – and that it could be terminated at any time by our simple act', Halifax reminded the Attorney General that they were allies, and not enemies. It was a world-wide principle and generally recognized that messages of this kind should be sent without interference.

At this point Berle intervened to say that he thought he could speak on behalf of the State Department and that they had never heard of any such principle, nor had they recognized it.

What we do recognize is the right of an embassy to communicate by secret code with governments overseas. In our own arrangements we have always insisted that the intelligence communications carried on between ourselves and friendly countries are under the control of embassies. We rely for the observance of hospitality on the honour of the embassy and on the usual diplomatic responsibility. But here Lord Halifax is asserting a principle in respect of communication by a non-diplomatic source as to the nature of whose activities Lord Halifax professed ignorance.

To this the Ambassador replied that he thought Colonel Donovan claimed the same right in Britain. But Berle at once pointed out that the chief of the Donovan group in London was attached to the United States Embassy there, and that the Embassy thus assumed responsibility for it. It would seem accordingly, Berle went on, that British messages transmitted 'back and forth' should either be known to the US Government or should go through the Embassy channel, subject to Embassy responsibility. 'Lord Halifax smiled,' Berle noted, 'and let it go at that.'

Bringing the meeting to a close, the Attorney General repeated that he had discussed the matter in Cabinet and with the President, saying 'the President had indicated some very real concern'. He expressed the hope that the conference between Hoover and Stephenson, which he undertook to arrange forthwith, would 'get somewhere on a co-operative basis' and that the future activities of BSC would be confined to liaison only. He added, in an implied reference to the registration, that he would be 'glad to try to work things out, if possible, on that basis'.

On their way out of the Embassy the Attorney General observed concisely: 'Someone has been doing some tall lying here.' On Berle asking where, on the evidence he had, Biddle thought the lack of frankness was, the Attorney General, according to Berle, said 'it was pretty plain that Stephenson had given inaccurate information to the Ambassador. Stephenson has assured me that the imformation that he gave Halifax was absolutely accurate. Berle's *aide-mémoire* concluded:

We chatted a little and made one surmise. Stephenson has probably transferred a very considerable number of his agents in this country to Donovan's payroll, on the excuse that they are to be used in 'recruiting personnel' for some of the overseas work in which Donovan is engaged. It is obvious that either the Ambassador or Stephenson has at once taken up the whole matter with Donovan, in an endeavour to protect the situation.

Broadly speaking, this surmise was correct. It only remains to add that a conference took place between Stephenson and Hoover on the lines Biddle had suggested. But, as will be seen, British SIS covert activities continued as before, though more discreetly than hitherto. Meanwhile I had the unenviable task of going through the list of BSC staff with the Attorney General and specifying the nature of each person's duties, so far as I was able to do so. At the same time, I think that when the McKellar Bill was passed in its revised form and became law, which it did on 1 May 1942, it was largely owing to my efforts and arguments with Biddle and other officials of the Justice Department that BSC was relieved of the earlier measure's crippling provisions and was not obliged to disclose its secret records and accounts. I also had to see Berle, and became quite friendly with both men, Biddle and I exchanging copies of legal biographies which we had both written, with cordial inscriptions, while Berle on one occasion invited me to a pleasant afternoon garden party at his Washington house. I also continued to see Hoover, who expressed his thanks for my wife's contribution in instructing selected members of the Bureau's female staff in the techniques of the secret opening of mail as practised in Room 99.

While the meetings between Biddle, Berle, and Halifax were taking place in Washington in February and March 1942, an important trial of a German spy ring was being staged in the Federal Court of the Southern District of New York. It was an example of the most valuable kind of liaison between BSC and the FBI, since the Bureau could not have collected the necessary evidence to indict the defendants without British help, primarily rendered by the Bermuda Censorship. This was the Ludwig or Joe K case, of which the details leading up to the arrest of Ludwig and his fellow spies have already been described. Ludwig, and six of the others, pleaded not guilty – they were, Helen Pauline Mayer (26), René Froehlich (30), Hans Helmut Pagel (20), Frederick Edward Schlosser (19), Karl Victor Mueller (36) and Dr Paul T. Borchardt (55). Ludwig's secretary, eighteen-year-old ex-high school girl Lucy Boehmler, pleaded guilty but turned State's evidence, testifying for the prosecution in the hope of receiving a lighter sentence when she was convicted. Carl Schroetter, the fishing-boat captain who spied on shipping, also pleaded guilty but refused to give any information or to testify against his fellow spies.

The case was tried by Judge Henry W. Goddard and a jury. It lasted five weeks, there were 300 documentary exhibits, and the transcript of the evidence ran to more than 2,000 pages. The genial sixty-seven-year-old judge was a Republican who had been appointed to the Federal bench in New York by President Harding in 1923, so that his judicial experience was considerable. Before the opening of the trial I was invited to discuss and advise upon that portion of the evidence – a substantial part – which had been supplied from British sources, and to assist generally in the preparation of the case against the accused. For this purpose I attended several meetings in the office of Mathias Correa, US Attorney for the New York Southern District, who was in charge of the prosecution, along with his principal assistant John Sonnett; I was consequently able to persuade des Graz and the British Censorship authorities in Bermuda to allow witnesses to come up from Bermuda to prove the correspondence which had been intercepted and which was to be put in evidence as exhibits at the trial. I was also present throughout most of the proceedings in court.

In his opening speech to the jury on 3 February 1942, Mr Correa described the Ludwig spy ring as concentrating on the gathering of military information, particularly about the position and movement of army troops and the location of military airports, and about army morale. The ring also gathered and transmitted to co-conspirators in Shanghai, Spain, Portugal, Argentina, and Germany, much information about shipping and defence factories, particularly those producing aircraft. With the aid of one Heinz Hillebrecht, a co-conspirator who went via Japan to Germany in May 1941, carrying much spy data in secret writing, Ludwig was able to recruit his ring from the Queens and Brooklyn areas, since Hillebrecht had been the leader of the local branch of the German-American Bund. According to the District Attorney, on a certain Sunday, Ulrich von der Osten, Lucy Boehmler (then his secretary), Ludwig, and another defendant Helen Mayer and her husband, who was now in Germany, had visited the Roosevelt and Mitchel airfields and the Grumman and Brewster aeroplane factories where they 'walked around and counted planes'. After Von der Osten's death in the accident near Times Square, Boehmler had become Ludwig's secretary, and together they had made an extensive tour of the Atlantic coastal states, gathering defence data and putting much of it in secret writing. 'They visited almost every naval base, airport and military establishment between here and Key West, Florida.'

After this brief summation and an equally brief reply by the leading defence attorney, the court adjourned for a short recess. I immediately received a message that the judge would like to see me in his room. Judge Goddard asked me to take a seat by his desk and then he reached down and opened a kind of drinks cabinet, upon which he invited me to join him in a whisky highball. After we had refreshed ourselves in this agreeable but, for me, unusual manner, the judge leaned back in his chair and said: 'May I ask you a question?'

'Go right ahead, judge,' I replied.

'Do you think these bastards are guilty?'

The question took me by surprise, as it was not one which an English judge might have been expected to put to me in similar circumstances. I replied cautiously, and I hope correctly, that this was a matter for the jury to decide, but that the evidence with which I was particularly familiar, consisting of the letters intercepted by the Bermuda censors, would certainly appear to incriminate Ludwig.

We then returned to the courtroom and after the judge had taken his seat on the bench, the District Attorney called Lucy Boehmler to the witness stand. An attractive young blonde, she professed to be a loyal American, for although she had been born in Stuttgart, Germany, she had lived in the United States for the past thirteen years. As secretary to Von der Osten and then Ludwig, she earned $25 a week, and had accepted the job because 'it sounded like a lot of fun'. She added that she never realized what she was doing. 'I just did what I was told,' she replied to the District Attorney's questioning. 'I never even thought about it.' Asked about the mail drops used by the ring to transmit information to Germany, she confirmed that they included a certain Manuel Alonso in Madrid, who was a most important intermediary for sending defence data abroad. 'That one was for a Mr Himmler in Germany,' she added. She went on to admit, when pressed by Correa, that the ring was responsible for an undisclosed number of Allied vessels being sunk in the Atlantic in 1941, the information leading to the sinkings having been gathered in New York by Ludwig, Pagel, Froehlich and Hillebrecht. She said that Ludwig once showed her a book in the back of which he 'had marked down the number of ships destroyed on the ocean', including sinkings resulting from the ring's espionage tactics. Boehmler also testified that Froehlich was an US army private attached to the medical corps on Governor's Island when he was arrested. According to the witness, Froehlich sent Ludwig lists of patients in the hospital, with full details of where they had come from, how many men were in their divisions, and what army morale was like all over the country. 'Ludwig also said that Froehlich had a good view of the harbour where he was, and jotted down the names of boats,' she told the court.

Boehmler also gave evidence about the secret writing used to transmit defence data, how to apply the script, and how she practised by writing with ammonium chloride, and then holding it over a stove which brought out the writing in brown. On one occasion, she said, she had taken some of the pyramidon pills to Dr Borchardt, who analysed the data. Referring to her trip along the east coast with Ludwig, she stated that Von der Osten would have accompanied Ludwig but for his death in the street accident. She went along instead, and the trip, which lasted several weeks, cost $1,500 and was apparently financed by 'money brought here for Ludwig' by a co-conspirator named 'Bill'; she understood he was a Nazi intelligence worker who took some of the material obtained back to Germany. She also testified that the defendant Helen Mayer had told her, during a conversation she had had with her on the beach the previous August, after Ludwig had gone to the Pocono mountains, that she had a short-wave radio transmitter in her basement home in Queens. Mayer had also asked for pyramidon since, so she said, she had some vital information to be sent quickly to Germany. They both visited Ludwig in the Poconos and Ludwig had told Mayer to memorize the information and 'give it to the right people in Germany', as she was planning to go to Berlin and meet her husband Walter there.

Cross-examined by counsel for four of the defendants, Boehmler said she never told her family the kind of work she was doing, but that, so far as her relatives knew, Ludwig was in the leather business and she did typing for him.

A considerable amount of prosecution testimony followed, implicating the various defendants and describing how Ludwig was trailed across the continent to Washington state where he was arrested. FBI agents testified about the material they found belonging to Ludwig, including the short-wave radio receiving set in his car, together with a mass of photographs of aircraft and defence plants and maps of different parts of the country. One of the photographs showed Brooklyn Bridge with the Federal Court-house in the background. 'That's getting close to home,' the judge commented when he was shown this picture.

On the sixth day of the trial there was a surprise, when one of the defendants, Hans Pagel, who worked as a chauffeur for a brewery and whose babyish face caused him to be nicknamed 'Bubi' by his confederates, changed his plea to guilty. This was because of FBI testimony that a large assortment of defence data had been found in the back of his car in Brooklyn, where he lived with his family. However he made no statement in court except when he was asked if he knew what he was doing: he answered meekly, 'I do.' He thereupon left the court under escort and returned to prison, there to await sentence.

Two days later there was a further surprise when Mr Charles Watkins-Mence, controller of the Imperial Censorship in Bermuda, appeared in court with three members of his staff. I had arranged for their transport and they had flown up from the island the previous day. The controller, who took the stand first, explained how the Censorship operated, each bag being divided into various categories and sent to the section dealing with that classification. He added that certain letters, which had seemed suspicious, were picked out by the sorters and sent to the head of the appropriate section (the Special Examiners) where they would be given to a particular examiner. Anything of special interest to the United States would be sent to the appropriate authorities there (i.e., the FBI through BSC). Watkins-Mence was not cross-examined.

He was succeeded on the witness stand by Miss Nadya Gardner, my former assistant in the special branch. She identified eleven letters and envelopes addressed by Ludwig and Von der Osten, nine of which were originals and two photostats, all being Government exhibits in the case. Some of the envelopes contained newspaper clippings and others single-spaced typewritten pages. The photostats were reproduced from originals which had been forwarded to their destinations after being photocopied. Some of the letters, she pointed out, were streaked with various colours, from the effects of laboratory testing for secret writing. Four similar letters were identified by another Bermuda Censorship examiner, Leslie Poole. Finally, Dr Charles Dent, the chief technical officer in the Bermuda Censorship, testified that he had developed secret writing in twelve of the letters and that he had analysed the material used for the secret ink and had 'decided that it was an aqueous solution of pyramidon'. He did not add, which he might have done, that it was the persevering Miss Gardner who had urged him to make the test for pyramidon, which at first he had declined to do on the grounds that it would be a waste of time.

The letters intercepted by the Bermuda censors were read to the jury, and the FBI technical and handwriting expert Charles Appel testified that the letters were typed on typewriters used by Ludwig and Von der Osten, the machines having been obtained by the Bureau, as already described. In one letter Ludwig expressed concern about the Bermuda censors holding up mail, and indicated that he would be sending some material by the American Export Line instead of by Pan American Clipper. This was why Nadya Gardner had allowed two of Ludwig's letters to go forward after copying them, since she naturally did not wish the members of the spy ring to be put on their guard. One letter introduced in evidence, from Von der Osten alias Konrad and addressed to Lisbon, dated 3 March 1941 (about a fortnight before his fatal accident), contained the following in German:

> My journeys through the country have shown me that this beautiful country is really in earnest . . . The government has the country entirely behind it and is seriously preparing for war . . . The American Federation of Labor is almost solidly behind the government . . . I also believe that, at least in the case of emergency, the Congress of Industrial Organizations will willy-nilly have to follow the example of its fellow trade union.

Much of this letter dealt in great detail with aircraft production throughout the United States, and listed the orders being filled, describing minutely the different types of planes.

In the last letters sent by Joe K to Berlin, Ludwig wrote that he wished to return to Germany because he was 'lonely here' and thought he could be of more help synthesizing espionage information in Berlin; also that his stomach was 'on the blink' and that the American food was not 'nearly as good as the European food'.

When the defence opened, Ludwig did not take the stand since he preferred not to testify, so that with the elimination of Hans Pagel, who had changed his plea to guilty, the only defendants who gave evidence were Mayer, Froehlich, Schlosser, Borchardt and Mueller. They were not particularly convincing. Mayer repudiated a statement she had made to the FBI at the time of her arrest, that she had suspected Ludwig of sending information to Germany. She was tired and hungry at the time, she said, and worried about her parents. She admitted, however, that she had often met Ludwig and that he was a frequent guest at her house,

together with other members of the ring. But she denied that aircraft and other defence data were discussed there, contrary to
Lucy Boehmler's evidence.

Froehlich, who denied giving any defence data to Ludwig in
magazines, said he had got mixed up with the ring through his
love for Lucy Boehmler, which was not returned. 'She stood me
up twice,' he said bitterly. Schlosser, accused of collecting shipping data for the ring, insisted that the statement he signed for the
FBI was wrong and that he had been forced to sign it under
duress. Mueller swore that he had done no more than give newspaper clippings to Ludwig, and had addressed three letters for
Ludwig which he later mailed without knowing what they
contained. Borchardt, who claimed that he was a Jewish refugee
from Nazi Germany, was accused of being a fake refugee, intend-
ing to return to Germany if he could and convince the Nazis of
his worth. As a military geographer, Borchardt, whose code-
name was Robert, had also tried to get into American Intelligence.
One of Ludwig's intercepted letters reported that 'Robert had
connections with our competitors, who offered him a position,
and I told him to take any decent job he could get'. Perhaps this
knowledge made Ludwig jealous. At all events the two men did
not like each other, since another of Ludwig's intercepted letters,
to Himmler, belittled Borchardt's abilities and complained of his
lack of co-operation. Borchardt also had a mysterious friend
whom he said was an official in the German government whom
he had known for years. Asked by Correa whether he had ever
written to his friend about Ludwig, he said he had done so only
once, the previous April, on the subject of procuring secret-
writing materials from Ludwig. Thereupon the District Attorney,
with a dramatic gesture, produced a letter dated 17 July 1941
from his German friend, which had been withheld until that
moment. Thus Borchardt was caught lying, while Borchardt and
Ludwig were shown as having spied on each other. No doubt
Borchardt had the average German military man's contempt for
the Gestapo.[8]

The jury did not take long to find all the prisoners guilty. In
passing sentence Judge Goddard told them that 'your sentences

should be such as not only to punish you but to indicate to others like you that such acts as these will not be tolerated in this country'. He sentenced Ludwig, Borchardt and Froehlich, each to the maximum term of twenty years, while Mrs Mayer, Pagel and Mueller got fifteen years and Schlosser twelve. With regard to Helen Mayer, the judge observed that 'the people sunk by torpedoes on the ocean get no greater mercy from the Germans because the data that resulted in the sinking came from a woman'. As they passed through the outer corridor to the elevator, Ludwig and Mayer were greeted by hisses and cries of 'Shame!' from the spectators.

Schroetter, the fishing-boat captain who had pleaded guilty, was given ten years, in spite of his vigorous protest that he was the victim of circumstance and against what he considered to be the excessive severity of the sentence. 'I was more or less pushed into the case. I don't think I've done anything detrimental to the United States . . . I agreed to do something, but when I was contacted I refused to go through with it.' He added that he was coerced because he had a sister in Germany. Finally, Lucy Boehmler, who pleaded guilty and then turned informer, was sentenced to five years or 'at least the duration of the war'. Ten days later Schroetter, who was sent to the Atlanta Federal penitentiary, committed suicide by slashing his wrists with the diaphragm of a radio receiving set and hanging himself with a bed-sheet attached to a vertical water-pipe.

Thus ended a dramatic espionage trial, the first to take place after the United States entered the war. However, because the spying had been done before Pearl Harbor, the spies escaped the death penalty which could not be imposed in peace time. The next lot of spies to be caught were not so lucky.

Meanwhile, on 16 March 1942 I received a gratifying letter from the District Attorney, Mathias Correa, who had been in charge of the prosecution:

> Now that the Ludwig case is finally and successfully concluded, I wish to take this opportunity of expressing to you my appreciation of the most friendly and helpful co-operation and

assistance which you and your associates rendered us in that case.

In my opinion the testimony and exhibits furnished by Mr Watkins-Mence and the other members of the Imperial Censorship stationed at Bermuda contributed very largely, in the case of some of the defendants almost wholly, to the successful outcome of the case.

Finally, I wish to thank you for the friendly spirit of co-operation in which you helped us at all stages of the case with which you were concerned. I look forward to a continuance of that pleasant relationship, however our official paths may cross. [9]

Coincidentally with the Ludwig spy trial in New York, another trial was taking place in Washington DC, that of the notorious pro-German propagandist George Sylvester Viereck on a charge of violating the Foreign Agents Registration Act by failing to inform the United States authorities of the details of his activities as an agent of Germany. Viereck, aged fifty-seven at this time, had been born in Munich; his father Louis Viereck had been a Socialist member of the Reichstag and was reputedly the illegitimate son of King William I of Prussia by an actress. George had been brought to New York by his parents at the age of eleven, and when his father became naturalized young Viereck automatically obtained American nationality. A lifelong admirer of the Hohenzollern dynasty in Germany, he was on friendly terms with the ex-Kaiser William II, and it was established that since the beginning of World War II he had received more than $100,000 from German sources in America for his propaganda work. However, initially there was no evidence of his connection with the propaganda division of the German Foreign Office. Fortunately, while the trial was going on I recalled that a letter had been picked up in Bermuda from Viereck to Dr Hans Heinrich Dieckhoff, a former German ambassador to the US and, at the time of the intercept, chief of the propaganda division in the Wilhelmstrasse. The letter contained proofs of a book entitled *Who's Who among the War Mongers* by Rush Holt, ex-Democrat Senator for West Virginia and an extreme isolationist, with corrections in Viereck's handwriting. Fortunately it had been turned over for examination in Bermuda to Nadya Gardner, before being sent on via Stephenson's New York office to the FBI. As Miss Gardner was still in New York for the Ludwig trial, I proposed that she should go to Washington as soon as possible and testify accordingly. Permission was given, but when Miss Gardner reached the Washington courthouse with me, the defence was submitting to the trial judge that he should direct the jury to acquit the defendant, since the Government had failed to prove that he had any case to answer. However, when Miss Gardner was allowed to take the stand, her sensational evidence changed the whole atmosphere. She testified that in the previous July she had examined the letter with the proofs of the ex-Senator's book, together with various newspaper clippings. The letter had been addressed to 'Signor Hoyningero Hueneras', an alias for the German Ambassador in Lisbon, for onward transmission to Dieckhoff in Berlin. She had also examined similar letters from Viereck, she added.

'What was Mr Viereck's signature on the letters?' asked William Maloney, the Attorney-General's special assistant in charge of the prosecution.

'It was Sylvester with a square,' she replied.

'Have you ever seen that before?'

'Yes, on various occasions,' she said. 'Sometimes it was GS with a square, and at other times it was George S with a square.' *Viereck*, she added for the information of the court, was a German word meaning 'square' or 'quadrangle'.

Viereck was convicted on three of the five counts in the indictment, and was sentenced to three terms, of eight months to two years, each term of imprisonment to run consecutively, in addition to a fine of $500. He appealed against his conviction and, on his appeal being rejected by the Court of Appeals, he asked the US Supreme Court to review the conviction. In the event the Supreme Court set aside the verdict of the court of first instance, on the ground that the trial judge had misdirected the jury, in that prior to the amendment of the Act in 1942, the Act only required the defendant to disclose his activities on behalf of a foreign principal and not in addition those he carried out on behalf of himself. A new trial was consequently ordered. Some of the prosecutor William Maloney's remarks to the jury in the first trial were also described as 'highly prejudicial' to the course of justice. In the second trial another of the Attorney General's special assistants, George A. McNulty, led for the prosecution, and undertook to establish that all the acts proved in the first trial had been committed by Viereck as an agent of the German Government and in no respect for himself.

The second trial opened in the Federal District Court in Washington before Associate Justice Bolitha J. Laws and a jury on 25 June 1943. At my instance, Nadya Gardner again came up from Bermuda and took the stand for the prosecution, which was conducted by George McNulty assisted by Albert Arent for the Attorney General. She identified many letters and articles in the form of newsletters which Viereck had sent to Dieckhoff and other German officials, which had not been introduced at the first trial. The following is an extract from one Viereck news-letter, put in evidence by Miss Gardner dated 18 July 1941:

> Legally we are still at peace . . . but the issue of war and peace will not be decided by the people . . . It will be decided by a few hundred men in Washington, most of whom are owned by the Administration. Whenever it suits Mr Roosevelt's personal promptings, his political advantage, he can have his war; when that moment comes the entire country, including the opposition, will be behind him. There will be a terrific reaction afterwards which may sweep men like Wheeler and Lindbergh into power.

Fortunately the reaction which Viereck forecast did not come to pass after Pearl Harbor, although Britain's prestige in the United States declined, as we have seen. Viereck was convicted and this time he was sentenced from one to five years, of which he served four-and-a-half years in various Federal penitentiaries, being released shortly after the end of the war, as were Ludwig and the other spies in their case.

When the second Viereck trial had finished, I was invited to visit the Attorney General's office in the Department of Justice where I was personally thanked by Francis Biddle. At the same time the chief prosecutor sent me an equally complimentary letter. 'Mr Arent and I want to express our thanks and the thanks of the Department to you and the British Security Co-ordination for the assistance which you have rendered in the Viereck case,' wrote Mr George McNulty. 'I am sure that you must be gratified that the material intercepted by the British Censorship has been put to such effective use. Miss Gardner deserves great credit both for the quality of her work and her shrewdness as a witness.'

The Ludwig and Viereck cases were excellent examples of the kind of liaison with the Justice Department in which I enjoyed participating, and one result of this liaison was that my relations with the FBI were always most friendly, particularly with Sam Foxworth, head of the Bureau's New York Office, and with Hoover himself. (Foxworth was an outstandingly able law enforcement officer who specialized in counter-espionage and sabotage operations, and it was a great tragedy when he was killed in an aeroplane crash in January 1943 at the comparatively early age of thirty-six.) Hoover would always see me if he was in Washington and I asked for an appointment, and he never forgot the help my wife had given the Bureau in training girls in Room 99 techniques. When asked to suggest a rough test for selecting girls likely to possess the manual dexterity needed for the job – the test to be used before the girl was taken on and sworn to secrecy, prior to being trained – Dorothy replied that experience had shown that girls with neat ankles as a rule proved the most suitable. Prospective recruits, being interviewed by a senior Bureau official who kept looking at their legs and ankles, some-times mistook the purpose for which they were required, which subsequently proved a source of considerable amusement in my office.

I remember going to see Hoover in his headquarters shortly after the capture of German saboteurs who had been landed on

Amagansett shore on Long Island in June 1942 and who had been tried *in camera* and found guilty, six afterwards being executed in the electric chair and two, who had been of particular help to the prosecution, being sentenced to long terms of imprisonment. This was an American operation in which the British took no part, but on the occasion of my visit Hoover gave me some interesting details of the case and showed me some of the exhibits at the trial in the shape of German marine fatigue uniforms, social security and identity cards which were exact replicas of the genuine United States articles, and quantities of detonator fuses and explosives, which had been buried in the sand on the Long Island beach. He also spoke of the way the saboteurs had been 'handled'. It was not necessary to employ any third-degree methods, he said, as the men had made full statements. He added that great precautions had been taken to interrogate them individually and not permit any communication between them. Although they showed some semblance of courage collectively, he said, they completely broke down individually and 'behaved with consummate cowardice'. In particular, Haupt, one of the saboteurs who was executed, showed the utmost disregard for the welfare of his fellows and was only concerned with trying – unsuccessfully, as it turned out – to save his own skin.

The purpose of my visit on this occasion was to discuss the publication in the New York press of details of short-wave radio messages sent by German agents, and in particular by an arrested agent named Johannes Kroeger. Kroeger, it was stated in the New York press, had seen ships in Port-of-Spain harbour, Trinidad, and had sent particulars to Nazi agents in Brazil who had relayed them by short-wave radio to Germany. I emphasized the great danger which, in my view, premature publication of such details of enemy communications constituted to British work in the field of counter-espionage.

Hoover replied that he fully appreciated my argument, but as he was not familiar with the details of the Kroeger case he would ask his assistant Mr Tamm to have a report prepared by his New York office. He immediately called Tamm to this effect by telephone.

'As a matter of principle,' he went on, 'I am inclined to keep enemy agents under observation for as long as possible, provided that their communications can be effectively covered. Once an arrest has been made, however, and criminal proceedings have been instituted, a certain amount of publicity is inevitable, and when the case comes to trial there is no machinery for preventing the publication of evidence unless it can be shown that by doing so the interests of the United States Government would be injured.' He pointed out that the US District Attorneys in charge of these cases were inclined to court publicity, 'hence the prominence which such proceedings received in all their stages in the press'.

The FBI chief then made the point that where the prosecution was founded in any measure on evidence supplied by British sources, such as the Ludwig and Viereck cases, no further steps would be taken without consulting British Security Co-ordination. 'In fact,' he concluded, 'I would be prepared to advise the Attorney General that in all future trials for espionage, where British interests are likely to be affected or where the prosecution has acted in whole or in part on information derived from British sources, no evidence shall be put in except after consultation with competent British authorities.' So far as I know he kept his word.

Finally he introduced a completely different subject, stating that he was particularly interested in any preparations which the Axis powers were making for the use of bacteriological methods of warfare. His organization had practically no information on this subject, and he would greatly appreciate, *'as a personal favour'*, any data which could be supplied to him from British sources. 'I feel it is very likely that such methods will eventually be used,' he added.

I told him that before the war I had written a book, *Air Defence and the Civil Population*, in which I had discussed this possibility.[10] I also mentioned that the British were manufacturing gas shells, filled with phosgene gas, and that there was an Inter-Service Committee on Chemical Warfare sitting in London, which the United States Military Mission there doubtless knew about. But I doubted that the Germans would dare to use bacteriological weapons for fear of retaliation on their civilian population. However, I undertook to obtain all the information I could for him on the subject, but I imagined that it did not amount to very much, which was indeed the case.

In the light of criticisms made by Berle and others, it is as well to remember that in 1941 alone the FBI received from Stephenson's staff no less than 100,000 reports, memoranda, and other documents on a range of subjects considerably wider than security and counter-espionage matters, such as chemical warfare in which Hoover was so particularly interested. Hoover disliked Colonel Donovan intensely and he resented the fact that Stephenson, particularly in the early days of Donovan's activities, supplied him with much information which Hoover thought was done at his Bureau's expense. But this was not so, and although many of Stephenson's internal operations were unorthodox, Intrepid took the view that they were justified in the light of events, as indeed, in my view, they were.

Nevertheless it was in gratitude for the information supplied by Stephenson's organization that early in 1941 the FBI, on Hoover's orders, had placed at the exclusive disposal of BSC a radio circuit to carry BSC's coded traffic between Washington and London. Except in a few rare instances when atmospheric conditions interfered with the operation of the circuit, it carried for the next eleven months all Stephenson's office traffic, which would otherwise have gone by commercial cable or radio, thus saving the British Government approximately $50,000. Then, following the altercation between Hoover and Stephenson at the time of the McKellar Bill and the discussions between Biddle and Halifax, the FBI decided to close down the station.

I had a great admiration for Hoover and his agents, and an affinity with them, our mutual relations always being most cordial. At the same time I was not blind to Hoover's failings. 'Mr Hoover is an extremely able and energetic administrator,' I wrote in a report for Stephenson in the spring of 1943, 'but he has a touch of the prima donna in his temperament and he is not unmindful of the benefits and joys of publicity for himself and his organization. He suffers no rivals and he is not overscrupulous either in his methods of removing them or overcoming other obstacles.' My report continued:

Although responsible for the collection of secret intelligence and the combating of enemy espionage and subversive activity in the US, the FBI is still inclined to regard these questions primarily from a police point of view and the Bureau is still principally more concerned with compiling a dossier and apprehending the individual enemy agent rather than unravelling the wider network and observing its movements and ramifications. This tendency is becoming less marked as the Bureau's members gain experience and wider knowledge of intelligence operations, and there is no doubt that this improvement is due in great measure to the Bureau's close association with the Stephenson organization. Of particular value to the Bureau during this period [after Pearl Harbour] was the detailed information on Axis espionage in North Africa which enabled the US Chiefs of Staff to take appropriate security measures following on the landing of the US invading forces in that area in November 1942.[11]

One of the troubles with Hoover and his G-men was that, while they were first rate at catching spies, they never mastered the technique of running double agents, unless they were of the relatively low-level type like William Sebold. The Donovan organization, which learned the technique from BSC, did better, but its members, too, were never quite as adept at a function in which the British were masters.

One of the most important of the British double agents during the war, whom I got to know quite well (and who incidentally clashed with the FBI), was a young Yugoslav of good family and education, Dusko Popov, code-named 'Tricycle'. Indeed Graham Greene, who himself worked for a time in MI6, regarded him as the most successful as well as the most important double agent in the British field. Tricycle hated the Germans who had arrested him and thrown him into prison, when he was a law student in

Dusko Popov, code-named 'Tricycle', an outstandingly successful double agent who worked for the British and the Germans.

Germany before the war, because in the course of political discussions he had been overheard praising the advantages of political freedom and democratic rule in contrast with the oppressive Nazi regime. When he was approached by a representative of German military intelligence (*Abwehr*) in Belgrade early in 1940, he agreed to work for the Germans, but at the same time he got in touch secretly with British Intelligence, getting to know Menzies, who realized his worth and took a strong liking to him. As a result of careful handling by the Twenty (XX, i.e. Double Cross) Committee, which controlled all the British double agents under Sir James Masterman, an Oxford don, Popov was built up as a valuable source in the eyes of the Germans, and during 1940 and the first half of 1941 he operated successfully between London and Lisbon.[12] He was undoubtedly clever and always showed himself absolutely loyal to his British employers. His taste in clothes, women, and entertainment were expensive – for example, he had a passionate affair with the French actress Simone Simon – but then the Germans were largely paying for them.

In August 1941 the Germans sent him to the United States with the object of forming a spy ring to replace the Ludwig ring, following the arrest of Ludwig and his principal associates. At the same time Popov brought with him a detailed questionnaire for military information, of which one-third was concerned with Hawaii and particularly Pearl Harbor, which the Germans told him the Japanese planned to attack before the end of the year. He also brought with him the secret of a remarkable new method of communication which the Germans had begun to use with its secret agents – the microdot. This was a speck the size of a pinhead which, when enlarged 200 times, could convey quite a long typescript message. 'You are the first agent to get it,' the *Abwehr* representative told Popov. 'This little dot will revolutionize our espionage system.' Thanks to Popov news of this invention was passed on to the Bermuda censors, who soon began to find microdots concealed beneath postage stamps and the flaps of envelopes.[13]

All this information was handed over by Tricycle to the FBI, who had helped to get him a passage from Lisbon to New York and consequently insisted on taking him over and running him themselves. Both Stephenson and the Twenty Committee in London had strong reservations about this arrangement, which in the event were fully justified. Tricycle disliked the comparatively unsophisticated G-men who controlled him, and he was worried by their inability to produce the requisite strategic information for him to pass on to the Germans. The FBI, on the other hand, disliked what they regarded as his extravagant mode of living, and kept making the impossible request that he should reduce his personal expenses. However, in spite of these difficulties, eight letters with secret writing in invisible ink containing the right kind of data (most of which were produced by Stephenson and Ellis), were dispatched by him to Germany in the autumn of 1941, although by a mistake one of the letters was picked out by the Bermuda censors and tested for secret writing, which made its onward transmission impossible.

In November 1941 Popov flew to Rio de Janeiro and saw Alfredo Engels, the head of German Secret Intelligence there, whose cover was that of director of the major German electrical manufacturers in Brazil. Tricycle's cover was that he worked for the Yugoslav Ministry of Information, for there were thousands of Yugoslav immigrants in Brazil. Engels also operated a powerful transmitter, code-named Bolivar, and much of the *Abwehr* traffic for the Americas was channelled through him. He told Popov that he had complete confidence in him and instructed him to return to New York and build a short-wave radio for communicating with Rio, Lisbon, and Hamburg. Of course, this suited Hoover's book since the Bureau would necessarily control the radio's use.

Tricycle returned to New York by sea, and when his ship, which was Portuguese, stopped at Trinidad he set off to explore the island with a ballerina named Dora whom he had met on board. However he was intercepted by Freckles Wren, whom Popov knew was the local MI5–MI6 representative and who asked him to spend a day with him which he did, excusing himself to Dora. Wren had been advised of Popov's coming and had been told to get a full account of his doings in Rio. After lunch, at which they were accompanied by Wren's secretary whom Popov found 'sensationally beautiful', feasting his eyes on her while she returned his glances with what Popov called 'a knowing smile', Wren dictated a long cable to the secretary.

'I'll have to run down to the office to code this,' Wren said when he had finished dictating. 'It will take a couple of hours, but I'll leave you Jane here as a substitute for your ballerina!'

'Sorry about the ballerina,' Jane said, as soon as Wren had left. But Popov knew she wasn't. At all events, as Popov told me afterwards, Jane proved a great compensation. 'If anything, she overcompensated. Or we did!'

Shortly after the ship sailed, news of the Japanese attack on Pearl Harbor came through on the ship's radio. After his arrival in New York I had several talks with Tricycle, and I could see how angry he was with the FBI whom he was convinced had never taken any action on his earlier warning about the Japanese and Pearl Harbor. He protested to his immediate controller, who merely said, 'Things can go wrong,' and later to Sam Foxworth, head of the FBI New York office, who advised him that 'searching for truth beyond your reach may be dangerous'.

Throughout the first three months of 1942 the FBI regularly transmitted to Germany messages which purported to come from Tricycle over his short-wave radio, but they gave Stephenson and Ellis in BSC no copies of these and no details about how they were being received. Tricycle was not even taken to see the radio station which had allegedly been built for him, with the result that he was in constant danger of being caught out by a snap question from a genuine German agent in America, or by a request to send a message at short notice. Soon I learned from Tricycle that the Germans were complaining that his reports lacked 'meat', and they must have begun to suspect that he was working under control, particularly after Engels was arrested in Brazil. It was a miracle that Tricycle was not completely blown by this time. Eventually, after a strong protest by Stephenson to Hoover, the latter appointed one of his more experienced officers to take charge of the double agent and undertook to obtain a more regular supply of suitable information from the United States armed forces for him to send the Germans; this was supplemented by data which Stephenson was able to obtain with the help of the British Army Staff Mission to Washington, to which I was attached at that time.

Nevertheless Hoover's men were unable to shed their characteristic gangbusting methods in handling Tricycle. For instance, when the Germans sent over some money for him, instead of allowing it to reach him without interference, the FBI attempted to draw the courier into a trap, which would of course, if it had been successful, have notified the Germans that Tricycle was at least under the gravest suspicion. The last straw for Popov came after the war, when he returned to New York in connection with his law business and saw an article in *The Reader's Digest* for April 1946 entitled 'The Enemy's Masterpiece of Espionage' by J. Edgar Hoover, in which the FBI chief claimed the credit for having obtained the secret of the microdot by capturing a spy, whom he described as 'a Balkan playboy', although he did not mention Popov by name. The article was illustrated by a memorandum of a telephone message from the Brazilian Ambassador to the Yugoslav government-in-exile, Alvis de Sousa. The memo only indicated a hotel-room number and the date: the recipient's name had been cut off. Popov immediately recognized the memo as having been sent to him by de Sousa when he was staying in Rio, a fact confirmed by de Sousa who happened to be in New York at the same time as Popov in 1946 and who upbraided Popov for having 'involved him in unwanted publicity'. The memo was said to have been found in the hotel room in Rio by an FBI agent who had surreptitiously gone through Popov's belongings and found the telephone memo which turned out to have a microdot on it, subsequently reflected by the light when examined in the FBI laboratory.

Popov telephoned headquarters and asked Hoover to call him back. But he did not do so. Popov called again, with the same negative result. He then flew to Washington and went straight to the FBI building at Ninth Street and Pennsylvania Avenue. When Popov explained his business to the assistant who received him, the agent said that Hoover was too busy to see him. 'You go tell Mr Hoover he'll see me right away,' Popov replied, 'or I'll hold a press conference.' The upshot was that Hoover decided he had time to see Popov after all, although when he entered his office Hoover angrily told Popov he would have him 'kicked out of the country'. However, according to Popov, Hoover eventually calmed down, and when he realized that Popov was serious in his threat to talk to the press, he undertook to get into touch with *The Reader's Digest* and try to stop publication in their Spanish and Portuguese editions. Whether he succeeded, Popov never discovered as he did not trouble to check up.

To return to 1942. By the summer of that year the FBI decided to have nothing further to do with Tricycle on the ground that he was a liar and was too expensive to justify his retention. In fact, it was a tacit admission of their incompetence in this particular instance, and an instructive illustration of how to spoil a good double agent.

Eventually Tricycle went back to London where he continued to do valuable work for the Twenty Committee right up to D-

Day, when another agent, who was in Portugal, was tricked into going to Germany where he was interrogated, no doubt under torture, and almost certainly disclosed that Tricycle was really working for the British.

I once asked Popov if there was anything particular in the way of a reward for his sterling work which he would like after the war. He replied that the only thing he would like would be to be appointed Honorary British Vice-Consul in his native Dubrovnik. But, alas, that was not to be. Marshal Tito had no use for Honorary Vice-Consuls in Dubrovnik or anywhere else in Communist Yugoslavia. So Dusko Popov never went back to his native country. Instead he married and went to live in France with his wife and four sons. 'Secret agents do retire,' he later wrote. 'At the end of the war, I was issued with two suits of mufti and a change of linen, and I said good-bye to it all. I had a life to make and a living to earn.'[14]

Secretary of State Cordell Hull's frigid reception of the Vichy French Ambassador Gaston Henry-Haye on his arrival in Washington in the autumn of 1940 has already been noted. Through a confidential source in the Embassy, Stephenson learned that one of the Ambassador's first acts had been to call the staff together and address them about their duties. 'Our prime objective is to establish the fact that Britain betrayed France and is therefore her real enemy,' he told them. 'Every means at our disposal must be used to convince American officialdom and the American public that this is true.' At this time there were many influential Americans who had social connections and invest-ments, or both, in France, and who were inclined to support the aged Marshal Pétain, who had become head of the government in unoccupied France after the armistice. They and their French friends felt bitterly towards the British for refusing to send any more planes to France in the last days of the fighting, and many of them were distinctly anti-British by reason of the attack on the French fleet at Mers-el-Kebir and Oran, which had put several French ships out of action and led to considerable loss of French lives. Henry-Haye and his Embassy exploited these feelings. They also did their best to neutralize support for General de Gaulle and his Free French movement, organizing a kind of Gestapo for the purpose, as has also been noted. The Ambassador's personal assistant Jean-Louis Musa was closely concerned with the Gestapo and also with anti-British propaganda.

As a first step towards exposing these activities, Stephenson asked me to make some enquiries about Musa. I discovered that although he had been born in Switzerland of a French mother by an Italian father, he had been a United States citizen for more than twenty years, having once worked as a waiter in the Hotel Lafayette on 9th Street in New York where he was called 'Nino', a nickname by which he was still known in the Vichy Embassy. He was delighted when he heard that Henry-Haye was coming to Washington as Ambassador, since they had had business dealings together in the past, and so he got into touch with him as soon as he arrived. In the result Musa became Henry-Haye's personal assistant and *homme d'affaires*. A tall, swarthy man in his early fifties, with dark, fluid eyes and a fondness for bow ties, Musa soon made himself extremely useful to the new Ambassador and the Embassy generally. As Henry-Haye himself said, he was exactly right for the job.

At the outset of his employment by the Ambassador, Musa was paid a salary of $300 a month, with an additional $200 expenses, a sum quite inadequate for a man of his tastes, particularly after his Belgian wife and daughter had joined him in the two-room suite which he had taken in the Hotel Navarro in Central Park South, and for which he paid a weekly rental of $75. He confided to another of Stephenson's agents, who had deliberately cultivated his acquaintance, that the Ambassador paid him 'a perfectly ridiculous sum'. The agent then took offices in mid-town Manhattan, where he ostensibly ran a trading company, and suggested to Musa that they should go into business together, offering to put an office and a secretary at Musa's disposal. Musa jumped at the suggestion and at once settled in to his new office, where Stephenson had already had hidden microphones installed. In the result, all Musa's conversations, whether on the telephone with Henry-Haye and others or with visitors to the office, were recorded; his papers were examined daily, and where necessary discreetly photographed; and the contents of his safe were regularly inspected, since Musa's 'business partner' had no difficulty in learning the combinations. In fact there was little, if anything, about Musa's work for Henry-Haye and his business and private life that Stephenson and I, as well as the 'business partner', did not know.

For instance, we knew the details of Musa's plan to buy the controlling interest in a company which had the exclusive rights to manufacture the Bren gun in the United States; also the details of the Vichy Government's project to erect, in conjunction with the Western Union's Cable Company, a powerful radio station on the French island of St Pierre off the south coast of Newfoundland. Western Union had five cables running into St Pierre from its 34,000 offices in the US, and the proposed new station on land provided by the Vichy Government – St Pierre had not yet been taken over by de Gaulle – would be capable of communicating anywhere in the world by radio-telegraph, while at the same time avoiding all British Censorship controls. For this privilege Western Union agreed to pay the Vichy Government a fixed royalty. 'I hope that you will give the necessary instructions,' Musa wrote from his New York office to Henry-Haye in Washington, 'so that this project of the greatest interest takes shape and progresses as fast as possible.' Fortunately both projects were knocked on the head by Stephenson. The Bren gun deal was stopped by Purvis of the British Purchasing Commission when it appeared likely that Musa would obtain blueprints of the weapon, while Stephenson's friend Vincent Astor, who was a director of Western Union, was able to put a stop to the St Pierre project with President Roosevelt's approval.

The watch kept on Musa's office revealed many other characteristic activities. For instance, he assisted the Embassy Military Attaché, Colonel Georges Bertrand-Vigne, in evading both the American currency-freezing regulations and the British blockade by paying dollars on the Colonel's behalf to Louis Arpels, the New York jeweller, while Arpel's company, Van

Cleef & Arpels, paid the equivalent in francs to the order of Bertrand-Vigne in France. He likewise conducted a regular business through a Portuguese intermediary in Lisbon for the purchase of food parcels for transmission to the German Occupied Zone in France. He dabbled in the passport racket, and some of the visas he obtained were for known German agents. He sold exit permits from unoccupied France for considerable sums. He also collected information from French girls, former employees of the French Purchasing Commission whom he had placed in various French and American business firms. He succeeded in persuading a French-language newspaper in Montreal not to engage Pierre Lazareff, the French journalist and editor of *France-Soir*, whom he suspected of supporting de Gaulle. Finally, he acted as a procurer of women for the Ambassador. On one occasion a shapely female manicurist in New York's Plaza Hotel was observed drinking champagne with Henry-Haye in the Stork Club, to which establishment he had invited her as his guest. To Musa the Ambassador said: 'You are in charge of the love department!'

Musa himself had a mistress, one Christine Bittmar, who used to telephone Musa's office at all hours making appointments to meet him. Here is one characteristic conversation which reflects their relationship. It was monitored in July 1941:

Musa: Are you behaving yourself?
Bittmar: Oh, very much.
Musa: May I drop in any time from now on?
Bittmar: Well, in a little while.
Musa: Ha, ha! What do you mean?
Bittmar: Well, I'm getting dressed.
Musa: Oh, you had better get undressed.
Bittmar: No.
Musa: Huh?
Bittmar: No, no.
Musa: I want to look at you.
Bittmar: No.
Musa: I want to look at you . . .

No doubt he succeeded in doing what he wished, as he left the office shortly afterwards for Christine's apartment.

Stephenson asked me to write a comprehensive report on Vichy French activities in the United States at this time, and to include transcripts of Musa's telephone conversations and photocopies of his letters, accounts, and other compromising documents. The report was given to President Roosevelt, who read it as 'a bed-time story', and described it as 'the most fascinating reading I have had for a long time' and 'the best piece of comprehensive intelligence work I have come across since the last war'. Stephenson thereupon asked the President's permission to publish a suitably edited version in the American press. The President agreed, provided that the State Department had no objection. The State Department proved amenable, but emphasized that the operation of discrediting Vichy policy in the United States must not be such as to cause a break in diplomatic relations between the two Governments. While Under-Secretary Sumner Welles had some reservations, Secretary of State Cordell Hull, who regarded Henry-Haye with contempt, let it be known that he hoped Stephenson would go ahead and 'blow Vichy sky-high'.[15]

In BSC the daily newspaper most suitable for publicizing the anti-Vichy operation was considered to be the *New York Herald-Tribune*. I was able to contact a sympathetic reporter on this journal, Ansel E. Talbert, and he agreed to co-operate by writing a story, or rather a series of stories, if I could supply him with selections from the basic material. This I was able to do from my report which had so intrigued the President, although I did not divulge the secret of Roosevelt's having read it.

The first story appeared on 31 August 1941, which was a Sunday, when the *Herald-Tribune* came out with headlines splashed across three columns of the front page in large type:

VICHY EMBASSY IN U.S.
SHOWN AS HEADING CLIQUE
OF AGENTS AIDING NAZIS

Charge Vichy Envoy Aids Nazi Spies, Saboteurs Here

Spokesmen here for the Free France of Gen. Charles de Gaulle, declining publication of their names for fear of reprisals, yesterday charged that Nazi spies, propagandists and "goon squads" in New York and Washington are speaking French this season—with an official French accent and with the knowledge and support of Ce...

Text of Letter Signed by Vichy Diplomat in U.S.

A Second Letter, Unsigned, but Likewise Addressed to 'My Dear Nino,' Follows...

Linked to Vichy Espionage Move

Henry-Haye Sought Radio Link To Vichy Under French Control, But Western Union Refused Deal

Ambassador Offered Concession for Transmitting Station on Island of St. P...
Conference Tomorrow on H...

Vichy Agents Sought Plans Of Bren Gun

Tried to Get Blueprints of Weapon Defending Britain From Invasion

Balked Mass-Scale Production in U.S.

F.B.I. Impersonator Now in Prison; Talked With Musa and Henry-Haye

Vichy Embassy in U.S. Shown as Heading Clique Of Agents Aiding Nazis

Jean Musa, Ex-Waiter, Called Chief Aid in N.Y. in 'Information' Work

Henry-Haye Cited As Guiding Hand

Plans for Dakar Attack Reported Smuggled

Three Men of Vichy

The headlines that marked the start of the successful campaign which exposed the Vichy French agents in Washington (September 1941).

Underneath there were smaller captions such as:

Jean Musa, Ex-Waiter
Called Chief Aide in N.Y. in 'Information' Work

and:

Henry-Haye Cited As Guiding Hand

The story, which bore a Washington dateline, bluntly accused the Vichy Embassy of operating a secret intelligence organization inside the United States with funds blocked by the US Government, the object being to help the Nazis to make France a vassal state of Germany. The three men in charge of this underground work were stated to be Colonel Bertrand-Vigne, the Vichy Military Attaché in the Washington Embassy, Captain Charles Brousse, the former Press Attaché, and Jean Musa. An accompanying photograph showed Ambassador Henry-Haye in conversation with Bertrand-Vigne and Musa in the Embassy garden.

Besides the Gestapo activities already described, there was a reproduction of a compromising letter from Bertrand-Vigne to Musa which had been photographed by Musa's 'business partner'. The story also revealed how the Vichy authorities had been able to thwart General de Gaulle's plans to capture Dakar in the previous year. Apparently the plans of the ill-fated Free French expedition to the west coast of Africa were smuggled into the United States in the fuel tank of a car shipped to Hoboken on a Greek steamer. Also in the tank were lists of French army and naval officers and air-force pilots who had joined the Free French movement.

During the same week three more articles appeared in the *Herald-Tribune* with headlines such as VICHY AGENTS SOUGHT PLANS OF BREN GUN with the sub-heading: 'Tried to Get Blueprints of Weapon Defending Britain from Invasion'. The articles were reproduced in more than a hundred newspapers in the United States and Canada, including the *Washington Post*, the *Baltimore Sun* and the *New York Daily Mirror*. Mr Henry Morgenthau, Secretary of the Treasury, voiced the general acclaim when he expressed a desire to meet the *Herald-Tribune* reporter who had produced such a brilliant series of articles. He said he wished to compliment him personally on such an outstanding journalistic feat.[16]

It was, of course, a tremendous scoop for the *Herald-Tribune*, since the articles were widely discussed throughout the country and provided the substance of many newspaper editorials. Henry-

Haye reacted by summoning a press conference and stating that he was going to protest to Secretary of State Hull. This he did, but to no effect. Meanwhile Stephenson had arranged that a pro-British reporter should attend the press conference and I primed him with embarrassing questions to put to the Ambassador. This resulted in more unfavourable publicity for the Vichyites, since Henry-Haye's feeble and evasive explanations were completely unconvincing. 'The Ambassador speaks as a representative of the French people, a friendly power,' wrote the *Herald-Tribune* in an editorial next day; 'yet the government he represents has repeatedly done everything it could to promote the German victory, which the United States has declared to be profoundly inimical to its vital interest, and to embarrass the British resistance to which the United States is pledged to render every aid in its power.'

The effect of this concerted newspaper campaign was altogether to discredit the Vichy regime's diplomatic representation in the United States. The Free French were naturally jubilant. Not the least satisfactory result was that Musa's 'Gestapo' largely ceased its activities, although Musa himself continued to be retained by the Ambassador. Privately Henry-Haye described the whole affair as 'a de-Gaullist-Jewish-British-FBI intrigue'.

Musa was arrested in July 1942 for having failed to register as an agent, as required by the McKellar Act. He was arraigned before Judge Goddard, who had presided at the trial of Ludwig and his fellow spies, and was released on bail. Following consider-able legal argument, the charge was dropped, apparently on Henry-Haye's intervention on the plea that Musa was an employee of the Vichy Embassy – although he had no diplomatic status, his name did not appear in the Diplomatic List, and he was paid out of the Ambassador's secret funds.

But Henry-Haye's days were numbered. A few months later, following the United States invasion of North Africa which was launched on 8 November 1942, the Vichy Government, now headed by Pierre Laval, immediately broke off diplomatic relations with Washington, whereupon the United States replied in kind. Henry-Haye and his staff were given their passports and the Vichy French Embassy was closed down. At the same time President Roosevelt publicly stated that Laval, by his action, was 'evidently still speaking the language prescribed by Hitler'. The President added that no act of Hitler, or any of his puppets, could sever relations between the American people and the people of France. 'This Government will continue as heretofore to devote its thought, its sympathy, and its aid to the rescue of the forty-five million people of France from enslavement and a permanent loss of their liberties and free institutions.'

Eighteen months before Henry-Haye's departure, the Vichy Embassy itself was penetrated by the Stephenson organization. Although the full story of this operation and its aftermath has been related elsewhere, it is interesting to recall its main features here. The person responsible for this penetration was an enterprising young American woman in her early thirties, born Elizabeth Thorpe, the daughter of a major in the US Marines. She had married a British diplomatist Arthur Pack, from whom she separated and whom she was in the process of divorcing when she was recruited by British Secret Intelligence, being code-named Cynthia. In the spring of 1941, posing as a newspaper-woman, she met Charles Brousse, the Press Attaché. Brousse fell for her and she willingly became his mistress. She had already slept with a number of men in the line of duty.

In July 1941 the Vichy Government decided to abolish Brousse's post, although Henry-Haye agreed to retain him as a member of the Embassy staff, paying him a greatly reduced salary from his secret funds. Cynthia saw her chance and put it bluntly to her lover that she was a US secret agent; as he detested Laval, he could best help France by supplying her with information, naturally for a monetary consideration. Brousse agreed, and gave her copies of all the outgoing and incoming Embassy telegrams, besides writing a daily report of what went on in the Embassy, giving details of the Ambassador's appointments and what happened at his interviews. Finally, by persuading the Embassy nightwatchman to let them use the Embassy premises for making love, she was able, with Brousse's connivance and help, to obtain access to the Vichy French naval ciphers. These she temporarily

Vichy, le 13 Décembre 1941 à 14 h 55.

Reçu le 16 à 19 h 54.

No. 2886.

A la date du 11 décembre, l'Ambassade des Etats-Unis m'a remis trois notes par lesquelles son Gouvernement demandait à être fixé sur les intentions de la France en ce qui concerne les points suivants:

1). Position de la France au regard du conflit qui vient d'éclater entre les Etats-Unis d'une part, l'Allemagne et l'Italie d'autre part.

2). Mouvement éventuel de nos navires stationnés aux Antilles.

3). Confirmation des dispositions précédemment affirmées en ce qui concerne la non-utilisation de la Flotte et de l'Afrique du Nord.

Je vous communique sous les trois numéros suivants le texte des notes remises à l'Amiral Leahy en réponse à chacune de ces (communications)./.

DIPLOMATIE.

Photocopy of the carbon copy of a telegram abstracted from the Vichy French Embassy archives in Washington by the ex-Press attaché Charles Brousse, and handed by him to his mistress, the British agent Mrs Elizabeth Pack, code-named 'Cynthia'.

The telegram is from Marshal Pétain to the Vichy French Ambassador in Washington, informing him that the US Ambassador in Vichy (Admiral William Leahy) had asked to know what the French intentions were regarding, 1) the conflict which had just broken out between the US and Germany and Italy; 2) the movement of French naval ships stationed in the West Indies; 3) confirmation of the previous agreement that Pétain had no intention of permitting the Axis powers to use French bases in North Africa and to have the assistance of the French fleet.

The telegraphed replies to these questions were 1) Vichy France intended to remain neutral; 2) no French naval ships to be allowed to leave any French port in the western hemisphere; 3) agreement was confirmed.

removed from the Embassy safe, after its combination had been discovered and the safe had been cracked, and surreptitiously photographed. The success of this operation was to prove of the greatest help to the American authorities at the time of the invasion of North Africa.

Although I was not her controller, I knew Cynthia at this time and with my wife Dorothy was closely concerned with the Embassy safe-cracking operation. Twenty-odd years later, after Cynthia had married Charles Brousse and they were living in a medieval château in the eastern Pyrenees, I was able to renew my acquaintance with her as their guest at the château, and we talked over old times in the war. [17]

'I hope and believe I was a patriot,' she said to me on this occasion. 'There is no rule of thumb for patriotism. I was able to make certain men fall in love with me – or think they had, at any rate – and in exchange for my 'love' they gave me information. Ashamed? Not in the least! My superiors told me that the results of my work saved thousands of British and American lives. Even one would have made it worthwhile. It involved me in situations from which 'respectable' women draw back – but mine was a total commitment. Wars are not won by respectable methods. One tries to win *any* war, in *any* way!' [18]

In October 1942 the London headquarters of MI6 telegraphed Stephenson that I had been promoted from captain to the rank of major, and I was informed accordingly. It is always something to reach field rank in the army, but in practice it made no difference to my SIS work, although it increased my standing with the British Army Staff Mission in Washington and in the supernumerary job I was to undertake of lecturing to the American army and censorship units on intelligence matters. My friend Charles des Graz, the British Censorship chief in the United States, was particularly pleased about my promotion which he considered long overdue. 'It should have been a grade higher,' he wrote to me at the time, 'but at any rate it is some recognition of the splendid job you have been doing. I hope it will not be the last.' In the event, it was not. At the same time, for various administrative reasons my work in Washington was gradually being phased out and Stephenson thought I should return to New York; but I wanted to go much further afield and was to tell him so.

Pat Buckley, a friend who had recently joined the Censorship in Bermuda, wrote to me about a leading article which had recently appeared in Henry Luce's *Life* magazine, belittling about, and slanted against, the British. My reply enabled me to say some of the things which were on my mind:

The *Life* article which you mention was, as I expect you know, written by Russell Davenport, Willkie's campaign organizer in the 1940 presidential election [and managing editor of *Fortune*, another of Luce's magazines]. It has proved a decided boomerang for its sponsors, as *Life* had to give our people such as Vernon Bartlett [broadcaster and staff writer on the London *News Chronicle*] the chance to refute it and in addition it brought most of the leading columnists, radio commentators, and so on, vigorously on our side.

At the same time this article is only symptomatic of a great deal of what is passing unnoticed in the press and other publicity channels here. The British love, perhaps I should say weakness, for understatement is being constantly used for our detriment contrasting as it does with the perennial American habit of 'high lighting' their case. As a result the British achievements in Libya and Madagascar have not received their fair share of credit, whereas American achievements so far in North Africa have been regarded as the most remarkable strategic feat of American arms by everyone here, while the fact that the operation could not have been carried out but for adequate naval and air support from ourselves has as usual been overlooked. What is even more alarming in my judgement is the disasters which the Americans are suffering in the Solomons are being glossed over and the news of US losses only allowed to trickle out by degrees.

For some time Stephenson has been very anxious for me to

return to New York . . . However, recent events, and particularly the operation which is now beginning in North Africa, make me most anxious to leave this hemisphere from which I think the war is rapidly moving away. On personal grounds I don't like leaving Stephenson as he seems to have a great many worries on his shoulders at the present time. On the other hand, I think his organization is now far too large and that I might perhaps set a good example by being one of the first of the old hands to get out.

Consequently I appealed as strongly as I could to Stephenson to release me from BSC. 'I am sure you will readily appreciate that as one of the younger members of the staff as well as a serving military officer, I should be stationed nearer the theatre of war where there is a chance of seeing some fighting,' I wrote to him from Washington on 28 November 1942. 'I am therefore asking you to be good enough to transmit to our London headquarters my request to be transferred to another station, preferably in the Near or Middle East.' I went on:

Should it not be possible to effect such a transfer, then I would like to resign altogether and return to the Intelligence Corps in the Army for a course of training in operational intelligence duties with a view to being posted to a fighting unit as a brigade or divisional intelligence officer.

Dorothy will be prepared to remain in her present position for the time being until my arrangements are clarified. She would of course like to join me eventually if this were practicable, but I am well aware that it may not be so.

You and I have now been associated for rather more than two years, and during the greater part of this time it has been my privilege to work for you. I have also enjoyed working for you and I have liked the work itself immensely. I need hardly add that I shall miss my colleagues and friends, particularly those of the Joint Intelligence Committee and the Criminal Division of the Department of Justice. At the same time I am sure you will realize my desire for service in a more active sphere of duty, and I look to you with a feeling of confidence to promote it.

But it was not to be. Stephenson begged me not to desert him and BSC in such persuasive terms that I felt I could not refuse my support at a time when he was having many difficulties with the American authorities, particularly the FBI, and ought to stay on at least for the time being. In addition to representing SIS and SOE in the Western Hemisphere, he had recently taken on the representation of the security service MI5, and he asked me to deputize for him in this capacity, certainly until MI5 appointed a representative of their own. I agreed, with some reluctance, to be responsible for counter-espionage within his territory when I returned to New York at the end of the year; but it was largely a desk-job and I was always happier working in the field on specific assignments, such as the *coup* in Bolivia.

One of my duties was to liaise with the British Information Service, which had initially been based in New York under the directorship of the historian C. K. Webster but which had not been conspicuously successful. The US entry into the war after the Pearl Harbor attack, and the change in Anglo-American relations to which I have referred, made it essential for the service to be placed in charge of a professional with a wider knowledge of the political world. The academically accomplished Webster was not loath to retire in favour of Mr (later Sir) Harold Butler, a Fellow of All Souls, Oxford, a former Director of the International Labour Office at the League of Nations in Geneva, and more recently, on the outbreak of the war in England, one of the regional commissioners for civil defence. Although approaching retiring age – he was now fifty-eight – Butler was an outstandingly able man, with a socially gifted Irish wife and three children, and he welcomed the opportunity of doing important and really worthwhile work in the information field. For this work he had been given the diplomatic rank of Minister in the British Embassy in Washington. As his personal assistant he brought out with him from England Captain Michael Crawfurd, a young soldier of twenty-five who had been through the hell of the

Dunkirk evacuation and latterly had been serving with Northern Command in Yorkshire. It fell to him and his chief to make arrangements to counter such falsities as were contained in the *Life* article I have mentioned.

One day when young Crawfurd was lunching with me in Washington, I showed him a copy of a book by a Frenchman Henry Torrés called *Campaign of Treachery*, which I had recently bought at Scribner's bookshop in New York. The sales assistant had told me that it was the last copy, adding that there would be no more since the publishers had decided to withdraw it. Crawfurd subsequently wrote to me from the Embassy that Mr Butler was very anxious to know the reason for this action. He went on in the same letter:

> As a matter of principle we have always imagined that it was impossible to prevent a book to which we took exception being published in this country. If it can be done, we should very much like to go about it, particularly as V. Sackville West is shortly having a new book of hers entitled *Grand Canyon* published over here, and as far as we can make out the book is the last thing in the world we want, talking in terms as it does, of a defeat of Great Britain and subsequent mediation on the part of the American Government between Germany and ourselves.

I found out from Charles Scribner, whom I knew slightly, that the Torrés book had been withdrawn because a Jewish gentleman named Wilde had threatened a libel suit over some passages which he considered offensive. As for Victoria Sackville-West's book, this was a novel, and although it might have annoyed Butler nothing could be done to stop it. It duly came out both in Britain and the United States.

On 19 November 1942, Crawfurd rang me up to say that the US Office of War Information, the British Ministry's counterpart, were 'starting on a nation-wide security publicity campaign'.

For this they are trying to rake up as many examples as they can find of leakage of information through bad security, careless talk, and so on. This afternoon they asked me if I could check the truth of one particular story of the sinking of the *Royal Oak* at Scapa Flow in the early months of the war. According to OWI, an article appeared in the May 16th issue of *The Saturday Evening Post* of this year in which it was stated that the sinking of the *Royal Oak* was wholly due to the successful activities of the German espionage service. Apparently this article mentions that a German naval officer was landed at Scapa Flow and there, in the guise of a hairdresser, I believe, he was able from careless talk to get all the necessary information about the openings to the boom. He then returned to the German Navy and as a result of the information he had acquired, a German submarine had no difficulty in passing through the boom and torpedoing the *Royal Oak*.

I told the OWI that I thought the story was a complete myth. But they were very keen in reproducing it and I eventually promised I would have it checked. So could you do this for me?

I immediately got on to my friends in British Naval Intelligence, who came back with the answer a few days afterwards that there was no truth whatever in *The Saturday Evening Post* story. 'The facts are that the defences of Scapa Flow were incomplete, with the result that a submarine was able to come through an opening,' I replied to Crawfurd on 24 November. 'This opening could plainly be seen by air reconnaisance and there is little doubt that its exact position was obtained by the enemy in this manner.' This was subsequently confirmed by German sources, from which it was learned that the operation of penetrating Scapa Flow through the swirling waters between two submerged blockships was carefully planned by the German Flag Officer Submarines, then Admiral Dönitz, and carried out by the 'redoubtable' (as Churchill called him) Lieutenant Günther Prien in the U-47. This achievement resulted in the loss of the battleship and 786 officers and men including a Rear-Admiral. Furthermore, Prien and his U-boat were able to make a successful withdrawal through the gap before it could be closed by another blockship.[19]

Next day I wrote to Crawfurd again, this time asking for his help in connection with Mrs Lisa Paravicini (as she then was), daughter of the writer Somerset Maugham. As usual I sent this letter to the Embassy, but I doubt whether he ever received it. Apparently he did not go to the Embassy from his apartment in 16th Street on that day, and it was not until several more days had passed that his absence was remarked on. One of the Embassy secretaries in the Chancery, suspecting that something was wrong, let himself into the apartment on 30 November with a pass-key and was horrified to discover Crawfurd lying face down on the floor of his living-room. Apparently he had been dead for about twenty-four hours. There was a bullet wound in his right temple and a British .38 calibre revolver was clutched in his right hand. It was plain that he had taken his own life, and the Washington Coroner issued a certificate of suicide. He left behind nothing in the shape of a note to explain his action.

'As you may imagine,' Harold Butler wrote to me in reply to my letter of sympathy, 'Michael's death is a great blow to us all.'

He was almost one of the family. We knew that he was subject to fits of depression, and one of the reasons which induced me to bring him out here was that he seemed to be unhappy at York, though he had a good and interesting job with Northern Command. I think he was deeply affected by Dunkirk.

Lately he had again been depressed and was pulled down by a bout of influenza, but we had no idea that his mind was so deeply disturbed. If he had only talked to me, as he had often done, we might have been able to save him.

Of course his loss to me will be irreparable. He was doing splendid work and I had come to rely on him for many things.

I was likewise appalled by the tragedy. I did not know Michael Crawfurd at all intimately, and I was unaware from his behaviour with me that he suffered from depression, especially as our lunchtime meetings were always quite cheerful affairs. His death may, of course, have been due to a sudden impulse, although the maid who regularly cleaned the apartment stated at the inquest that the last time she had done so she saw the gun on a table and noticed that it had four cartridges in the chamber, while it usually only had two.[20]

The subject of my last, unanswered, letter to Crawfurd is worth recalling. In the previous May, Merle Oberon had rung me up to ask if I could help her friend, twenty-seven-year-old Lisa Paravicini, who had been working voluntarily in the New York office of the British Information Service while her husband, a Swiss who had become a naturalized British subject, was serving with the British forces in Libya. Merle explained that Mrs Paravicini's residence permit had expired and she had consequently been summoned to appear before the Immigration authorities on Ellis Island, on a certain date in the near future, to show cause why she should not leave the country; she was also told to bring her luggage with her. I told Merle that I thought I could help by appealing to my friend Mathias Correa, the New York District Attorney, but that I ought to be in a position to state that I was acquainted with Mrs Paravicini whom in fact I had never met. Merle therefore brought her along to my New York apartment, where I talked to her and found her very pleasant but at the same time considerably alarmed by the ominous instructions about bringing her luggage with her to Ellis Island. Both her parents were living in the United States at this time and she had a child, who was with her mother. I promised to do what I could to help her remain in the country and after she had left I telephoned the District Attorney, who said he would let me know what he could do.

Shortly afterwards Correa called me back to say that Mrs Paravicini must go to Ellis Island for an interview with the Immigration officials but that she need not take her luggage with her, news which came as a great relief to her when I passed it on. She duly presented herself at Ellis Island on the appointed day, when she was questioned at some length. Afterwards Merle told me something of what happened.

'I see from your original application to enter the United States that you were born in Rome in 1915?' her interrogator asked, evidently under the impression from her married name that she was an Italian and knowing that the US was now at war with Italy.

'Yes,' Mrs Paravicini agreed.

'Why was that?' the Immigration official went on.

'Well, my mother happened to be living in Rome at the time.'

'Oh, yes,' said the official. 'You also stated that your father is a writer?'

Mrs Paravicini again nodded in agreement.

'What sort of things does he write?' asked the official, who had obviously never heard of Somerset Maugham.

'Novels, short stories, articles, and such like,' replied Mrs Paravicini.

The Immigration official eyed her suspiciously, as he asked his key question. *'Does he write revolutionary literature?'*

After she had repeatedly assured the official that her father had never given the slightest hint in any of his writing that he wished to overthrow the United States Constitution, Mrs Paravicini was given permission to return to Manhattan, and remain there until the end of October, when she could renew her application for a further stay. In my letter to poor Crawfurd I had pointed out that, as she was still registered with the State Department as an employee of the British Information Service, I should have thought that it would have been possible for her to remain in the US so long as this status continued, without her being obliged to apply for extensions of stay every few months. No doubt someone in Butler's office eventually sorted this out with the Immigration people, as I heard no more about it.[21]

Of course, it was not work for me all the time. Leaves in the army and BSC were not ungenerous, and I spent two of mine in Mexico where I had become interested in the lives of the ill-fated Emperor Maximilian and his equally unfortunate wife Carlota, who went mad, and lived on after his execution for fifty-nine years in placid insanity. On the second occasion I managed to finance part of my journey by acting as a temporary King's Messenger and carrying a diplomatic bag from Washington to the British

Legation in Mexico City. By this date Peter Smithers, whom I had first met when he briefly disembarked with Lord Lothian from the Pan American Clipper at Bermuda in December 1940, had become Acting Naval Attaché in Mexico and the Central American Republics, where he proved most helpful to Stephenson's representatives in that area.[22] 'We are looking forward to your visit, and are saving up our energies to keep pace with you in the Mexican food and drink!' he wrote to me when he heard I was coming. 'We also have one or two nice attractive German girls on ice for you, if you want to do some investigation.' I need hardly say that I did not meet any of the latter, but I enjoyed the former, particularly in the hospitable house at Cuernavaca, which belonged to George Conway, a scholarly Englishman who ran Mexico's electricity system in addition to collecting rare antiquarian books and manuscripts. As a small return for Conway's kindness I was to dedicate *Mexican Empire*[23], my biography of Maximilian and Carlota, to him.

I returned on this occasion by way of California to Washington where I wrote my thank-you letter to Stephenson's man in Mexico City:

The passenger control at Los Angeles is certainly pretty hot – hotter than Miami which I always thought was the tops in the way of inquisition. One chap took away all my papers and then another fellow came up and asked me if I had anything with which to identify myself. The only thing I had happened to be my War Office pass, and in an unsuspecting moment I handed it over, forgetting that it was signed by the Director of Military Intelligence. This evoked the following pleasantry ·from the examining magistrate: 'Ah, I see you are a British Intelligence Officer.'

The Mexico City-Los Angeles flight is about the longest I think scheduled by Pan American Airways. By the time the inquisition was over and I had driven the odd 20 miles or so to Beverley Hills [where I had been invited to stay with Merle Oberon], I was feeling a little weary. Merle, in the good old Hollywood style, had got together an enormous party includ-

ing the Fred Astaires and a lot more of the movie people, and I
was expected to keep it up until the small hours – which I must
say I did and fortunately got my second wind early in the
evening.

Before leaving Washington to take up my new assignment in
New York, Dorothy and I gave a cocktail party for about a
hundred guests in the Mayfair Hotel, at which we tried to blend
the British and American services. Colonel Donovan's OSS was
represented by David Bruce, a future US Ambassador in London,
who was to write a graceful foreword to *The Quiet Canadian*, the
English version of my biography of Stephenson; also by my name-
sake the ebullient Henry Hyde and his charming French wife
Mimi. The FBI agents included Charlie Appel, the Bureau's
handwriting expert, who was a particular friend of Dorothy's and
who had been an expert witness in the Ludwig spy trial. Among
those who came from the British Embassy were two outstanding
Fellows of All Souls College, Oxford, John Foster and Isaiah
Berlin, both later knighted. At this time John Foster was the
Embassy legal adviser, while Isaiah Berlin was its political
commentator.

Berlin's political commentaries on American affairs were
characteristically brilliant. Winston Churchill was so impressed
by them that he asked who was their author. On being told that it
was Mr I. Berlin, he gave instructions that I. Berlin should be
invited to lunch at Downing Street when he came to London. The
secretary mistook this I. Berlin for Irving Berlin, the American
composer of songs and musicals, whom I had met with Alex
Korda. The result was that when Irving Berlin arrived in London
shortly afterwards, he was bidden to lunch and warmly
congratulated by the Prime Minister on his work. The composer
looked puzzled but eventually concluded that Churchill had taken
a fancy to his hit-song of the period, *I'm Dreaming of a White
Christmas*. (Incidentally the last word was changed by the wits
among the American troops in North Africa to *Mistress*.) However, it was soon evident from the visitor's complete ignorance of
political commentaries that it was the wrong Berlin, and everyone

had a good laugh – except perhaps the unfortunate individual responsible for the error. The right Berlin got his invitation later.

The first six months of 1943 I found pretty boring, for my counter-espionage job kept me most of the time in the BSC headquarters in Rockefeller Center, with occasional trips to see des Graz on censorship matters in his down-town office. At Stephenson's request I wrote the history of his organization from the time of its inception, being careful to specify the leading personnel by their numbers in the service, most of which I have now forgotten except Stephenson's (48000), Ellis's (48905), and my own (48910).[24] Otherwise I spent my time in the office exchanging letters and telegrams with London and the Security Service representatives in Newfoundland, Bermuda, and the Caribbean.

In June 1943 Sir David Petrie, the new Director-General of the Security Service (MI5), telegraphed Stephenson that he was sending out a civilian in the person of Mr G. C. Denham to take over the representation of the service's interests in the western hemisphere. He would be accompanied by Colonel Vivian (Vee-Vee), Menzies's titular deputy in MI6, and Maurice Jeffes, Director of Passport Control in London, and Petrie hoped they would all co-operate with Stephenson to make the necessary adjustments so as to effect a 'smooth and speedy transfer'. Like Vivian, Petrie, a Scot educated at Aberdeen University and aged sixty-four, had spent most of his earlier career in India, where he had been Director of Intelligence in the Home Department of the Indian Government before returning to England to succeed the Security Service's founder, Vernon Kell, as Director-General in 1940, following the complete breakdown of Kell's health. Petrie's initial, and perhaps most notable, achievement was to establish a much closer liaison with the sister Secret Service than had hitherto existed. For example, he appointed Roger Hollis, who had been in business in China and was the son of an Anglican Bishop, to head the section dealing with Communist affairs, his opposite number in MI6 ironically being Kim Philby, who dealt with Soviet affairs. (Suspicion was later to fall upon both men as being Russian agents, but while Hollis, who was later promoted to head MI5, was cleared, Philby's guilt was established by his defection to Moscow.)

Petrie appeared to have a particular liking for representatives who had worked in the East, since Mr Denham had come from a business house in Singapore. Denham, a genial middle-aged business type, seemed to have only a hazy conception of what his new duties involved, since at our first meeting he admitted to having no idea of the amount and variety of work being done by BSC for MI5, particularly as regards the security of British shipping. Denham's reaction was that he saw no reason why the transfer should not be 'smooth' but he doubted very much whether in the circumstances it should be 'speedy'. He was quite right, and he was immediately sent off on an educational tour of Canada and the Caribbean. He did not return for about six weeks, when I was glad to hand over to him so that I could get off with des Graz and Ellis to Miami, where an extremely important British-American conference on censorship and counter-espionage was to take place.

The conference was opened on 16 August 1943 by Mr Byron Price, the US Director of Censorship, an able and friendly man in his early fifties who had been the chief executive news editor of the Associated Press agency before being appointed to his war-time post, in which, thanks largely to des Graz's help, he had rapidly picked up the censorship techniques.[25] Upwards of a hundred delegates attended from Britain, Canada, Bermuda, the West Indies, and South Africa, besides BSC, while in addition to the US censorship, the American agencies included the FBI, OSS, and military and naval intelligence. 'We are not undertaking here anything particularly new or revolutionary,' said Byron Price in his opening address describing the objectives of the conference. 'Counter-espionage has been one of the chief concerns of all censors since the earliest days of history.' He went on:

We know that many of the present day methods of the spy are either adaptations or outright repetitions of formulas used in the last great war, and even earlier. Like every other art, of course, espionage seeks improvement, and now and then hits upon something new. We must undertake, therefore, a two-fold task; we must try to devise better methods of dealing with old tricks, and also to discover an effective answer to the new ones.

As a rule I dislike conferences, but this one was perhaps the most lively and informative I have ever attended. Every aspect of the subject was covered, from 'watch lists' of suspected names and addresses to microdots and secret inks, besides a variety of case histories. Ellis spoke of the history and role of BSC, MI5, and MI6; I made two contributions, one on the organization and characteristics of the German espionage system in the eastern hemisphere, and the other on the use of censorship material in US courts of law; des Graz, besides intervening in most of the discussions, wound up the conference with his usual flair. One of the most interesting talks, I thought, was given on Japanese espionage by Giles Playfair, who had been in charge of sound broadcasting in Singapore and described in fascinating detail his personal experiences before and during the fall of the island, from which he managed to escape in the nick of time to join BSC via Java, Australia, Panama, Jamaica, and Liverpool.[26]

As a member of the English Bar I had been invited by the President of the American Bar Association, Mr George M. Morris, to the Association's annual meeting which that year was held in the Drake Hotel, Chicago. The guest of honour was the English Attorney General, Sir Donald Somervell. The other British guests were John Foster, the British Embassy's legal adviser, Maurice Bathurst of the Information Service in the Embassy (later a judge), and Wilfred Gallienne, the British Consul-General in Chicago (later Ambassador in Cuba). On my first day in Chicago I went to listen to the proceedings of the Association's Committee on Legal Aid.

The chairman of this committee related a somewhat touching story which illustrated the kind of work on which this particular committee was engaged. A British seaman serving on a ship of the Royal Navy, which had put in to Philadelphia for repairs, met an American girl whom he married in a very short space of time. He subsequently discovered that she was pregnant by another man. It now appeared that the American wife would have preferred to marry the father of her future child but had been unable to discover his whereabouts. The seaman's Captain got in touch with the Bar Association, and as a result a divorce was arranged; the Association with considerable difficulty succeeded in locating the father-to-be and the second marriage took place a few days before the arrival of the child. Meanwhile the seaman was able to return to his ship, relieved of what, to say the least, might have proved a very serious embarrassment to him. In fact it was the first case of this kind involving a British seaman in the US, and it impressed me as an excellent example of the Association's activities in the field of legal aid.

The same afternoon the English Attorney General invited the Association President and a few others to tea at which the other English visitors were included. On this occasion I met Homer Cummings who had served as US Attorney General in President Roosevelt's first two administrations, having previously refused the Governor-Generalship of the Philippines. Cummings, who was then seventy-three and had retired in 1939, told me that he had known many former Presidents and had been a great friend of William Howard Taft, the famous pre-World War I Republican President who had failed to secure re-election in 1913 because of the split in the the Republican vote which let in Woodrow Wilson. I asked him why he had not written his memoirs. 'For a man to write his autobiography,' he replied, 'he must be either very stupid or very conceited.' However, Cummings agreed that biographies written by other hands were desirable, although he added that they might also be 'dangerous'. In particular he instanced a biography of Taft which included some stories that in his opinion were 'scandalous'.

By a coincidence, while in the Drake Hotel lobby I ran into the current Attorney General, Francis Biddle, with whom I had worked over BSC's position as a foreign agency. Biddle, who was not attending the conference but had looked in for a few minutes, told me he had just returned from a day's visit to Bismark, North

Dakota, where he had inspected a prisoner-of-war camp. 'We think nothing of making long journeys in this country,' he said. 'Today I have done 1600 miles and I am flying back to Washington this afternoon.' He went on to say that he had asked one of the German prisoners whether he had anything to complain about in the conditions at the camp. The prisoner replied that he did not get enough butter.

'How much butter do you get?' asked Biddle.

'So much,' said the prisoner, holding up his fingers and adding, 'three times a day.'

'Gracious me,' the Attorney General told him, 'that's as much as I get.'

'Yes,' the prisoner retorted, 'but according to the rules' – apparently he had made a careful study of the Geneva international agreement governing the treatment of POWs – 'we are to get as much as the US army.' Biddle, as a good lawyer, was obliged to agree that this contention was correct.

Donald Somervell, whose address was entitled 'Law and Liberty', referred to the part he had taken in the British House of Commons in the passing of the American Visiting Forces Act, which gave US military authorities in Britain the power to try members of their Forces by court martial for all offences against the local law, including murder. Occasionally this jurisdiction was waived in the case of the latter and the accused was tried in an English court, but by no means invariably. Some years later, when I was a member of the House of Commons and active in the campaign to abolish the death penalty for murder in Great Britain, I had occasion to meet Albert Pierrepoint, the public hangman, and asked him what were the cases he most disliked having to deal with in the course of his official duties. He replied that they were invariably those of servicemen, whom he was called upon to execute at the American-base military prison in Shepton Mallet. For some reason these executions took place in the middle of the night, about 1 a.m., instead at 8 or 9 o'clock in the morning as in Britain. Furthermore, as the condemned man stood shivering on the scaffold before being launched into eternity, he had to listen to the Provost-Marshal reading a lengthy document which set out the details of his crime and the sentence, before being asked if he had anything to say – the whole process taking up about six minutes. This was a refinement of cruelty which even the hardened Pierrepoint, a strong supporter of capital punishment, considered unnecessary, particularly since on the occasion of his first execution at Shepton Mallet the Provost-Marshal had fainted and collapsed on the floor of the scaffold.

On my return to New York I again tackled Stephenson on the subject of my release to serve nearer the European war theatre, and this time he agreed. I had a fair amount of accumulated leave, and while Dorothy went down to Bermuda to ply her old craft (since the Bermuda Censorship was very short-handed at this time), I returned to Mexico to collect some additional material for my biography of Maximilian and Carlota. After that Stephenson kindly allowed me to pay a short visit to England to get fixed up in a new Intelligence appointment, which I did. I flew on to Northern Ireland to see my parents whom I had not seen for four years, only to find when I reached their home in Belfast that they had gone off on a visit to Dublin. British army personnel were not allowed to visit neutral Eire unless their homes were there, and then, of course, only in civilian clothes. Fortunately I was able to persuade the military authorities in Belfast that my parents had migrated to the south for an indefinite period, and I was allowed to cross the border – where I noticed that there was a strict security check at the frontier railway station. After a happy reunion with my father and mother, as well as many other relations, in Dublin, I went back to New York, travelling in the liner *Queen Mary* with relatively few other passengers, in contrast to the east-bound voyages which used to accommodate about 17,000 American troops at this time.

It now only remained for me to wind up my affairs in New York, official and private, and to say good-bye to the many American friends I had made in both these categories. Mr J. Edgar Hoover, who had heard that my wife and I were leaving the country for

To my very good friends
Dorothy & H. Montgomery Hyde
With most cordial regards
J. Edgar Hoover

1.20.44

J. Edgar Hoover, Director of the FBI. The picture was given to the author when he and his wife left the United States early in 1944 to return to England.

good, asked to see me before our departure. The meeting took place in his Washington headquarters in the afternoon of 20 January 1944. I knew that he had had what was an extremely trying morning testifying before a Congressional Committee and that he must be feeling exhausted, so that I did not expect our farewells to last for more than a few minutes. In the event our talk went on for an hour and a half, ranging over a wide variety of subjects. It was largely a monologue on Hoover's part in which my occasional interjections merely served to elicit or develop some point and sometimes to divert him to some other topic.

The FBI Director began by saying how extremely sorry he was that I was leaving and how personally grateful he was for the assistance which I and my wife, particularly my wife, had been to the Bureau. As I was being posted to London, he spoke about some of the changes he was making in the personnel of the Bureau there. He hoped, he said, that the closest possible liaison with the corresponding British agencies would continue now more than ever, since, with the prospect of the invasion of Europe clearly defined, it was necessary that the appropriate representatives of both countries should work together in the field of counter-espionage and the detection of subversive activities generally aimed at the Allies' combined work effort. He went on to say that in this field, and also in the field of secret intelligence, he did not envisage the cessation of the Bureau's work after the war. He referred openly to his agents in Lisbon and he expressed the hope that their work would continue, together with that of agents in any part of Europe where it was 'necessary to collect information affecting the security of the Western Hemisphere'. These agents, he explained, nominally worked as attachés in the US missions overseas. But they did not have their own forms of code and cipher communication and had to use their respective missions' facilities. Hoover stated that this was unsatisfactory; he felt that the Bureau should have its own communications, just as BSC had.

Here I must digress briefly to record what my old Oxford friend and university contemporary, Hugh Cox, the US Assistant Attorney General, told me at this time. Cox had recently spoken about Hoover's desire to have his own communications to a member of the US Embassy in London, who had told him that he thought Hoover might have other representatives besides the attachés unknown to the Ambassador, possibly in the code-room. 'I would not mind at all,' this official added, 'if Hoover had his own cable communications, provided that I could be certain that he was not reading ours!'

A further reason why the FBI Director attached particular importance to the continuance of the strongest Anglo-American liaison in security matters, I gathered, was his interest in Communism and its ramifications. This was to become almost a pathological obsession with him. He told me that he anticipated that the Communists would 'cause a great deal of trouble' in the United States after the war. 'It does not seem to matter whether these people receive their orders from Moscow or not,' he said. 'The fact remains that they are pledged by the political beliefs to which they subscribe to overthrow the established Constitution of the United States. As a law-enforcement agency which is pledged to uphold the Constitution, the Bureau must be prepared to take strong counter-action against the members of the Communist Party operating in this country.'

Not only the security of the United States but that of Canada and the whole of Latin America might be similarly threatened by the operation of the Communist Party, he went on, and in the general interest it behoved all those who might be affected, particularly the intelligence organizations of Great Britain and the United States, to pool their resources and exchange their views freely. (This was always a favourite topic of Hoover's, and he was still at it fifteen years later when his book, *Masters of Deceit*, about the menace of Communism, became a best-seller.)

I raised the question of those who had access to information on western hemisphere security matters using them as the basis for sensational publications, and I remarked that he must be prepared for a spate of such literature after the war and possibly before its ultimate conclusion. He agreed warmly, adding how harmful H. O. Yardley's book *The American Black Chamber* had been and what assistance it had given to the Germans and Japanese. He said that, of course, he could not speak for the officials of other agencies, but so far as the Bureau was concerned, confidential information of a comprehensive character – 'the whole picture' as he called it – was in the hands of a few trusted members of his organization and he could rely on them not to make use of their knowledge, at any rate without his express approbation. He also spoke of the damage caused by writers who only got half the story correct and distorted or invented the remainder, instancing two works in particular – *Under Cover* by John Roy Carlson, an American who managed to gain entrance to many of the subversive organizations operating in the US before Pearl Harbor, and *Passport to Treason* by Alan Hynd, which described the activities and eventual breaking-up of various Axis spy groups which had worked in the US since 1938. Here I detected what I thought was a hint of jealousy that Hoover had been scooped by two private investigators, since he might be said to feel that he had what was more or less of a monopoly in expressing himself in print on the subject. At all events he regretted that there was no statute in the United States Code which corresponded to the British Official Secrets Act and which could be applied 'against authors who gave free rein to their knowledge as well as imagination in the field of security and counter-espionage'.

Speaking of sabotage, Hoover said that with the exception of the eight Nazi saboteurs who had landed on US territory in the summer of 1942, there had been no act of sabotage committed in the United States which had been directly traceable to enemy action. Several thousand cases of sabotage had in fact occurred, but they had been traced to other than enemy-inspired causes.

Mention of the eight Nazi saboteurs, which it will be recalled Hoover had briefly mentioned to me when I met him shortly after their capture, induced the Director to expatiate upon the German mentality as evinced by the cowardly behaviour of the German agents when they had been caught. The Japanese, on the other hand, according to his experience, were tough and cruel. He doubted if anything, even physical violence (to which, he added by way of an aside, his agents never resorted), would obtain any worthwhile results from them. He also referred to the difficulty the Bureau had experienced in obtaining counter-intelligence about Japanese activities, for the same reason that US forces in the field had captured relatively so few Japanese prisoners – the fanatical desire to die for the Emperor rather than be captured.

While on the subject of the activities of enemy agents in the United States, the Director mentioned the celebrated McNab decision, handed down by the US Supreme Court, making it illegal for an FBI agent to hold any suspect for questioning before arraignment; if any confession were obtained from the suspect, it might not be put in evidence at his subsequent trial. This decision, which was actually the work of Justice Felix Frankfurter, exhibited, in Hoover's judgement, 'too fine a desire to preserve the letter of civil liberties in the face of wartime expediencies'. Time and again, Hoover asserted, promising cases had been spoiled by the Bureau's having been compelled to release a suspect before evidence could be obtained in the shape of a confession on which an indictment might later be founded.

It is a scandal that our hands should be tied in this manner simply because the judges in the Supreme Court live in a rarefied atmosphere remote from present-day wartime actualities and thus construe the constitutional principles of civil liberty inherent in the Constitution.

'A lot has been said in certain quarters about the methods by which these confessions have been obtained,' said Hoover in this context. 'It is not our practice to employ the third degree. I do not believe in third degree. I am convinced that proof can be obtained much more readily, by humane methods of questioning.'

The Director gave me to understand that this view was not held by most of the State police authorities. He cited a number of cases where a man had been arrested on charges of violating both Federal and State laws, and for some reason (such as the McNab decision) the Bureau had been obliged to drop the Federal charge: the accused person had often begged not to be handed over to the State authorities. Hoover went on to say that in a number of instances he had actually obtained an assurance from the State District Attorney concerned that the accused should be decently and humanely treated.

The Director seemed anxious that I should appreciate that

whatever criticisms might be levelled at the Bureau, its word could always be depended upon, whether in dealings with colleagues or with those enemies of society whom it was its prime object to defeat. He spoke at length of its record as a law-enforcement agency, particularly in connection with the suppressing of kidnapping which became a Federal offence after the abduction of the Lindbergh baby in 1932, and of other rackets which the gangster underworld had operated in the past. He touched on the history of various gangs led by such notorious characters as Al Capone and John Dillinger, and he described in some detail the apprehension of the Tuohy gang, the last gang operating on an extensive scale in Chicago to be 'cleaned up'. Hoover said he had personally directed the operations which led to the arrest of this gang in their hideout in Chicago's north side. It was he himself who announced through a loudspeaker, which was installed in an apartment directly opposite that in which the gang members were concealed, that they would have five minutes in which to come out 'backwards with their hands up' or else he and his men would go in and shoot it out with them. 'In that case,' he went on, 'none of them would have come out alive!'

Apparently Roger Tuohy, the leader of the gang – 'Terrible Tuohy' as he was called – was not as formidable as his principal assistant whose name was Banghart. Mr Banghart, in appearance an extremely quiet and well-spoken individual, was in reality a ruthless killer, said Hoover, who frequently tortured his victims by burning the soles of their feet and that kind of thing. Hoover went on to relate some of the sordid details of the private lives of these men. One curious revelation intrigued me. Apparently all the gangsters had women on whom, when times were good, they lavished mink coats and fancy jewellery, but who, 'when the boys were on the run', were expected to provide them with hideouts and food. These 'molls', as Hoover called them, were all either redheads or peroxide blondes. They were never brunettes.

The Supreme Court, according to Hoover, was not his only obstacle in the field of law enforcement. Congress, or rather its Committee system, also impeded the Bureau's efforts. That very morning he had been before the Congressional Committee investigating the Federal Communications Commission and he had been obliged to cite, although he had not shown it to the Committee, a memorándum which he had received from President Roosevelt, 'forbidding me to testify on matters pertaining to national security'. The Chairman of this Committee, Mr Clarence F. Lea, a Democrat from California, had asserted that messages from the western hemisphere had been surreptitiously transmitted to the Axis powers by radio, and Hoover was questioned as to what steps in the way of interception of these messages by monitoring had been taken.[27]

'I told one of the members of the Committee, off the record,' Hoover went on, 'that, although officially we had no one in South America, in fact we had a considerable number of agents there and it was their duty to concern themselves with such matters. However, you will understand that it is hardly a subject which can be publicly aired before a Congressional Committee!'

Another instance, which he cited, of lack of understanding on the part of the Legislature, was its initial opposition to the measure which, had it been passed, would have made the handing over of a ransom to kidnappers illegal. The payment of ransom in any case frequently facilitated the detection of the kidnappers, he explained, since the notes could often be traced and the appearance of this 'hot money' often gave a lead to finding those who were passing it.

'But law enforcement cannot be regarded entirely as of national interest,' the FBI Director emphatically declared. He expressed in the strongest terms the hope that after the war there would be the closest co-operation between the law-enforcement bodies of the world in the work of detecting international criminals, thus anticipating the coming into being of the International Criminal Police Commission (Interpol) with headquarters in Paris, on which the police of nearly fifty countries are now represented by senior officers of their criminal investigation departments.[28]

'Before the war such attempts as were made to put this work on an international basis were undertaken by the German and Austrian police; this system naturally broke down. Communications by ship and aeroplane are going to be so fast after the war that all countries must, in their own interests, co-operate in some such scheme if they are to prevent large-scale international criminals from escaping from the scene of their crimes to other areas of jurisdiction without fear of apprehension.'

Finally, Hoover expressed the view that prospects in the field of law enforcement in the US after the war were not encouraging. The Director envisaged a wave of crime spreading over the country and a great increase in offences of various kinds, partly as a result of servicemen returning from overseas and not settling suitably down into civilian life, and partly owing to the appearance throughout the country of a reckless and irresponsible youth with no feeling for the safety of human life, either their own or that of others. Already there had been a great increase in juvenile crime, he said, and in his opinion this augured very badly for post-war American life. (Hoover's prediction was to be realized in the post-war years, as I was myself to appreciate when I made a tour of American penitentiaries and other correctional institutions in the 1950s and learned that there were approximately four times more prisoners in custody in the US than there were in the United Kingdom, having regard to the relative proportions of the countries' populations.)

As I was leaving his office, Hoover shook me warmly by the hand and gave me a photograph of a drawing of himself which he had inscribed in kind words for my wife and myself. I responded by sending him an autographed copy of my book *Judge Jeffreys*, which described how justice was administered in seventeenth-century England, a copy of which I had already given to the Attorney General Francis Biddle. My inscription seems to have been appropriate, since the Director wrote in thanking me for the gift: 'I was pleased to find your splendid comments on the flyleaf and you may be sure I will keep it in my personal library.'[29]

A few days later Dorothy and I gave a farewell drinks party to our New York friends in the Twenty-One Club ('Jack and Charlie's') which had been a celebrated speakeasy in Prohibition days, and where we had enjoyed many excellent meals and much hospitality from Alex Korda and others. It was a nostalgic leave-taking – and also an extremely cheap one. We were only charged

$75, barely enough to pay for a lunch for two these days, although we had around a hundred guests.[30]

I left for England in a Liberator bomber, a convenient way of crossing the Atlantic at that time, although the aircraft was un-heated and the cabin was not pressurized so that I had to wear an oxygen mask throughout most of the journey. In order to obtain the necessary supply of oxygen one had to keep the mask securely fastened across one's face. On a recent journey Alex Korda had allowed the mask to slip down, with the result that he rapidly be-came unconscious. Another passenger, sitting opposite and noticing that Korda's face had turned blue, rushed across and adjusted the mask. When Korda came to, he was so grateful to the man who had saved his life that he offered him a job with his motion-picture company in London after the war. 'But I don't know anything about films,' the man protested. 'Never mind,' said Korda, 'what do you know about?' 'Sailing,' was the answer. 'Well,' Korda told him 'you can be captain of my yacht,' which in fact was what he became – an easy assignment, since Korda only used the yacht for a few weeks in the year. I was also to get a post-war job with Korda but in the more exacting role of legal adviser. However, that is another story.

The last letter I received before leaving New York for Montreal to catch the bomber was from my kinsman Sir Mayson Beeton. 'You have certainly got hold of a war job which is bringing you much adventure,' he wrote, 'and I hope you are not forgetting to keep a rough diary of your wanderings and doings – and the people, places and things you have "contacted" as the Yanks say.' The fact that I was able to do so, however roughly, has helped to make possible the writing of this book.

'I want you to know that I found our association a very happy one,' Bill Stephenson, my old chief in BSC, wrote from New York some time later, after I had become a Legal Officer in the Allied Control Commission for Austria. 'All of us here enjoyed working with you and regretted your departure. I wish you every success in your present post and in whatever new experience may lie ahead of you.' These experiences were to be numerous and varied, but that again is another story.

General William J. Donovan

Appendix

THE STORY OF OSS
by Sir William Stephenson (Intrepid)

From a hitherto unpublished tape-recording in the author's possession, of an account by Stephenson dictated to an American friend who was collecting material for a history of the US Office of Strategic Services during World War II.

The following abbreviations are used:

BI = British Secret Intelligence Service
BSC = British Security Co-ordination
CIA = US Central Intelligence Agency
COI = US Co-ordinator of Information
FBI = US Federal Bureau of Investigation
OSS = US Office of Strategic Services
SOE = British Special Operations Executive

It may be that you have thought of me as primarily a regional representative of a certain organization which you and I know as BI. My original charter went beyond that and indeed was soon expanded to include representation of all the secret and general covert organizations – nine of them – also security and communications. In fact this latter division of my organization BSC was by far the largest of its type in operation, exchanging over a million groups a day, and then acting as a sort of yo-yo between the summits that eventually made BSC the only all-encompassing secret security organization which has ever existed anywhere, and myself the repository of secret information at all levels beyond that of any other single individual then involved. I know that, with you in possession of it, this tape will be sacrosanct and I shall chatter away without concern and refrain from putting any limitation upon what to decide, if anything, to use for the history of OSS.

Perhaps we should start at the end and go back to the beginning. On 1 December 1952, the then head of the CIA (General Walter Bedell Smith, Chief of Staff to General Eisenhower) said to an enquiring editor of *Maclean's Magazine* (in Toronto): 'General Donovan said that Bill Stephenson taught us everything we ever knew about foreign intelligence operations.' Neither you nor I would go as far as that. But up to a point in time it might have been valid . . . There can be no story about the CIA organization that is not the story of the man (General William Donovan) and his activities from the outbreak of war in Europe and the creation of OSS.

I needn't enlarge too much upon what my principal concerns were upon my arrival here (in New York). Obviously the establishment of a secret organization to investigate enemy activities and to institute adequate wartime security measures in the western hemisphere in relation to British interests in a neutral territory were of importance, and American assistance in achieving this objective was essential. The procurement of certain supplies for Britain was high on the list, and it was the burning urgency of the attempt to fulfil this requirement that made me instinctively – I don't think it can be rated much higher than that – concentrate on a single individual who, despite all my contacts in high places, might achieve more on the official or sub-official levels which had so far been unproductive.

My assessment was proved correct, in the event. Donovan, by virtue of his very independence of thought and action, inevitably had his critics, but there are few of them who would deny the credit due to him for having reached a correct appraisal of the international situation in the summer of 1940. At that time the US Government was debating two alternative courses of action. One was to endeavour to keep Britain in the war by supplying her with the material assistance of which she was desperately in need. The other was to give Britain up for lost and to concentrate exclusively on American rearmament to offset the German threat. That the former course was eventually pursued was due in a large measure to Donovan's tireless advocacy of it. Immediately after the fall of France not even President Roosevelt himself could

feel assured that aid to Britain would not be wasted in the circumstances. I need not remind you of the dispatches from the US
ambassadors in London and Paris threatening that Britain's cause
was hopeless, and the majority of the Cabinet here in the US were
inclined to the same conclusion, all of which found expression in
organized isolationism with men like Lindbergh and Senator
Wheeler.[1] Donovan, on the other hand, was convinced that, provided with sufficient aid from the USA, Britain could and would
survive. It was my task first to inform him of Britain's foremost
requirements so that he could make them known in the
appropriate quarters, and secondly to furnish him with concrete
evidence in support of his contention that American assistance
would not be improvident charity but a sound investment.

In June of 1940, very shortly after I arrived here, he arranged
for me to attend a meeting with Knox and Stimson[2] where the
main subject of discussion was Britain's lack of destroyers; and
the way was explored towards finding a formula for the transfer,
without legal breach of US neutrality and without offence to
American public opinion, of fifty over-age American destroyers
to the Royal Navy. It was then that I suggested that Donovan
should pay a visit to Britain with the object of investigating conditions at first hand and assessing for himself the British war
effort, its most urgent requirements, and its potential chances of
success. He referred to Knox and they jointly referred to the
President, who agreed.

Donovan left by Clipper on 14 July 1940. I arranged that he
should be accorded every opportunity to conduct his enquiries. I
endeavoured to marshal my friends in high places to bare their
breasts. He was received in audience by the King. He had ample
time with Churchill and those members of the Cabinet concerned.
He visited war factories and military training centres. He spoke
with industrial leaders and with representatives of all classes in
the community. He learned what was true – that Churchill
defying the Nazis was no mere façade but the very heart of
Britain, which was still beating strongly. He flew back in early
August and shortly after his arrival I was to inform London that
the visit had been everything I had hoped for, and that Knox and

he were pressing the destroyers-for-bases case strongly with the President, despite what I described at the time as strong opposition from below and procrastination from above. At midnight on 22/23 August, I was able to report to London that the destroyer deal was agreed and that forty-four of the fifty destroyers were already commissioned. It is certain that the destroyers-for-bases deal could not have eventuated when it did without Donovan's intercession, and I was instructed to convey to him the warmest thanks of the British Government.

Then there were other supplies that he was largely instrumental in obtaining for Britain during the same period and by the same means, among them 100 Flying Fortresses for RAF Coastal Command and 1,000,000 rifles for the newly formed Home Guard. My work with him up to this time can be described as covert diplomacy inasmuch as it was preparatory and supplementary to negotiations conducted directly by HM Ambassador (Lord Lothian). When Donovan returned from London, there was widespread publicity for his view that Britain would hold. He wrote a series of five articles dealing with German fifth-column tactics which appeared in important newspapers and were broadcast by him over a nationwide hook-up, the first ever accorded a speaker other than the President. Of course, we provided the information upon which these were based.

During the early winter of 1940, the British Government was especially concerned to secure assistance from the US Navy in convoying British merchant shipping across the Atlantic. This was a measure of intervention that the United States Government was understandably reluctant to take. Donovan pleaded our case at a meeting in December 1940 with Knox, Stimson, and Hull.[3] The whole story is too long to set upon this tape, but that conference led one way and another to his second trip. However there was more to it than that, as incidentally Churchill wanted an influential American to apply some subtle delaying tactics in Bulgaria and Yugoslavia, which might even slightly affect the timetable of Hitler's attack on Russia. You will have all the details of his very important achievements in these objectives, including the stripping of the emissary in the Royal Palace of every-

thing but his pants. This was his second visit since the beginning
of the war to Britain, and an important one too.

I accompanied him to London, where we talked with Churchill
and others who appreciated the significance and potentialities of
the second visit of one who had justified my build-up of him prior
to his first visit. The visit to the Balkans might be described as
somewhat of a diversion as far as the original terms of reference
by Hull, Stimson, and Knox were concerned. They particularly
required information about the situation in the Mediterranean
and Middle East garnered by their own observers. This was forthcoming in full measure. He had the whole precarious position laid
before him without restraint and when he returned to Washington on 18 March 1941, he had a very comprehensive situation
report with which to enlighten his sponsors. The following morning, at breakfast with the President, he was assured of active
support of a step that was at that moment as water to a parched
man dying of thirst – direct transportation to the Middle East of
war materials. Two weeks later the ships were loading. He talked
of his visit with those concerned in the Mediterranean and all that
surrounded it, and said that he had never been treated in such
royal and exalted fashion and that the red carpet had been thicker
and wider than he thought it was possible to lay. He had
been preceded by a signal from their Lordships at the Admiralty
sent through the Director of Naval Intelligence,[4] which made it
abundantly clear that he was the most important emissary that
they were ever likely to encounter, in this world or the next. I
know because I dictated every word of it myself in the presence of
the DNI in his office. The sentiments were worthy, and the
results more than justified a little hero worship. Well, those are
some of the highlights of the pre-COI days but I think not
irrelevant to the background.

Now for COI. From the beginning – that is June 1940 – I had
discussed and argued with Donovan the need for the US Government to establish an agency for conducting secret activities
throughout the world, an agency with which I could collaborate
fully by virtue of its being patterned in the matter of co-ordinated
functions after my own organization. Early he agreed in principle

and on his first two visits to England he spent some time in the BI, SOE, and other similar agencies, both at their headquarters and field-training stations. In April of 1941 President Roosevelt began to give serious consideration to the question, but no decision was made for some time, despite various pressures.

Parenthetically I may say that I enlisted the help of several avenues of influence at the White House. Winant and Sherwood were the most persistent and effective, I think.[5] There were others who kept the subject alive. Vincent Astor was one who comes to mind, but he leaned towards the Hoover camp.[6] Along with the efforts to create an opposite number to BSC in the US was the equally difficult task of creating in London a mind pattern of an acceptable order of attitude of our friend. There was quite naturally a certain aura of suspicion understandably associated with an old established organization (BI), whose life-blood is the undiluted quintessence of cynicism. At one point it became necessary to enlist the support of the great man at the top (Churchill), who fortunately for me always saw eye to eye with me on all matters relating to British-American exchanges, and in his immediate entourage there were some who kept an eagle eye on any suggestion of deviation from the great man's orders in relation to our friend by the departments concerned. Pug Ismay was one and Desmond Morton was another.[7]

Nonetheless, had it been comprehended in that building opposite the tube station[8] to what extent I was supplying our friend with secret information to build up his candidacy for the position I wanted him to achieve here, there would have been such a cold blast of horror sweep through it that on your first visit to it you would have had to find your way over one corpse after another. Donovan began to send up to the summit papers designed to stress the lack and need of establishing undercover services in secret intelligence, special operations, psychological and economic warfare, external counter-espionage, and other related activities. Of course my staff produced the material for these papers and they were usually sent up in practically their original form. There was always only one objective so far as he was concerned, which was that, 'I must garner all that I can from any source which might be of help to my country in what I see so clearly lies ahead of it.'

The idea that our friend (Donovan) himself should direct the new agency that we envisaged did not at first appeal to him. Nor was it by any means a foregone conclusion that he would be offered the appointment. Yet I was convinced that he was the obvious man for the job. In the first place he had the confidence of the President, the Secretary of State, and the civilian heads of the service departments. In the second place he had made some study of it and had given considerable thought to the conduct of secret activities. Thirdly, he had all the requisite vision and drive to build swiftly an organization of sufficient size and competence to play an effective part in the war. Lastly, he had already shown his willingness to co-operate fully with BSC and the worth of his co-operation had been abundantly proved.

On 18 June 1941, our friend saw the President and accepted the appointment of co-ordinator of all forms of intelligence including various covert offensive operations. By Presidential Executive Order of 11 July, he was appointed head of the Office of Co-ordinator of Information. The presidential directive was necessarily vague in its terminology, but in fact our friend had been entrusted with responsibility not only for collecting intelligence but for co-ordinating this work with preparations to conduct special operations and subversive propaganda. Thus COI was in effect, if not in name, the American counterpart of BSC. That night I took five instead of the usual four hours of sleep.

Collaboration began at once. Indeed, together we drew up the initial plans for his agency both as regards establishment and methods of operation. On 9 August 1941, I noted that our friend's organization was rapidly taking shape. Central offices in Washington had been established and were functioning, understanding with the Chiefs of Staff had been satisfactory, and he felt confident of their co-operation. He had several competent assistants, he had the beginnings of a working apparatus in Washington and New York, and I felt he should be able to safeguard secret documents. To secure the closest possible day-to-day working liaison between BSC and COI, I set up an office in

Washington to which I attached experienced officers of all branches, and he in turn established an office in New York.

The establishment of COI five months before Pearl Harbor represented more the promise than the fact of American participation in secret activities abroad. From my point of view COI was essentially a long-term investment, and for some time it required far more help than it could give us in return. This was inevitably so for four main reasons.

First, there was the obvious one that COI was a pioneer body, lacking previous experience of its own upon which to draw. Secondly, so long as the US remained at peace, Donovan's position was equivalent to Hoover's in the intelligence field, that is to say, he had responsibility without power. For example, to conduct propaganda operations he needed among other things control of short-wave radio facilities. But broadcasting in the US is a private industry, and before Pearl Harbor the owners of short-wave stations could not be ousted or even coerced. In many instances they refused to follow COI directives or to use COI material. Again the State Department was reluctant to risk identity with an agency whose covert functions clearly endangered US neutrality and, despite initial promises to the contrary, largely withheld its co-operation which was needed to provide cover for its operations abroad.

Thirdly, the older agencies, whose collaboration he required to carry out his task of correlating intelligence, were at the outset somewhat hostile, partly through scepticism regarding the work of an organization which of necessity was staffed by amateurs, and partly through fear that COI would infringe on their own prerogatives. This was particularly true of the FBI and to a lesser extent of the service departments. Lastly, when war came, our friend was expected by the Chiefs of Staff, as justification for the continuance of his organization, to produce immediate results despite the fact that he had insufficient time and authority to make adequate preparations. It is fair to say that if our friend had not been able to rely on BSC's assistance, his organization could not have survived; and indeed it is a fact that before he had his own operational machinery in working order, which was not until several months after Pearl Harbor, he was entirely dependent on it.

The provision of such assistance was the ensuring of COI's full collaboration. To indicate its comprehensive character some points may be enumerated briefly:

1. The bulk of COI's secret intelligence before Pearl Harbor, and for several weeks thereafter, was supplied by my organization BSC from its various sources.
2. BSC controlled through its intermediaries two short-wave radio services, one for broadcasts to Europe and Africa, the other for broadcasts to the Far East. These were made available to COI immediately after Pearl Harbor and they were the foundation of all American short-wave radio propaganda.
3. COI officers of all divisions, as well as COI agents, were in the beginning trained at BSC schools in Canada.
4. BSC supplied COI with all the equipment which it needed for some period after Pearl Harbor, when such equipment was not yet in production in the United States.
5. In September 1941 I made arrangements for senior COI officers to spend three months studying all SOE training and operations at first hand.
6. In January 1942 I had senior officers of SOE sent to set up the Special Operations division of COI.
7. In October 1941 I arranged for the lecturers in communications in all BI to come to Washington to assist in the establishment of a world-wide system of clandestine communications for COI. The head of my own Communications division, who was probably the most experienced in the field, continued to act as adviser to COI.[9]

These are but a few instances of assistance rendered to the nascent COI. In short, BSC had a considerable part in the upbringing of the agency of which it was in a sense the parent. The effort thus expended would only have been wasted if COI, to carry the metaphor a little further, had never grown to man's estate. In fact, from the story of OSS which follows, that development proved extremely rewarding. For not only was Donovan's organization eventually equipped to discharge its responsibilities, but since it owed much to our efforts it was inevitably prepared to work in fullest accord with us.

And now for OSS. The period during which Donovan's organization was largely dependent upon us (that is BSC) may be said to have ended in June 1942 when, in that month, an Executive Order abolished COI and established two new agencies in its place, the Office of War Information and the Office of Strategic Services. The former was entrusted with responsibilities *inter alia* for all overseas propaganda other than black, that is covert, propaganda. Under Donovan this was one of COI's remaining functions. OSS's sphere of operations was restricted to exclude the western hemisphere and Donovan was placed directly under the Chiefs of Staff. Parenthetically it may be said that Bob Sherwood was responsible for the amputation from COI of the propaganda section and he and Donovan wasted no time on fare-wells. You may have noted that Sherwood's reference to me in his book *Roosevelt and Hopkins* refers to my close association, co-operation, and operations with Hoover, but there is no mention of Donovan. [10]

The Executive Order, while limited to the scope of Donovan's activities, yet considerably strengthened his position and removed the causes of friction which had hitherto existed between his organisation and other US intelligence agencies, notably the FBI. At the same time, by establishing OSS as an arm of the US services, this resulted in Donovan being above suspicion of being an instrument of presidential policy and made his organization an essential part of the war effort.

At the time the Order was issued both Donovan and I were in London and it was therefore the occasion for discussions concerning secret collaboration between OSS and its British equivalents. These resulted in agreement between OSS and BI and between OSS and SOE, as follows:

1. Between OSS and BI it was decided that there should be as

free an interchange of information as possible but no integration of OSS with BI. Thus Donovan's organization would be free to adopt its own methods of collating intelligence and would operate independently of BSC. This agreement, which was formalized in an exchange of letters, remained valid for the duration of the war.

2. Between OSS and SOE for Special Operations the world was divided into various zones, British zones, American zones, and British-American zones. It was decided that in British zones SOE should have command and in American zones OSS should have command, while in the British-American zones such as Germany both organizations would be free to operate independently, although wherever possible activities should be closely co-ordinated. This agreement, known as the London Agreement, was with certain minor alterations subsequently approved on the American side by the US Chiefs of Staff and on the British side by the British Chiefs of Staff and the Foreign Office.

Thus provision was made by OSS and BI for independently pooling their resources in the field of secret intelligence and by OSS and SOE for a working partnership in the field of special operations. Furthermore, OSS decided to follow the example of BI by establishing a separate division to undertake counter-espionage, and as far as Europe was concerned it was agreed that this work should be administered jointly by BI and OSS from London.

Parenthetically I might here interject that all the products of cryptographic operations were also made available to OSS, after strong opposition of American service agencies was overridden. This affair was a comparatively low-level subject in the British cryptographic organization (GC & CS). Of all our exchanges, the only routine material that I was specifically barred from passing to Donovan was the high-level cryptographic product (Ultra). On numerous occasions when he consulted me about the reports which were destined for the highest level in various departments of OSS, for example Research and Analysis, I would suggest alterations based upon knowledge of the real, rather than the deduced, situation as evidenced by the deciphered enemy communications. He always followed my advice in this, and I assumed that he shrewdly guessed what actuated it. I endeavoured to the end to get the Combined Chiefs of Staff to authorize that Donovan should be made privy to this, by far the most important source of secret intelligence. But it was never agreed. I always felt uncomfortable about it, but I think that because of his important prior reference on important appreciations I was able to remould somewhat some incipient real bloomers. Thus by my interjections there was Anglo-American co-operation in all forms of secret activity outside the western hemisphere, which steadily increased in scope and value. And while its emphasis inevitably shifted from OSS in the United States to various operational theatres, BSC had the responsibility of maintaining and co-ordinating liaison with OSS headquarters. Its work in this regard may be briefly summarized as follows:

Secret Intelligence. Immediately following the agreement made in London, I appointed a special liaison officer with a staff to OSS headquarters whose responsibility was to pass to me information of American origin and to advise OSS on such matters as the management of agents, methods of operation, and the evaluation of intelligence reports. In the result, BSC received a large number of reports made by OSS agents throughout the world. Latterly an OSS office was established in London and it was arranged that this office should pass intelligence reports direct to BI headquarters. BSC kept an eye on this new channel, however, and always drew London's attention to intelligence on the theory of double-checking the switchman (on a railway). The OSS headquarters establishment was separate from the Secret Intelligence division, which produced useful intelligence and with which my offices maintained regular contact. Among them were the Survey of Foreign Experts and the Research and Analysis branches. These provided *inter alia* essential information concerning potential bombing objectives throughout Europe. The work of the Research and Analysis branch in producing strategic surveys and maps was generally regarded as second to none. It made its compilations available to me and I made certain that they reached those most directly concerned without a moment's delay.

Special Operations. Shortly after the conclusion of the London Agreement I arranged for SOE to send to Washington four experts with real experience in the different theatres where OSS was operating. They maintained liaison with OSS on a planning level in regard both to organization and methods. At the same time my supply experts were attached to OSS to advise on the production of special devices and weapons. They made available various specifications and new developments, and they assisted OSS to establish its own production schedules. Subsequently, their task was to establish close co-ordination both with OSS and SOE with regard to the production of devices already in use, and to the development of new devices. The research and development procedure adopted by OSS was largely based on SOE–BSC practice. The material purchased from OSS included much that could not otherwise have been obtained. In May 1943, for example, we acquired three ships with a minimum range of 3,000 miles, a maximum speed of at least sixteen knots, and four tons of cargo space, for irregular operations in the North Sea. Donovan persuaded the US Navy to release to OSS three hundred-foot sub-chasers which were fitted with AA guns, K guns, depth charges, and radar. They ran the German blockade to and from Sweden, carrying not only valuable material, such as ball bearings, but a number of passengers who were considered important to the war effort, including the Manhattan Project.[11]

Of course, BSC supplied OSS with all its requirements during the period when they were not yet in production in the United States. We provided Donovan, for example, with all the equipment he used in the Torch operation preceding the invasion of North Africa.[12] On the other hand, OSS obtained from the US War Department for BSC high-powered items including radio equipment and cameras, and such special items as kayaks, of all things! However, we produced for OSS out-of-the-way items too, such as land mines camouflaged as camel dung. There were all sorts of curious exchanges, one in 1943 which only Donovan and two of his officers knew about . . . to do with the exchange of dollars between the British Treasury and the US Treasury,

Donovan and I acting as intermediaries. The amounts involved were $18,000,000. We wanted those of 50 and 100 dollar denominations and the equivalent value in small bills. This was to do with pre- and post-invasion affairs. If the transaction had been direct between the two Treasuries, too many people.would have been involved. Everything went smoothly until experience proved that $1,000,000 could go into one bag, but the same amount in small notes required thirty or forty bags and because of the shortage of aircraft cargo space the flow from east to west did not equal the flow eastwards. The US Treasury turned off the tap, and a somewhat urgent temporary dilemma was solved by OSS borrowing from the Treasury on its own notes until we could deliver this massive freight from London to Washington.

Now to wind up. It can be said for certain that OSS was comparable to the combined efforts of BI and SOE – in short, a commendable accomplishment when it is remembered how little time Donovan was afforded to build up his organization, and how many serious obstacles he faced at the outset. Qualitatively too, much of OSS's work was without doubt of first-class importance by any standard. As such, one example it is pertinent to recall is that the head of OSS's office in Berne persuaded an official of the German Foreign Office to provide him with all telegrams which passed through his hands. For some time BI thought it was a plant, a situation which irritated Donovan and which persisted until I raised a riot in London and enlisted the assistance of the head of the cryptographic factory (at Bletchley Park) who was soon able to establish beyond question, by checking against his own findings, that the material was completely reliable.[13]

The work of OSS fully convinced United States views of the need for preserving a foreign intelligence service (CIA) which had to be built on the foundations laid by OSS. Under the Presidential Order of 20 September 1945, OSS was abolished. As President Truman wrote to Donovan on that day:

Timely steps should be taken to conserve those resources and skills within your organization which are vital to our peace-time purposes. I want to take this occasion to thank you for the capable leadership you have brought to a vital wartime activity in your capacity as Director of Strategic Services. You may well find satisfaction in the achievements of your Office and take pride in your contribution to them. Great additional reward for your efforts should lie in the knowledge that the peacetime intelligence services of the Government are being created on the foundation of the facilities and resources mobilized through the Office of Strategic Services during the war.[14]

Sources and Notes

The principal source used in this work is the author's collection of private correspondence, memoranda, reports, and miscellaneous papers now preserved in the Archives Centre in Churchill College, Cambridge. Printed sources used are included with the notes under the respective chapter headings, together with references to other MS sources.

Chapter 1. To War with a Steam Kettle

1   Winston S. Churchill, *Thoughts and Adventures* (London, 1947), pp 58–59.
2   F. H. Hinsley, *British Intelligence in the Second World War*, Vol I (London, 1979), p 16 *et seq*. See also Admiral Sir William James, *The Eyes of the Navy* (London, 1955), on Hall. Some papers on the origins and early history of the SIS are still retained in the Cabinet Office and are not generally available for research, although Professor Hinsley and his assistants were allowed to see them.
3   Richard Deacon, *A History of the British Secret Service* (London, 1969), p 174. Compton Mackenzie, *My Life and Times*, Octave Seven, (London, 1968), p 98. Mackenzie said that Cumming had died in June or July 1922. Actually he died in June 1923, aged 64.
4   *Dictionary of National Biography*, sub Walsingham.
5   *The Diary of Samuel Pepys*, Vol IX, ed. R.C. Latham and V. Matthews (London, 1976), p 70.
6   ibid, pp 401–402.
7   Eric Maschwitz, *No Chip on my Shoulder* (London, 1957), p 127. Maschwitz died in 1969, aged 70.
8   H. Montgomery Hyde, *Baldwin* (London, 1973), p 282.
9   Sir Alexander Cadogan, *Diaries* ed. David Dilks (London, 1971), p 202.
10 Private information.
11 Walter Schellenberg, *The Schellenberg Memoirs* (London, 1956), p 82 *et seq*.
12 Cadogan, p 226.

13 ibid, p 232.
14 ibid, p 234.
15 Schellenberg, p 110.
16 Earl Jowitt, *Some Were Spies* (London, 1954), pp 40–76. Richard D. Whalen, *The Founding Father* (New York, 1964), pp 309–320. Winston S. Churchill, *The Second World War*, Vol I: *The Gathering Storm* (London, 1948), p 345. Statement by Clare E. Hoffman of Michigan in the House of Representatives, Washington; *Congressional Record*, 25 October 1945. James Leasor, 'Spy in the Net': *Sunday Express* (London) 18 November 1962.
17 Hugh Dalton, *Memoirs. The Fateful Years 1931–1945* (London, 1957), p 366 *et seq*.
18 Bruce Page, David Leitch and Phillip Knightley, *Philby* (London, 1968), p 121.
19 Kim Philby, *My Silent War* (London, 1968), p 86.
20 Page, Leitch and Knightley, pp 123–25.
21 Maschwitz, pp 129–30.
22 Liddell left Gibraltar in 1941 to become Inspector-General of Training in England. He was later Director and Acting Chief Commissioner of the St John Ambulance Brigade, and Governor of the Royal Hospital Chelsea. He died in 1956, aged 73.
23 Brigadier Charles Newman French later became Secretary of St Luke's Hospital and wrote its history. He died in 1959, aged 84.
24 Sir Edwin Herbert, Director-General of Postal and Telegraph Censorship from 1940 to 1945, was created a life peer as Lord Tangley in 1963. He had previously been President of the Law Society. He died in 1973, aged 74.
25 Charles des Graz, CBE, later Director of the Western Area of Censorship, bought a property in Bermuda during the war, to which he intended to retire when he left Sotheby's. Unfortunately he did not live very long to enjoy it, as he died suddenly in 1953, aged 60, while reading a book in bed in his London bachelor chambers in The Albany. He was a close friend of mine during and after the war, and lent me these chambers on one occasion in 1942 when I was on leave in England.

On 12 July 1944, I wrote thanking him for sending me a copy of his valedictory address to the Bermuda Censorship: 'We both arrived in Bermuda almost on the same day in August 1940, and having watched the organization there grow and in some measure having participated in it and promoted it, I have always had its welfare and fortunes very much at heart. And this feeling has continued even though my personal connection with the Station ceased before the peak of its achievement was reached. I hope that in quieter times when you, as I am sure you will, set about writing the full history of those exciting years, we shall be able to meet in some calmer atmosphere and exchange ideas and recollections of what, I think, must rank as one of the foremost and outstanding achievements of the war. Incidentally, I was very glad to see in the recent debate on the ministry of information vote in the House of Commons, the Parliamentary Under-Secretary paid a warm and well-deserved tribute to the work of the censorship units, particularly in the Western Hemisphere.'

Des Graz would have been the ideal person to write the history of the postal and telegraph censorship during the war, and it was a great tragedy that his relatively early death prevented him from doing so.

26 Walter (Freckles) Wren died in 1971, aged 69.
27 Sir Mayson Beeton died in 1947, aged 82. Before his death he wrote a foreword to my biography of his parents, *Mr and Mrs Beeton* (London, 1951). His daughter Audrey married Surgeon-Commander Murray Levick, who accompanied Captain Scott's ill-fated Antarctic Expedition as medical officer and zoologist. He and his wife later founded and ran the Public Schools Exploration Society. Murray Levick died in 1956 and his wife in 1980. Their only son Rodney inherited the Beeton collection of papers and books.

Chapter 2. The Bermuda Triangle

1 Peter Fleming, *Invasion 1940* (London, 1958), p 15.
2 Bickham Sweet-Escott, *Baker Street Irregular* (London, 1965), p 36. Francis Ogilvy died in 1964, aged 60.
3 General Grand was Director of Fortifications and Works at the War Office from 1949 to 1952, after which he retired. He died in 1975, aged 77.
4 Chapman Pincher, *Their Trade Is Treachery* (London, 1981), p 161 *et seq*.
5 General Sir Denis Bernard retired as Governor of Bermuda in September 1941, when he was succeeded by Lord Knollys. He died in 1956, aged 73.
6 Cordell Hull, *Memoirs*, Vol I (London, 1948), pp 733–36.
7 Minutes' of Legislative Council 9 October 1940: Bermuda Archives.
8 *New York Times* 10 October 1940. Vollard's house and picture gallery were at 28 Rue de Martignac, formerly the residence of the Princesse de Ligne. See Ambroise Vollard, *Recollections of a Picture Dealer* (London, 1936).

9   HMS *Belfast*, now part of the Imperial War Museum, is at present anchored in the Pool of London and is open to the public.

10   Typescript by Edward Pearce in the author's possession.

11   H. Montgomery Hyde, *The Quiet Canadian* (London, 1962), p 97.

12   Alexander Kerensky, Russian lawyer and politician, was Prime Minister of the Provisional Government in Petrograd at this time. He went into hiding during the Revolution in October 1917 and escaped in a British destroyer. He spent his later years in the United States, where he taught for a time in university. During one of his occasional visits to England, I was introduced to him by his nephew Sir Frank Soskice, later Lord Stow Hill. He died in New York in 1970, aged 89.

13   Robin Maugham, *Somerset and All the Maughams* (London, 1966), p 207. Somerset Maugham died in 1965 within a few weeks of his 92nd birthday. I was among those members of the Garrick Club who gave him a dinner to celebrate his 80th birthday on 25 January 1954.

14   Lord Bearsted, who succeeded his father as 2nd Viscount in 1927, died in 1948, aged 66. His third son, Anthony, also served in the Intelligence Corps during the last war.

15   J. R. M. Butler, *Lord Lothian* (London, 1960), pp 311–12.

16   To comply with American law, Stephenson's organization was registered under this title (BSC for short) with the State Department in January 1941. Its overt purpose was publicly expressed as follows in *The Quiet Canadian* by Hyde, p 58:

> Consequent upon the large-scale and vital interests of the British Government in connection with the purchase and shipment of munitions and war material from the United States, coupled with the presence in this country of a number of British official missions, a variety of security problems has been created, and these, affecting closely as they do the interests of the British Government, call for very close and friendly collaboration between the authorities of the two countries.
>
> Thus, for example, the presence in large numbers of British and Allied ships engaged in loading explosives and other war materials, and the existence of large quantities of similar materials in plants, on railways, and in dock areas throughout the country, presenting as they do a tempting target to saboteurs and enemy agents, constitute in themselves a security problem of considerable magnitude.
>
> With a view to co-ordinating the liaison between the various British missions and the United States authorities in all security matters arising from the present abnormal circumstances, an

organization bearing the title *British Security Co-ordination* has been formed under the control of a Director of Security Co-ordination, assisted by a headquarters staff.

17 R. W. Logan, *Haiti and the Dominican Republic* (London, 1968), *passim*.

Chapter 3. British Security Co-ordination

1   Oakes was mysteriously murdered during the night of 7/8 July 1943, at Westbourne House. The crime was never officially solved, although Oakes's son-in-law Alfred de Marigny was tried for it and acquitted. Christie was staying in the house at the time, but he had nothing to do with it. For a detailed account of the case, see 'Who killed Sir Harry Oakes?' by H. Montgomery Hyde in *Crime Has its Heroes* (London, 1976), pp 178–190.
2   Michael Pye, *The King Over the Water* (London, 1981), p 98.
3   Winston S. Churchill, *The Second World War*, Vol IV (London, 1951), p 789.
4   Oliver Jensen, '880 Censors in Bermuda': *Life* (New York), 10 May 1941.
5   Hyde, *The Quiet Canadian*, p 80 *et seq*.
6   Stephenson to Hyde, 8 May 1945: Author's papers.
7   *The Times*, 16 July, 21 July 1975.
8   Maschwitz, p 143.
9   ibid, p 144.
10 Hyde, *The Quiet Canadian*, p 183.
11 Chapman Pincher, op. cit., pp 161–72.
12 Ellis Papers, In the possession of Ellis's daughter.
13 William Webb Ellis (1807–1872), who went to Rugby School and Brasenose College, Oxford, later entered the church and for many years was Rector at St Clement Danes, London, where there is a tablet to his memory erected by the Royal Air Force Rugby Football Union. He never married and died in Menton, France. It is remarkable that his name does not appear in the British *Dictionary of National Biography*.
14 Paul Schwarz, *This Man Ribbentrop* (New York, 1943), pp 202–203.
15 Chapman Pincher, p 171.
16 *The Times* 27 April 1981.
17 Hyde, *The Quiet Canadian*, p 139 *et seq*.
18 Hull, I, p 821.
19 Sir Courtenay Forbes retired on pension in 1945 and during his

retirement he joined a well-known firm of turf accountants (or bookmakers) in London, being the only former diplomatist in the British foreign service ever to have done so. He died in 1958, aged 69.

20 Sir James Dodds, later Ambassador to Peru, retired in 1951, and died in 1972, aged 81.

21 *New York Times*, 20, 21, 22, 24 July, 1941.

22 Hull, II, p 1388.

23 Sumner Welles, *Seven Major Decisions* (London, 1951), p 101.

24 In 1929, when Churchill and his son Randolph met Chaplin for the first time, they were equally captivated. 'You could not help liking him,' Winston wrote to his wife. 'He is a marvellous comedian – bolshy in politics and delightful in conversation.' Among others whom he impersonated on this occasion were Napoleon, Uriah Heep, Henry Irving, and John Barrymore as Hamlet. Martin Gilbert, *Winston S. Churchill* Companion Vol V. Part 2, *The Wilderness Years* (London, 1981), p 97 and note.

25 Betty Grable died in 1973, aged 56. She had long since been superseded by Marilyn Monroe.

26 Michael Korda, *Charmed Lives* (London, 1980), p 156. Sidney Skolsky in *Washington Times-Herald*, 11 February 1943.

27 Merle Oberon's second husband, whom she divorced in 1949, was Lucien Ballard, a Hollywood cameraman. In 1958 she married a wealthy Mexican industrialist Bruno Pagliai, by whom she had a son and daughter. With her third husband she entertained lavishly in their luxurious house in Acapulco. This marriage eventually broke up and she married as her fourth husband a young Dutch actor Robert Wolders, who had co-starred with her in 1973 in the Mexican film *Interval* which she herself also produced and helped to edit and in which she made something of a comeback as an actress. She died in 1979, aged 68. Contrary to the press obituary notices, she was born in India and not in Tasmania, and her father's name was O'Brien and not Thompson, although the latter appears as her father in her entry in the British *Who's Who*, where she also gave the year of her birth as 1917 instead of 1911. There is some doubt about the legitimacy of her birth, and it is possible that Thompson, who came from Tasmania, married her mother. That Merle had some coloured blood comes out strongly in her portrait by Oswald Birley.

28 Otto Strasser returned from Canada to West Germany in 1955, when his German citizenship, of which he had been deprived, was restored to him. In 1969 he appealed to a West German Court for a state pension as a register of the Nazis, but the Court rejected his appeal on the ground that he had been a personal opponent of Hitler

rather than a principal opponent of Nazism. He died in Munich in 1974, aged 77.

Chapter 4. Good-bye to All That

1 Earl of Birkenhead, *Halifax* (London, 1965), p 480.
2 Hull, I, p 495. Berle died in 1971, aged 76.
3 J. Pierrepoint Moffat had been Chief of the European Affairs Division of the State Department since 1937.
4 State Department Archives: Berle Papers, VIII 2. 50–52. Tamm later became a Federal judge.
5 ibid, VIII 2, 125–28.
6 ibid, VIII 2, 138–45 (10 March 1942).
7 Francis Biddle, *In Brief Authority* (New York, 1962), p 145.
8 *Harper's Magazine*, Vol 185, No. 1105, (June 1942), pp 19–20, 'The Case of the Ten Nazis Spies' by Edward C. Aswell. This is an interesting article since Aswell was a member of the jury.
9 Author's papers in Churchill College, Cambridge, Archives Centre.
10 In collaboration with G. R. Falkiner Nuttall. Published in England in 1937. It later became the official textbook on the subject in the Irish Free State.
11 This report on British Security Co-ordination, dated March 1943, is in the author's papers in Churchill College, Cambridge.
12 J. C. Masterman, *The Double Cross System in the War of 1939 to 1945* (New Haven and London, 1972).
13 Dusko Popov, *Spy Counter Spy* (London, 1974), p 129 *et seq*.
14 Popov died at his home near Grasse in the South of France in August 1981, aged 69.
15 The MS report 'The Vichy French in the United States' is in the author's papers in Churchill College, Cambridge.
16 *New York Herald-Tribune*, 31 August, 2, 3, 4 September 1941.
17 H. Montgomery Hyde, *Cynthia* (New York, 1965, London, 1966), *passim*. Elizabeth Brousse's papers, voice recordings, etc., are in the author's collection in Churchill College, Cambridge.
18 ibid, p 5.
19 Churchill, I, p 385. The battleship *Royal Oak* was sunk as she lay at anchor inside Scapa Flow in the early hours of 14 October 1939. According to another unsubstantiated report, the attack was planned by a German spy named Alfred Wahring, a former naval officer, who had come to Britain on a Swiss passport, eventually becoming naturalized, establishing himself as a Swiss watchmaker under the name of Alfred Oertel, and keeping a jeweller's shop at

Kirkwall in the Orkneys, near Scapa Flow. He is said to have provided German intelligence with reports over many years: Deacon, *A History of the British Secret Service*, p 283.

20 *Washington Times-Herald*, 1 December 1942.

21 Mrs Paravicini was later divorced from her husband and in 1948 married Lord John Hope, MP, who was created Lord Glendevon in 1964.

22 Peter Smithers later became a Conservative MP, Parliamentary Under-Secretary at the Foreign Office, and Secretary-General of the Council of Europe. He was knighted in 1970.

23 *Mexican Empire: The History of Maximilian and Carlota* was published by Macmillan in England in 1946 and gained Macmillan Centenary Award.

24 A copy is with the author's papers in Churchill College, Cambridge.

25 Byron Price, later Assistant General Secretary (Administration and Finance) in the United Nations, died in 1981, aged 90.

26 See also the account by Giles Playfair in his *Singapore Goes off the Air* (New York, 1943).

27 The Federal Communications Commission Chairman Mr James L. Fly had refused to hand over to the FBI fingerprint records of more than 200,000 radio operators and workers in the face of repeated demands from Hoover and Biddle. 'The evidence is strong,' the Attorney General had written to the FCC Chairman on 2 January 1942, less than a month after Pearl Harbor, 'that messages have been surreptitiously transmitted to our enemies by radio, and that military attacks have been furthered or facilitated by these radio messages.' Biddle's letter repeated a request first made in June 1940 and many times reiterated. In his reply, dated 5 January, Fly stated that the radio employees' union leaders objected to having their fingerprints placed in the FBI records. *Washington Herald-Tribune*, 21 January 1944.

28 Interpol's function is not generally understood by the public. It rarely initiates the pursuit of criminals but is really a gigantic clearing-house for the exchange of information. It has a radio network broadcasting from Paris and covering all countries outside the Iron Curtain in Europe, over which requests for information and replies can be transmitted with great speed. The Secretariat of Interpol regularly circulates information about international criminals, as a result of which frequent arrests have been made. There is a branch office in Holland specializing in forgery and counterfeiting of currency. See Julian Symons, *Crime and Detection* (London, 1968) p 184, and Sir Harold Scott, *Scotland Yard* (London, 1954), p 96.

29 When Hoover was approaching the normal retiring age in 1964, President Johnson exempted him from the Civil Service retirement provision 'for an indefinite time'. Consequently John Edgar Hoover was still Director of the FBI when he died on 2 May 1972, aged 77, having served under eight Presidents and fifteen Attorneys General as Director for 40 years. The son of a Washington civil servant, he got a job as messenger in the Library of Congress to help support his family after his father died and he studied at night for a law degree at George Washington University. After graduating he joined the Department of Justice as an attorney, becoming special assistant to the Attorney General Mitchell Palmer in 1919. Two years later he became Assistant Director of the Bureau of Investigation, as it was then known, and Director in 1924. He never married.

30 Dorothy and I were divorced in 1951, much to my regret, since she had fallen in love with another member of MI6, Commander Wilfred Dunderdale, RNVR, whom she later married. Dunderdale was the officer upon whom Ian Fleming is said to have based his fictitious character James Bond in his novels of espionage. I remained on friendly terms with both Dorothy and her second husband until her death in 1978.

Appendix

1 Colonel Charles A. Lindbergh was the first man to fly non-stop from New York to Paris, which he did in May 1925, taking 34 hours. Senator Burton K. Wheeler, a Democrat, represented Montana in the Senate. Along with Lindbergh, he was a leader of the America First movement, which opposed US involvement in the war which would mean 'ploughing every fourth American boy on foreign battlefields for the benefit of a decayed British Empire'.

2 Franklin Knox, a newspaper publisher, and Henry Stimson, a former Secretary of State, were both Republicans, and had recently been appointed respectively Secretary of the Navy and Secretary for War by President Roosevelt in his otherwise Democrat Cabinet.

3 Cordell Hull was US Secretary of State from 1933 to 1944.

4 The Director of Naval Intelligence at this time was Admiral John Godfrey, who had hoped to be appointed Chief of BI (SIS) on Admiral Sinclair's death. As DNI his ability was outstanding.

5 John Winant, former Senator and Governor of New Hampshire, became US Ambassador to Britain in January, 1941, succeeding the defeatist Joseph Kennedy. He remained in his London post, where he was immensely popular and successful, throughout the

war. In 1947, in a fit of depression caused by overwork, he took his own life. Robert Sherwood was a well-known editor and dramatist, whose plays included *Reunion in Vienna* (1931), *The Petrified Forest* (1934), *Idiot's Delight* (1936), and, perhaps greatest of all, *There Shall Be No Night* (1940). During the war he became Director of the Office of War Information. He died in 1955.

6 Vincent Astor, son of John Jacob Astor, was head of the wealthy Astor family in the US at this time. His commercial and financial interests were considerable. As Director of the Western Union Telegraph Co, he rendered great help to Stephenson.

7 General Hastings ('Pug') Ismay was Churchill's Chief of Staff. Desmond Morton was Churchill's personal assistant, particularly in the secret intelligence field.

8 The tube station was St James's Park in London and was directly opposite BI headquarters at 54 Broadway.

9 Professor B. Bailey was Professor of Physics at Toronto University.

10 Sherwood's work appeared in England as *The White House Papers of Harry L. Hopkins* (London, 1948): see p 270, where the author refers to Stephenson as the 'quiet Canadian'.

11 The Manhattan Project was the American code-name for the development of the atom bomb in the US.

12 Torch was the code-name for the Allied landings in North Africa, and was the first major American offensive in the war.

13 The head of the OSS office in Berne at this time was Allen Dulles, a younger brother of President Eisenhower's Secretary of State John Foster Dulles. See his book *The Craft of Intelligence* (London, 1963); and on the Berne material (alternatively known as the Wood traffic) Andrew Tully, *CIA: The Inside Story* (New York, 1962), at p 421, and the present author's *Room 3603* (New York, 1963), at p 177. Allen Dulles virtually created the CIA, of which he was Director from 1953 to 1961. He died in 1969.

14 Corey Ford, *Donovan of OSS* (Boston, 1970), at p 343. Although Donovan has rightly been regarded as the father of the CIA, President Truman disliked him and had no further use for his services after the war. In 1953 President Eisenhower appointed him US ambassador to Thailand, but he was obliged to resign because of ill-health eighteen months later. He died in 1959, aged 76.

Index